WORLD INDUSTRY STUDIES 1

Collapse and Survival:
Industry Strategies in a Changing World

WORLD INDUSTRY STUDIES

Edited by Professor Ingo Walter,
Graduate School of Business Administration,
New York Universitity

Collapse and Survival:
Industry Strategies in a Changing World

Robert H. Ballance
Senior Industrial Development Officer
United Nations Industrial Development Organisation

Stuart W. Sinclair
Graduate School of Management
University of California at Los Angeles

London
GEORGE ALLEN & UNWIN
Boston   Sydney

**George Allen & Unwin (Publishers) Ltd,
40 Museum Street, London WC1A 1LU, UK**

George Allen & Unwin (Publishers) Ltd,
Park Lane, Hemel Hempstead, Herts HP2 4TE, UK

Allen & Unwin Inc.,
9 Winchester Terrace, Winchester, Mass 01890, USA

George Allen & Unwin Australia Pty Ltd,
8 Napier Street, North Sydney, NSW 2060, Australia

First published in 1983

British Library Cataloguing in Publication Data

Ballance, Robert H.
    Collapse and survival: industry strategies in a changing world.—
(World industry studies; 1)
1. Industrial organization (Economic theory)
I. Title   II. Sinclair, Stuart W.
III. Series
338   HD2326
ISBN 0-04-338107-3
ISBN 0-04-338108-1 Pbk

Library of Congress Cataloging in Publication Data

Ballance, Robert H.
    Collapse and survival.
(World industry studies; 1)
Bibliography: p.
Includes index.
1. Corporate planning. 2. Industrial organization (Economic theory).
3. Competition, International—Case studies. 4. Industry and state.
5. International division of labor. 6. International business enter-
prises. 7. International economic relations. 8. Economic history—
1971– . I. Sinclair, Stuart W. II. Title. III. Series.
HD30.28.B34 1983   338   83–7117
ISBN 0-04-338107-3
ISBN 0-04-338108-1 (pbk.)

Set in 10 on 11 point Times by
Phoenix Photosetting, Chatham
and printed in Great Britain
by Mackays of Chatham Ltd

Contents

List of Tables

List of Figures

List of Abbreviations

ACP	African, Caribbean and Pacific countries
AISI	American Iron and Steel Industry
ASEAN	Association of South East Asian Nations
BIS	Bank for International Settlements
BLS	Bureau of Labor Statistics
BP	British Petroleum
BRISCC	British Iron and Steel Consumers Council
CAD	computer aided design
CAM	computer aided manufacture
CAP	Common Agricultural Policy
CMEA	Council for Mutual Economic Assistance
ECE	Economic Commission for Europe
EEC	European Economic Community
EFTA	European Free Trade Association
GATT	General Agreement on Tariffs and Trade
GDP	gross domestic product
GM	General Motors
GNP	gross national product
IBRD	International Bank for Reconstruction and Development (World Bank)
ICL	International Computers Ltd (UK)
IDE	Institute of Developing Economies
IISI	International Iron and Steel Institute
IMF	International Monetary Fund
ISC	International Steel Cartel
ISIC	International Standard Industrial Classification
JAMA	Japan Automobile Manufacturers Association
JETRO	Japanese External Trade Organization
LDC	less developed country
MIJ	Machine Industries of Japan
MITI	Ministry of International Trade and Industry
MTTA	Machine Tool Trades Association
MVA	manufacturing value added
MVMA	Motor Vehicle Manufacturers Association (US)
NIC	newly industrialising country
NTB	non tariff barrier
NTT	Nippon Telegraph and Telephone

OECD	Organization for Economic Co-operation and Development
OMA	orderly marketing agreement
OPEC	Organization of Petroleum Exporting Countries
PAL	West European television – tube system
PME	public manufacturing enterprise
R & D	research and development
SECAM	West European television – tube system
SITC	Standard International Trade Classification
TNC	transnational corporation
TPM	trigger price mechanism
UAW	United Auto Workers
UNCTAD	United Nations Conference on Trade and Development
UNCTC	United Nations Centre for Transnational Corporations
UNIDO	United Nations Industrial Development Organization
USNWR	US News and World Report
VER	voluntary export restraint
VW	Volkswagen

Foreword

Recent years have seen wrenching changes in the structure of the world economy. Industries that were once the 'commanding heights' of their national economies have become mere shadows, kept alive by high levels of protection from imports and government subsidies. These same industries have evolved into the engines of economic development in growth-oriented emerging nations, counting on dramatic export drives to exploit their new-found competitive advantage. The required global economic restructuring is by no means painless, set against the creation of advanced, high-tech industries whose timing and resource needs rarely match the shifting production patterns among the traditional industrial sectors. Yet economic growth, both at the national and global level, requires effective public policies to come to terms with industrial restructuring in broad alignment with market forces.

The reasons for the unprecedented global restructuring at the industry level are rather apparent. They include accelerated technological diffusion, integration of capital markets, the rise of the multinational corporation as a dominant form of international economic organization, reduced information and transportation costs, and broad-based liberalisation of trade barriers. At the same time, volatility of interest rates and exchange rates, as well as prices of natural resources and energy, have 'shocked' industries and induced competitive shifts that are often by no means permanent. And over the years, governments have assumed social obligations that make market-driven structural adjustment increasingly difficult.

This series is designed to come to grips with these issues on an industry level. Each story is different, yet the basic questions remain the same. What are the causes of competitive change in an industry, and where are they leading? What kinds of shifts in market performance and industrial structure derive from the developments? How have public policies succeeded or failed to cope with them, and to what extent have the results deviated from the dictates of the free market? What are the costs and benefits of such policies, to the affected individuals and groups, to nations, and to the world as a whole? And where do we go from here? That is, what are the implications for corporate strategic planning and for government policy-making?

We live in a world of many goods and services and many countries, and one must be careful not to focus too strongly on narrow sectoral problems. But the fact remains that firms and governments do rely heavily on individual sectoral scenarios, and need to know where market forces are leading them – as well as the consequences of defying such forces.

This volume is the first in a series of global industry studies, each outlining the evolution of a single sector in an attempt to provide definitive answers to the foregoing questions. Unlike the volumes that follow, Messrs Ballance and Sinclair lead off the series with a broad overview of the issues. They clearly draw on the experiences of individual sectors, yet succeed in sketching a conceptual, and empirical and policy framework within which later volumes can be set.

INGO WALTER
New York University

Preface

During the last thirty years the map of world industry has changed completely. Whereas in 1945 a very few countries accounted for an overwhelming share of all manufacturing output, by 1981 their predominance had been significantly reduced. New capacity had emerged in a number of industries throughout the world to challenge the established industrial leaders. Until comparatively recently the closure of a shipbuilding yard in Glasgow, a textile plant in Lille or an oil refinery in Baton Rouge seemed to be no reason for undue alarm. Other plants and other jobs would take their place. But during the 1970s and certainly in the early 1980s this presumption appeared to be increasingly ill-founded. More people were spending time on the unemployment register after being laid off from industry, and they were spending longer and longer in each spell of unemployment between jobs. Moreover, workers were increasingly finding that the skills they had acquired in one industry were no longer of economic value; vacancies lay elsewhere.

For the managements witnessing the erosion of sales in long-established and seemingly inpregnable businesses, there was usually some warning. Many of the imports now entering major domestic markets had been arranged by firms that were based in those countries, although their production facilities were located elsewhere. But for firms not integrated into an international purchasing and distribution network, the first responses were to governments for aid and to business strategists for advice. Sometimes both were approached. Yet the problem with the former was that aid was by no means always forthcoming – it depended on a range of apparently capricious factors – while the problem with the latter was that advice was not always sound. The reassuring theme of 'going up-market' to secure a product niche with lower price elasticities sounded increasingly hollow as not just Japanese but other exporters were quickly arriving at the same frontiers of product development. Cutting costs was another path urged on management, yet from the late 1960s onwards the relatively poor record of productivity and investment in many established firms made this exceptionally difficult.

Although it is not often recognised, issues such as these are inextricably linked. Decisions about new auto assembly capacity in Spain – or even in South Korea – will have an effect upon other producers

in Europe, Japan and the USA. These effects, which will ultimately
make themselves felt on pricing, design and trade policy decisions in
the firms in the industry and their suppliers, inevitably impinge upon
the welfare of Detroit's assembly workers and Sao Paulo's engineers.

Indeed, it is the unmistakably international character of industry
which lies at the root of much of this book. Today, there are very few
industries that are not dependent in some way on foreign economies.
They may be reliant on imported supplies or intermediate inputs,
imports of capital equipment and technology, foreign labour or
foreign management, or they may supply foreign markets. The
degree of internationalisation, of course, differs between industries.
In some instances, the scope of analysis can be confined to North
America, Japan and Western Europe, while other industries are
practically worldwide when gauged in terms of the network of economic, political and policy considerations that link them. The book's
primary objectives are to set out the recent changes both in the world
industrial map and in the forces – economic and otherwise – that have
shaped it. The consequences of these shifts in industrial leadership
and competitiveness for individual firms are discussed, chiefly in the
context of five industries which have undergone particularly rapid or
convulsive change.

The emphasis on international differences in rates of growth, technological development and change leads naturally into a discussion of
policy – both public and corporate. In the 1970s, public policy was
recognised as an important determinant of industrial growth and
change. Indeed, a substantial portion of current industrial capacity –
even outside the communist bloc – owes its very existence to public
policy decisions. However, the growing involvement of the state was
seldom accompanied by new institutional arrangements to
co-ordinate the many decisions that began to fall within the
government's purview. Because of this failure – and for other equally
important reasons explored in this book – public policy has become
increasingly susceptible to pressure from special interest groups, the
composition of which may include producers, representatives of
labour, bureaucrats from the public sector, suppliers, consumers, or
others whose interests are associated with the future prospects of a
given industry. In using their new-found ability to influence public
policy, pressure groups have added another dimension – a political
one – to the range of economic and corporate issues that are
traditionally part of the firm's normal decision-making responsibilities.
As a result, corporate decisions are blended with various forms of
lobbying activities. Together, they give rise to a whole range of 'industry
strategies' which are described in this book.

Initially, interest in the idea of strategic planning and strategic management mainly stressed economic factors. Typical of the more widely used approaches was the Boston Consulting Group's 'business portfolio matrix', in which a firm's divisions were arrayed according to their relative market share and the rate at which the overall market is growing. The implication of the matrix is that low-yielding assets should periodically be weeded out of a business portfolio. This is indeed the interpretation of the post-1980 recession that many management consultants favour – that the spate of plant closures reflects, as much as intensified foreign and domestic competition, a deliberate abandoning of low-return assets. However, as more firms and affiliated industrial interest groups realise that they can affect both the rate of market growth and their own market shares by non-economic or political means, the nature of business strategy will naturally become more complicated. The last chapter of this book attempts to convey the flavour of precisely that complexity.

Among the people who have offered assistance and informed criticism in the preparation of this book are Tracy Murray, Professor of Economics at the University of Arkansas, Hans W. Singer, Professor of Economics, Institute of Development Studies, University of Sussex, and Paul Hallwood, Department of Political Economy at the University of Aberdeen. Robert Ballance is a senior industrial development officer in the United Nations Industrial Development Organisation, Vienna, Austria; the views expressed here do not in any way represent those of the organisation with which he is affiliated. Stuart Sinclair is currently at the Graduate School of Management, University of California at Los Angeles.

1

World Industry in Transition

Recent years have witnessed more than the usual amount of uncertainty and reappraisal in industries across the world. After relatively smooth and uninterrupted growth in manufacturing output from the end of the First World War, the early 1970s saw the appearance of new problems – as well as the reappearance of some older and still unresolved ones too. The abrupt change in energy prices after 1973; the marked fall in the rate of growth of productivity in virtually all industrialised countries; the enhanced awareness of new sources of industrial capacity outside the traditional centres of activity in the West; and the more awkward worldwide macroeconomic climate – these and other phenomena have come increasingly to preoccupy and puzzle industrialists, policy makers and economists.

This book examines the present position of world industry. It reviews the background of the exceptionally strong postwar growth of net manufacturing output.[1] It looks at the policy framework adopted to bolster this growth by governments in advanced countries – both western and socialist – and in the less developed countries (LDCs).[2] And it examines, in some detail, the recent experience of firms in five industries[3] which, for various reasons, have been in the forefront of the huge changes occurring since 1945. In addressing these subjects the book presents an analysis and an interpretation of world industry in transition. But it also attempts to go beyond this and to identify not only what developments have come about, but also some of the reasons why they occurred. For much of the post-war literature concerned with industry and industrialisation has either ignored the processes whereby industrial policies are formulated or has overlooked the fact that different policies imply different sets of costs and benefits for the individuals and groups involved. In discussing how certain policies have evolved, not necessarily because they were 'right' but because they reflected the preferences of various groups or interests, the book tries to throw some light upon the interactions between structural change and interest group behaviour.

This introductory chapter begins by reviewing very quickly the overall economic climate within which industries have had to operate in recent years. It then presents a short overview of the main controversies which have sprung up concerning the topics of industry, industrial development and industrial policy. Finally, it describes the layout of the rest of the book.

The world economy in the 1970s

After an unprecedented period of rapid growth and development, the world economy was seriously affected by the four-fold rise in oil prices in late 1973. This action, which ushered in the most severe postwar recession experienced by the advanced countries, exacerbated, but did not in itself cause, a number of difficulties with which many governments had been grappling since the late 1960s. Rising inflation, growing unemployment, decelerating productivity growth and greater than expected currency instability after the advent of floating exchange rates were among the most apparent difficulties. The slowdown in economic growth and in the growth of manufacturing output in virtually all countries of the world was, however, the factor which attracted most attention. After growing at an annual average rate of 4.7 per cent between 1963 and 1972, the expansion of GNP in the advanced countries slowed to only 2.8 per cent per year from 1973 to 1981 (IMF, 1982, p. 143). An even sharper drop in the growth of manufacturing value added (MVA) was experienced. As Table 1.1 shows, its growth rate in the advanced market economies was more than halved after 1970.

Table 1.1 *Growth of manufacturing value added* by economic grouping, selected periods (percentage)*

Period	LDCs	Socialist countries	Advanced market economies
1960–70	7.3	9.6	6.2
1970–81	5.8	7.0	3.0

Source: UNIDO, 1982a, Table 1.3
* at constant prices

An unmistakable consequence of this slowdown was the rise in unemployment witnessed in all advanced countries. After experiencing only moderate rates of unemployment in the 1950s, levels moved upwards and, after 1980, unemployment became the most serious economic problem in many countries. This upward trend was caused partly by demographic factors, in particular the fact that birth rates in advanced countries peaked between 1956 and 1960 and led to unprecedently large accessions of young job-seekers to labour markets during the late 1970s and early 1980s. But the increase in unemployment is widely thought also to have resulted from a fundamental shift in policy priorities. As the National Institute of Economic and Social Research (1979, p. 38) noted, 'economic policies in general tend now not to be much concerned with employment or economic growth objectives, but simply with the objective of reducing the rate of increase of prices'.

There is no doubt that the accelerating pace of inflation from the late 1960s onwards became increasingly worrisome to economists and politicians. After a brief spell of 3–4 per cent annual inflation in the late 1950s, price rises settled to below 2 per cent in the advanced economies in the early 1960s. But by 1970 the rate of increase was averaging over 5 per cent, and 1974 saw inflation reach the unprecedented rate of 13 per cent. After lulls in the mid-1970s, the 1979–82 period was one of renewed inflationary pressures, with even hitherto little-affected countries such as Austria, Switzerland and West Germany grappling with rates considerably above their accustomed norm.

The worsening of inflation in the 1960s was one of the factors which prompted a re-emergence of interest in monetary policies in all the advanced economies. In the heyday of the cruder versions of Keynesian economics, the importance of the size and funding of the public sector's financial deficits had tended to be overlooked. With the renewed interest in monetary theory, however, the monetary implications of demand management policy came to be examined more rigorously than before. By the late 1970s, a widely-shared consensus had evolved that, at root, monetary and fiscal policies were two sides of the same coin and could not be analysed independently of one another (Peston, 1981).

Inevitably, the deteriorating economic climate and the apparent end of demand management policies as successful regulators of economies spawned a number of different interpretations of what had gone wrong. Explanations ranged from growing discontent among a generation of workers who had not known the privations of the early post-war period (Runciman, 1972) to the inexorable growth of the public sector (Bacon and Eltis, 1976). Another view which commanded widespread sympathy focused on the long-run fall in the rate of return to industrial capital in the post-war years. After generally high rates immediately after the end of the Second World War and in the 1950s, the following two decades witnessed a tendency for these rates to decline. The extent of the decline and the timing of its inception naturally differed between countries, but the overall drift was unmistakable by the 1970s.

A long cycle in industry?

In the belief that this relatively prolonged slowdown in growth may be consistent with more fundamental factors than trade union behaviour, rising government expenditure or other such trends, some economists have returned with renewed interest to the notion of long cycles. Inspired by the pioneering work on 50- to 60-year cycles of economic activity by Kondratieff in the 1920s, they have pondered on the extent to which the problems of the 1970s and early 1980s reflect a downward phase in the long-term rate of world economic growth stemming from an absence of revolutionary product innovations. For, following the work of Schumpeter (1939) and, later, Mensch (1975), it has been suggested that until there is a fuller commercial diffusion of a new wave of innovations, such as those likely to be associated with microelectronics, a low rate of economic growth relative to the immediate post-war period is all that can be expected (Freeman, 1981).

Central to the notion of a long wave of activity is the manufacturing sector, its rate of growth and its rate of innovation. Drawing on the seminal work of Verndoorn (1949), Kaldor (1966) proposed that slow economic growth (in the UK at least, but by implication elsewhere too) was a consequence of industrial maturity, manifested in the exhaustion of the surplus of farm labour which had already contributed so strongly to the impressive post-war recoveries of other European countries. Arguing that this supply constraint had prevented a satisfactory growth of manufacturing output and, by virtue of Verndoorn's Law, had constrained the growth of industrial productivity, Kaldor put the case for tax incentives to shift labour back from services into industry. Although the view was much criticised (Gomulka, 1971; Rowthorne, 1975), it is interesting to observe that today a number of governments, notably in Austria, France and Sweden, are intent on a similar path and plan to oversee the expenditure of substantial sums of money in 're-industrialising' their economies.

A policy of re-industrialisation seems perverse to many commentators. Virtually all advanced countries have experienced similar growth paths since their industrial revolution, with the share of manufacturing within GDP initially expanding slowly, then accelerating. Later, the growth of manufacturing tends to decelerate and the sector's share in GDP may even decline. This was the pattern expected by such economists as Chenery and Sirquin (1975) and documented by UNIDO (1979, pp. 43–51). So firmly did this pattern seem to be established, indeed, that it began to be seen as immutable. But is it?

Both the debate over the long cycle, and another debate centring on the impact of oil revenues on industrialisation, have thrown doubt upon this deterministic view. First, research by van Duijn (1981, 1983) on specific industries within the manufacturing sector has suggested that although in the early stages of evolution there does appear to be a common pattern of growth, similar to a logistic curve, a decline in output is by no means inevitable once the stage of maturity or saturation is reached. Echoing some of the early literature from related fields such as marketing (Levitt, 1965; Wells, 1972), van Duijn has shown that the options for further growth, through product innovation, process innovation, price-cutting, or some other strategies, are considerable. Thus, far from following the paths suggested by earlier economists, who, in the light of the celebrated Engel's Law, tended to view industries' prospects strictly in terms of income elasticities of demand, it appears that adjustments and strategies may be pursued to evade decline. But this research also clearly implies that these options must be identified at the level of individual industries, and not at the aggregated level of the manufacturing sector as a whole.

Recently, a considerable literature on business strategies has grown up around the very idea that the problems and opportunities facing each industry are unique and must, in consequence, be analysed in isolation. One method of categorising firms' strategic options which has become widely used is the business portfolio matrix, as popularised by the General Electric Company and the Boston Consulting Group. This is an effort to help clarify companies' thinking about their various divisions (or, as they are known in the matrix, 'strategic business units') and the relationship which each bears to the overall fortunes of the firm (Kotler, 1980, pp. 75-90). Problems which may disrupt business units' progress have been analysed in terms of 'opportunity and threat analysis'. Other writers have concentrated on the choice of strategies open to firms under different circumstances. Among the better-known is Porter (1979, 1980), whose 'generic strategies' approach attempts to identify the least-risk profit-maximising path for firms to pursue under different circumstances. Strategies discussed in this context include 'harvesting', whereby a firm decides to make a carefully-timed tactical withdrawal from a market, and 'focus', whereby a firm attempts to intensify its hold over a smaller and more carefully segmented portion of its accustomed market. Few observers doubt the influence of this type of thinking in the 1980–83 recession. As a survey by the *Wall Street Journal* put it, many basic American industries are undergoing a period of 'deconglomeration', . . . 'directors are abandoning low-return assets in order to maximize their companies' long-term return on remaining assets' (*WSJ*, 15 Oct. 1982).

Another recent source of thinking on the subject of industrial development is the debate over oil and its impact on industry. Initially, there was widespread agreement that oil (or gas) exports from a new source would tend to undermine the manufacturing sector in the exporting country by virtue of the stronger exchange-rate that followed from the improvement in balance of payments. This so-called 'Dutch disease' was thought to have spread to Norway and the UK in 1980 and 1981, as they became net oil exporters for the first time. The idea provoked interest in the notion of de-industrialisation, whereby manufacturing output is reduced below the level sufficient to pay for the country's imports of manufactures. Although the term is an ambiguous one – it has, to quote Blackaby (1979, p. 1), 'gate-crashed the literature, thereby avoiding the entrance fee of a definition' – it is nevertheless widely used, particularly in connection with industries that are thought to be basic to a country's industrial 'survival'. In investigating this notion of de-industrialisation, Thirlwall (1982, p. 27) has shown that eight advanced countries experienced an absolute decline in manufacturing employment between 1966 and 1981. He argued that such a phenomenon is necessarily harmful, since 'manufacturing possesses certain growth-inducing characteristics that other sectors of the economy do not have'. Given this support from economic theory (as well as the more emotive appeals that such basic industries seem to enjoy in the public mind), one of the tasks of this book is to investigate the ways in which producers, employees, bureaucracies and other interests organise to 'defend' their industries from such erosion.

The international character of industry today

One of the appeals of the long-wave approach is that it offers an interpretation of industry's problems which is at root international. For a major objection to several of the more parochial hypotheses, which attempt to explain the deteriorating operating environment for industries country by country, is the overwhelming evidence that virtually all western countries and, in different ways, all the socialist countries, have experienced a similar set of phenomena, including decelerating industrial productivity growth and slower growth of output overall.

Naturally, the fact that manufacturing has become far more international in character over the last few decades has not gone unnoticed. As Chapter 2 will show, the spread of manufacturing capacity since 1950 has become extensive. There are very few industries that are not now dependent in some way on foreign economies, being reliant on imported inputs and supplies, imports of foreign capital, technology, foreign labour and management or foreign markets.

Among the LDCs, the growth of industrial capacity, both for export and for domestic consumption, was initiated in the 1960s, although it was not until the global slowdown in the 1970s that the phenomenon became widely discussed. It may be, as Turner (1982, p. 269) has argued, that the growth of industry in a number of LDCs is not 'posing fundamentally new problems to the world economy, but that (they have) emerged at the wrong time. . . . At a time of slow growth and high unemployment, there is obvious scepticism about the workings of the economic adjustment process'. Alternatively, it may be that the real – if usually exaggerated – problem of redeploying workers made redundant as factories close in the face of competitively-priced imports might have emerged as an issue at any time. Whatever the truth of the matter, there is no question that the diffusion of manufacturing capacity across continents, with the consequent diminution of various countries' positions of world leadership, has led to new tensions of various types. One of the tasks of the first five chapters of this book is to examine the ways in which official policies encourage this diffusion, and, in Chapters 6 and 7, to examine the ways in which certain interest groups are now intent on slowing down or reversing it while others try to accelerate it.

This evident growth of industrial capacity in the 'newly industrialising countries' (NICs) such as Singapore and South Korea, has also been replicated, although on a much smaller scale, in other LDCs. The NICs apart, there were 31 LDCs that each exported $100 million worth or more of industrially processed goods in 1975 (World Bank, 1979, p. 14). Even the 31 least developed countries, with an average *per capita* income in 1979 of under $100, experienced reasonably satisfactory industrial growth, with their MVA rising at an annual average rate of 5.1 per cent between 1970 and 1980 (UNIDO, 1982a, p. 11).

Quite apart from this growth of industrial capacity among a number of LDCs, it should not be forgotten that the past two decades have also witnessed substantial growth in industrial capacity in the socialist countries. Between 1960 and 1981 the share of these countries in world MVA grew from 14.0 per cent to 24.9 per cent – proportionately a far more significant increase than that achieved in the LDCs, whose combined share of world MVA rose from 8.0 per cent to only 10.3 per cent in the same period (UNIDO, 1982a, p. 4). Various aspects of the pattern of industrial development evidenced in socialist countries are discussed in Chapters 3 and 5, where the comparatively late retention of 'heavy' industries such as iron and steel within manufacturing is remarked upon. With regard to trade in manufactures, several socialist countries have experienced moderate success, although the share of these countries in world exports of manufactures, 8.1 per cent in 1980, was less than that attained by the LDCs and, in fact, represented a decline in comparison with the early 1960s.

So far, however, it appears that Western concern with the growth of socialist industry is meagre. Only in selected industries has there been much outcry, for instance over alleged dumping by Eastern European producers in Western markets, or objections to the practice whereby Western firms are obliged to receive payment in kind from the plant and equipment sold in socialist countries. An instance of this is the chemicals industry, where European producers have since the late 1970s periodically been aggrieved by shipments of very low priced basic petrochemical products from new Eastern European plants. Similarly, some European auto manufacturers fear that the additional capacity being developed for socialist producers with the help of Fiat and other European firms will lead ultimately to a rise in cheap imports. Although the auto exports of socialist countries to Western Europe have increased very quickly, reaching 150,000 units by 1981, they still account for only 1.5 per cent of the market.

Industrial policies in a changing world

A further area of investigation in recent years has been concerned with the design and execution of public policies as applied to industry. The importance of public policy in shaping industries all over the world has been brought to people's attention for several reasons. First, new-found interest has emerged from the realisation – albeit belated – that there are substantial portions of world industrial capacity, even outside the socialist countries, whose very existence is due to public policy decisions. Trends in industrial organisation have led to a gradual overlapping of activities in the public and private sectors, and to a blurring of the 'public' and 'private' character of a given industrial enterprise. As one observer has noted, 'more than ever, pricing and production decisions are arrived at, not with the help of Adam Smith's invisible hand, but through the interaction of corporate strategists, government planners and managers in the public sector' (Ballance *et al*. 1982, p. 224). The substantial involvement of the state, through holding agencies such as IRI in Italy or industrial development corporations and joint ventures in LDCs, has focused attention on the fact that private firms are a minority in many industries and by no means dictate the shape of the business environment.

Second, as the need to accommodate adjustment pressures has grown, public policy has come to occupy the very centre of a wide-ranging debate, being alternately pictured as a prime cause of many contemporary industrial problems or as a way out of an existing industrial dilemma. In the case of the USA, this field has been depicted as 'a hodgepodge of public policies bearing no direct relation to overall industrial health' (Reich, 1982, p. 874). Failure to co-ordinate American industrial policies is thought to have aggravated the adjustment problem by promoting the mobility of capital but not the utilisation of unemployed labour or under-used infrastructure. In Japan, the Structurally Depressed Industries Law permits explicit subsidies to firms that agree to scrap excess capacity but requires that the funds be used to retrain and relocate workers. Meanwhile, the French Government, inspired by the successful *dirigiste* policies of the Japanese, has declared that 'there are no obsolete industries, only obsolete technologies' (*WSJ*, 29 Mar. 1982). Accordingly, the government there has proclaimed a comprehensive and ambitious new industrial policy with consolidated firms acting as, to use Goran Ohlin's term, 'national champions'. In so doing France is clearly negating Raymond Vernon's forecast of 1974 that henceforth both the style and the substance of European industrial policies would converge (Vernon, 1974, pp. 3–24), although even at the time he acknowledged that France had always tended to pursue an atypical line in such matters.

In the LDCs, too, the question of industrial policy is now high on most agendas. Led by growing realisation of the fact that many LDCs survived the 1973 oil price-rises surprisingly well and maintained relatively satisfactory growth rates (Hallwood and Sinclair, 1981, pp. 162–76), the contribution of deliberate government policies to this success has come under scrutiny. In a survey of 55 LDCs, for instance, W. G. Tyler's work (1981) suggests that explicit policy decisions, particularly where concerned with liberalising countries' trade sectors, contributed strongly to their resilience in the face of oil price shocks. In Tyler's opinion, countries which neglect their export sectors through discriminatory economic policies are likely to have to settle for lower rates of economic growth as a result.

The importance and growing diversity of public policies in the manufacturing sector suggest the need to inquire further into the background to policy-making and the interest groups that formulate, and implement – or, indeed, oppose and obstruct – policies. Much of the theoretical analysis of decision-making processes, particularly in the field of neo-classical microeconomics, has traditionally taken assumptions of maximisation as a starting point. In the perfectly competitive models, there is only one policy open to firms – to maximise profits – otherwise they go out of business immediately. Moreover, since all firms in this paradigm are assumed to be price-takers from the larger market, are unable to extract any super-normal profit, and, in consequence, neither require nor possess any internal decision-making apparatus, there is no question of influencing the market through some type of informal political activity. Yet these assumptions seem somewhat out of place in a world where headlines are claimed by the dilemmas of Chrysler or AEG-Telefunken and their negotiations with the state. An appreciation of this gap between theory and reality prompted Cyert and Hedrick to remark that 'the real world still escapes our models; . . . we wonder whether economics can remain an empirical science and continue to ignore the actual decision-making process of real firms' (1972, p. 409). Given the traditional way of perceiving firm-level (and, by implication, industry-level) decision processes, it is not surprising that the real-world processes of lobbying and organising so as to affect the business environment were largely ignored by economists for a long time. As Gilpin (1975, p. 5) has written in another context, 'economists do not really believe in power; political scientists, for their part, do not really believe in markets'.

Alternative theories of the firm that stress the role of decision-making and admit the possibility of conflicts of interest have only appeared comparatively recently, paralleling the growing interest of political scientists in extra-parliamentary or informal decision-making organisations. Like economists, political scientists tended, until the 1960s, to focus on the more formal aspects of power and decision-making. However, in response to the growing authority and complexity of government intervention, those who tried to influence it also became better organised. Thus, studies of the lobbying phenomenon began to proliferate and 'the theory of representation (was) enlarged to include them' (Blondel, 1979, p. 158).

More recently still, there has been some investigation of the ways in which the size and age of industries can affect their willingness and ability to call for government controls to restrict entry or otherwise inhibit competition. Murrell (1982, p. 990), for example, has suggested that 'rigidities increase with the age of the industry' and that 'heavy industries . . . would be more susceptible to organizational rigidities . . . than light industries'. Insights gained from looking at the nexus between institutional organisation and industrial structure may eventually 'support a theory which may be valuable in promoting our understanding of nations' (p. 994). Given this growing awareness of the influence that interest groups can sometimes wield in shaping industrial policy, then, there is a clear need to assess the nature and extent of their actions.

One final point remains to be made. This book is being written during a fairly prolonged recession. Whereas previous recessions were characterised by a fall in both nominal and real interest rates that spurred the turnaround in inventories and consumer expenditure which typically accompanies the beginning of the upswing, the present recession, in contrast, has been characterised by extremely high interest rates. Not only has this hampered the growth of investment in industry and commerce generally, but it has had exceptionally severe consequences on a number of activities which are particularly interest-rate-sensitive. An implication is that, on top of the usual adjustments which take place during a recession – Schumpeter's gale of creative destruction – a protracted and unusually painful series of changes have occurred simultaneously in these particular industries. Two such industries, automobiles and steel, are investigated later in this book.

The book proceeds by examining, in chapter 2, the evolution of post-war priorities for industrial development in the advanced countries, both Western and socialist, and the LDCs. That discussion focusses on the broad thrust of national policy but, in chapter 3, the policy priorities applied to the manufacturing sector are examined. The early ambitions of planners and politicians in the LDCs to diversify away from economies dominated by agrarian and mining activities are traced, as are the policies adopted in advanced countries. In the latter case, the ambivalence which has always characterised thinking about extensive policy intervention in the manufacturing sector is noted. Chapter 4 then examines structural change in the manufacturing sector and considers various economic determinants of the pattern of development in the manufacturing sector. Manufacturing is contrasted with agriculture and services in these respects. In Chapter 5 there is a detailed analysis of the changes which have occurred since the Second World War in the composition of the manufacturing sector in different blocs of countries. The substantial nature of these changes is charted, and there is an initial discussion of the tensions to which they have sometimes given rise. Chapters 6 and 7 look at several specific industries: automobiles, steel, consumer electronics, advanced electronics and oil refining. That discussion highlights the nature and extent of the problems facing firms in advanced countries primarily. To some extent, however, firms in socialist countries and LDCs are also discussed. Particular attention is paid in these chapters to the way in which industry strategies have been adopted, and the ways in which various interest groups have attempted to shape the options open to each group of firms. Chapter 8 concludes the book with a discussion of three major themes which have emerged from the earlier analysis. These themes are the changing role of the transnational corporation (TNC), the influence of public policy on industrial structure, and the choice of industry strategies open to those involved in the industries covered in Chapters 6 and 7.

Notes

1   Two terms, net manufacturing output and manufacturing value added (MVA), are used interchangeably throughout this book. Both terms generally refer to the gross value of output less inputs such as the cost of materials, fuels, commissioned work done by others, electricity purchased and similar expenditures, where the costs of the inputs are evaluated on a 'received' or 'consumed' basis.
2   The term 'advanced countries' is used throughout this book to refer both to socialist countries, that is the seven Eastern European countries in the Council for Mutual Economic Assistance (CMEA), and to advanced market economies – which are defined to include all members of the Organization for Economic Co-operation and Development (OECD) (except Greece, Turkey and Yugoslavia) and South Africa. Unless otherwise indicated, the data and discussion exclude mainland China.
3   The definition of an 'industry' requires some elaboration. In so far as the discussion in later chapters is couched in terms of the International Standard Industrial Classification (ISIC), the term has a precise definition, being equivalent to each 3-digit designation. For practical purposes, the analysis of several industries (particularly in Chapters 6 and 7) could not be conducted strictly along statistical lines and a more descriptive definition is used.

2

The Industrial Setting after the Second World War

Although the end of the Second World War marked a watershed in the evolution of world industry, many of the basic forces that would later alter the institutional and policy environment had already emerged earlier in the century. By that time, the USA had surpassed the UK as the world's predominant economic and industrial power. For nearly a century the world had followed British leadership on economic and policy questions, but the 1920s and 1930s were years of uncertainty as the global role of that country was eroded while interests in the USA hesitated to exert their new-found influence. Chaos was added to uncertainty by the Great Depression which disrupted long-term patterns of growth and trade and led to drastic changes in macroeconomic policy. Further complications included the break-up of the advanced countries into three political groups: Western democracies, national socialist regimes and communist governments. Thus 1920–45 were years of economic and political instability. The world had passed through an unpleasant period; as a result governments, policy-makers and economists were particularly sensitive to the political implications of economic circumstances.

This chapter sketches the international policy framework that emerged after this period, and examines how this framework has adjusted to changes in the world industrial map. This is necessary for understanding the background against which the advanced countries and, later, the LDCs, pursued a variety of policies related to industrialisation.

The changing pattern of industrial leadership

With the culmination of the Second World War, countries embarked on a process of realignment. Among the advanced countries a form of bi-polar leadership, provided by the USA and the USSR, supplanted the ternary division of the 1930s. Table 2.1 shows the global distribution of manufacturing value added between 1938 and 1980. At the outset of the Second World War the advanced countries dominated the industrial scene. Together, Western and socialist countries accounted for over 95 per cent of world MVA in 1938. The LDCs were, for the most part, observers rather than participants in the industrialisation process, and indeed their share of world MVA changed very little between 1938 and 1953.

The pronounced concentration of manufacturing activity had a profound impact on post-war planning and economic thought. The development prospects of the LDCs received little explicit attention, either in the economic literature or in the policy deliberations of the

Table 2.1   *Estimated shares in world manufacturing value added, by country groupings and sub-groups, selected years*

	1938	1948	1953	1963	1970	1975	1978	1980
Advanced market economies	61.0	72.2	72.0	64.8				
of which:				77.3	73.4	67.5	66.8	65.2
old industrial centre[1]	41.0	58.7	55.2	44.5				
				46.1	39.6	35.7	35.0	33.4
recently-industrialised market economies[2]	13.8	6.5	10.4	14.0				
				22.9	25.8	24.2	24.5	24.3
others	6.2	6.9	6.4	6.2				
				8.3	8.0	7.6	7.3	7.5
Advanced socialist economies	34.5	22.1	23.2	28.5				
				14.6	17.8	22.5	22.9	23.8
LDCs, of which:	4.5	5.7	4.8	6.6				
				8.1	8.8	10.0	10.3	11.0
semi-industrialised countries[3]	3.3	4.0	3.2	4.4				
				5.5	6.0	7.0	7.2	7.7

Source: UNIDO, *Industrial Development Survey*, ninth edition (forthcoming)

Notes: Data for the years 1938–63 are in current prices. Data for the years 1963–78 are at prices of 1975. All data were compiled from national accounts sources for manufacturing value added expressed in US dollars.

1 The industrial centre is defined to include Belgium, France, Luxembourg, the Netherlands, Norway, Sweden, the UK, and the USA.

2 Recently-industrialised market economies are Greece, Ireland, Israel, Italy, Japan, Portugal and West Germany.

3 Semi-industrialised LDCs include Argentina, Brazil, Colombia, Egypt, Hong Kong, India, Malaysia, Mexico, Philippines, Singapore, South Korea, Thailand and Turkey.

advanced countries. Instead, most of the early 'development' literature was concerned with southern Europe. Few, if any, universities
offered courses on economic development and there were only a
handful of works on the subject.

Hindsight, however, shows that relations between the rich and
poor countries had already entered a period of rapid transformation.
The colonisation of Africa and Asia, which had taken over 300 years,
came swiftly to an end. The first wave of decolonisation took place
around 1950 when India, the Dutch East Indies and China asserted
their independence. The process, which was completed in subsequent
waves, did much to change thinking about industrialisation in LDCs,
as well as their relations with advanced countries.

The priorities in the advanced countries

In the years immediately following the Second World War, priorities
in the advanced countries focused on the reconstruction of Europe
rather than the development of Africa, Asia and Latin America.
Western governments took the initiative in creating an international
policy framework that was to shape later patterns of industrial
growth, trade and investment. The role of the 'Eastern block' in
shaping this framework was minimal. In many respects the West's
post-war economic policies were primarily intended to serve political
goals. By proposing an international system that closely linked the
Western economies, American policy-makers hoped to promote a set
of mutual interests that took precedence over national interests. A
compatible set of economic objectives – in today's parlance, an
extended degree of 'economic interdependence' – was expected to
facilitate agreements on foreign policy and defence. Accordingly, a
liberalised system was needed to permit an increasing flow of raw
materials, finished products, capital, labour and technology between
the Western countries. In this way, the self-interest of industrialists,
labourers and financiers in one country would be shared, to some
extent, with their counterparts elsewhere. Eventually, the concept of
interdependence proved to be most applicable to manufacturing processes where international links are more important, rather than in
agriculture or services.

Experience suggests that the impetus for a liberalised system
usually requires a powerful leader or regulator. In other words, the
internationalisation of economic relations will proceed most rapidly if
one nation has a virtual monopoly of power. Among Western countries this precondition was uniquely satisfied by the USA which
emerged from the Second World War as the dominant power in the

spheres of industry, trade and finance. According to Table 2.2, that country accounted for more than 56 per cent of world MVA.

Given its predominant position among Western countries, the American intention to create an integrated international economic system served national self-interests, although foreign policy objectives were the major determinants. The presumed Soviet threat was the overriding concern for fostering the integration of Western countries. The desire to integrate West Germany into European and world markets was another political consideration. Closer economic integration between France and Germany was expected to lessen the chances of renewed conflict. The failure of the post-1918 German arrangements was still fresh in the minds of many, prompting one leading economist (Hoover, 1946, p. 649) to speculate that the German 'economic problem' would persist well into the 1960s.

In the case of Japan, the US approach was somewhat different. There was no intention of re-integrating the Japanese economy with other Asian nations as in Western Europe. Ironically, negotiators originally intended the country to become more dependent on foreign trade. US policy was to provide unilateral trade concessions for Japanese exports of textiles and, later, steel, television sets, cameras, ships and other items. With economic assistance, and behind a military shield provided by the USA, the Japanese were to build a self-sustaining economy.

Table 2.2   *The share of the USA in world manufacturing value added and trade, selected years (percentages)*

Year	Share of world manufacturing value added		Share in world exports	Share in world exports of manufactures (SITC 5 to 8 less 68)
1948	56.7		21.9	—
1953	55.3		18.9	—
1958	34.2		16.4	20.4*
1963	32.6	29.7	14.9	17.3
1970		24.3	13.6	14.9
1975		21.3	12.2	13.9
1979		21.7	10.9	12.2

* SITC 5 to 8

Source: UN, 1963a; UN, *Yearbook of Industrial Statistics*, vol. I, various issues; UN, *Yearbook of International Trade Statistics*, various issues; UN, *Monthly Bulletin of Statistics*, various issues; UNCTAD, 1969; IMF, *International Financial Statistics Yearbook*, various issues; UNIDO, 1981a, and UNIDO, 1982b.

Notes: Value added shares for the period 1948–63 were compiled from data in current prices. Data for the period 1963–79 were based on information at constant prices. All trade shares were compiled from data at current prices.

Policies to foster economic interdependence changed over time but, in general, most were designed to facilitate foreign investment, the transfer of technology, and an international division of labour favouring the growth of productivity. The necessary institutional framework was created with the signing of the Bretton Woods Agreement, which provided for the establishment of the World Bank, the International Monetary Fund (IMF) and an international monetary system. Later, economic interdependence was fostered through more formal arrangements such as the European Economic Community (EEC).

Shortly after the inception of this institutional framework, the pace of industrial growth not only recovered its momentum but exceeded pre-war levels. During the years 1953–75, the West's MVA grew at an annual compound rate of 7.4 per cent. The growth performance of individual countries differed widely; manufacturing output in the recently industrialised countries (see Table 2.1) expanded by 12.7 per cent per annum compared to only 5.9 per cent in those countries which might be termed the industrial centre. This uneven distribution of growth marked the beginning of a long-term decline in the relative importance of the industrial centre, as illustrated by Table 2.1. These trends did not, however, jeopardise the efficacy of a political alignment based on economic interdependence. For the political, social and economic upheavals caused by the war and by decolonisation in the LDCs introduced a new dimension of adaptability in many Western countries, 'thereby providing those who sought change with the means of concrete expression' (Interfutures, 1979, p. 67). Although industrial growth was uneven, it flourished and under these conditions governments had no incentive to disengage themselves from the evolving Western system.

Industrial progress in socialist countries was even faster than that experienced in the West. Manufacturing grew at rates of almost 9 per cent during the 1960s and early 1970s. Moreover, structural changes in socialist countries were extensive; the manufacturing sector's estimated share in GDP rose from 36 per cent in 1960 to 51 per cent in 1975 (UNIDO, 1979, pp. 38 and 44). These developments had little impact on the LDCs, however, since contacts were limited to special relationships with specific countries, including at various times Cuba, Egypt, Ethiopia and Vietnam.

In the West, the encouragement of greater trade between partners was an important adjunct to the emphasis on interdependence. Explicit principles were endorsed when the charter for the General Agreement on Tariffs and Trade (GATT) was signed by twenty-three countries in 1947. These principles included a code of conduct for commercial policy, the practice of non-discrimination between countries, and the intention that trade barriers would be gradually reduced. Eventually, these negotiations, conducted under the auspices of GATT, came to focus on trade in manufactures. Under heavy pressure from farming interests, European negotiators succeeded in removing agricultural issues from much of the discussion. The Rome Treaty in 1958 and the development of a Common Agricultural Policy in 1962 eventually led to a common set of policies on agricultural pricing and marketing practices that, to a large extent, isolated that sector from external competition or pressure. Structural adjustments in agriculture thus became a regional issue rather than an international one. Accordingly, international tariff-reducing negotiations like the Dillon Round in 1961, followed by the Kennedy Round and the Tokyo Round, focused on manufactures; agricultural issues were largely shunted aside because their discussion was likely to be so difficult as to jeopardise the entire negotiation process (Diebold, 1972, ch. 8). The same would be true of other potential subjects such as foreign direct investment and foreign ownership.

The post-war policies of the USA were an important part of this institutional framework. Two initiatives are particularly noteworthy. The first, known as the Marshall Plan, was designed 'to force the European countries to view their separate economies as part of an integrated European whole and to cooperate in the formulation of economic policies' (Krause, 1968, p. 25). Begun in 1948, it was to continue for four years and to provide war-torn Europe with financial resources to rebuild its industrial capacity. In fact, economic assistance was reduced two years later with the outbreak of the Korean War, while military assistance to Europe was increased substantially. Most economists found the results of the programme difficult to evaluate, given its premature curtailment, although they generally regarded it as having a positive impact on European reconstruction.

The second US policy initiative, known as the Reciprocal Trade Agreements Act, has had a much longer life. Its legal foundation was established in 1934 as a means of overcoming the consequences of the Great Depression. The programme was based on fundamental propositions of classical economics. It endorsed the principle that more trade was preferable to less trade and that relatively unhindered trade would stimulate additional trade. The approach also stipulated that all trading countries should be treated equally.

The long-term significance that American policy-makers attached to trade in manufactures was firmly grounded in the experience of the advanced Western economies. For example, the manufactured exports of these countries had grown at a rate of 36 per cent per decade between 1876–80 and 1913 and rose to 48 per cent per decade for 1913–53 (Kravis, 1970, p. 862). Manufactures accounted for one-third of total trade of Western countries in the five-year period 1925–9 but about one-half in the 1950s.

Similarly, the West's emphasis on liberalising its trade by gradually reducing tariffs on manufactures coincided with long-term trends. Estimated tariff rates applied by Western countries to their imports of manufactures are shown in Table 2.3 for the period 1902–62. The only break in the downward trend was in the inter-war year, 1925, when European tariffs rose, but later resumed their decline. Thus, in the case of manufactures the West's tariff-setting practices have long

Table 2.3   *Estimates of nominal tariff levels for manufactures, selected years (percentages)*

	1902	1913	1925	1962
Denmark	18	14	10	—
Japan	9	—	—	16.1
Sweden	23	20	16	6.6
USA	73	44	37	11.5
EEC:				
Belgium	13	9	15	
France	34	20	21	
West Germany	25	13	20	11.0
Italy	27	18	22	
Netherlands	3	4	6	

Source: Little *et al.*, 1970, pp. 162–3.

differed from those observed for agricultural products and the trends occurring after the Second World War were not unique. Trade among Western countries thrived without wide-ranging disputes over access to markets, the security of raw material supplies, trade wars, or the creation of international cartels. As a result, the trading environment became decidedly less restricted than it was, for example, during the inter-war period, when about 42 per cent of world trade was cartelised or subject to similar arrangements, almost all of which concerned manufactures (Balassa, 1978a, p. 429).

Political considerations continued to influence economic policy in later years. The contrasting attitudes of the USA to the formation of the EEC and the European Free Trade Association (EFTA) suggest the extent to which economic policy served political goals. While the former effort at integration was warmly supported by the USA, the latter, which originally included the UK and neutral countries like Austria, Sweden and Switzerland, received little or no American support. As one former State Department official noted at the time, 'the American attitude toward the proposed Outer Seven Free Trade

Area project was explainable by the overriding political importance of the Common Market as a stage in the development of the political unity of the Six, whereas the Free Trade Area was viewed as a purely commercial arrangement' (Frank, 1961, p. 127–8).

The early push to industrialise in the LDCs

During the early part of this period the LDCs were of only marginal economic and political consequence for Western thinking. Among economists, there was a consensus that the economic aspirations of the LDCs could be met by a 'trickle-down' mechanism. The assumption was that, with concomitant institutional and policy adjustments in the LDCs, the rapid growth of the world's advanced countries would spread through international channels like trade, investment and the growth of world demand. This should bring about a corresponding growth in output and income in those LDCs involved in the international economy.

The fact that the LDCs accounted for only five per cent of world MVA in 1953 (see Table 2.1) was not lost on the government officials of the newly independent countries. They associated a large industrial base with economic and political power, control over natural resources and adequate financial capabilities. Rapid industrial growth was regarded as the key to economic prosperity and international influence. Understandably, in many (but not all) LDCs industrialisation became a top development priority. Although advocates provided a variety of supporting arguments for such strategies, the manifest post-war concentration of world industrial capacity in the advanced countries was an overwhelming factor in focusing the LDC's ambitions on industry.

Other explanations for the early emphasis in LDCs on industrialisation can be cited. Rapid growth promised to be a painless means of alleviating the material demands of poverty-stricken majorities and was also a readily palatable approach to the upper classes. If, instead, policy-makers in LDCs had chosen a more drastic course of redistributing existing income and wealth rather than merely redistributing the benefits of growth, the support of the upper classes would have been jeopardised. Given the political fragmentation and instability of many LDCs after decolonisation, their governments' preference for redistributing the benefits of growth was a strong one. This argued in favour of establishing industry, in the hope that it would grow faster than other sectors like agriculture or infrastructure. Carried to its extreme, the development strategies of many LDCs degenerated into an attitude of 'industrialisation or bust'.

The reasons for emphasising industrial growth in the LDCs were different from those of the advanced countries: domestic considerations were far more important than international ones. If anything, the previous experience in the international community reinforced an 'inward orientation'. The legacy of two world wars and a depression had led to a break in long-term trade patterns, so that between 1913 and 1953 the LDCs' exports of manufactures grew at only one-half of the rate recorded in 1876-1913 (Kravis, 1970, p. 862). The American emphasis on the post-war reconstruction of Europe had a similar impact by reducing the LDCs' access to international capital markets. For example, the commitments (disbursed and undisbursed) of the US-funded Export-Import Bank to Latin America totalled about $430 million during the war years. In 1946, however, almost one billion dollars was allocated to European borrowers while Latin America received only $30 million (Fishlow, 1978, p. 33–4).

Due to their tendency to adopt an inward orientation in the immediate post-war period, no international strategy equivalent to the West's approach of interdependence and expanded trade emerged among the LDCs. Thus, the relationships which sprang up in the 1950s were largely at the initiative (however limited) of the West and, as a result, were reminiscent of the earlier colonial approach. Development co-operation was limited to the West's provision of experts. They had little to do with commercial matters such as investment or trade, and served mainly as replacements for former colonial officials. Later, the provision of experts came to be supplemented by project assistance and financial aid, so that, by 1960, the value of aid transfers was about 0.5 per cent of the GNP of advanced Western countries. In later years, it fell to 0.3 per cent and has remained at roughly that level.

Links between the LDCs and the socialist countries were even more tenuous. Aid disbursed by the latter was equivalent to only 0.03 per cent of the GNP of socialist countries and was roughly one-tenth the level provided by Western countries (Interfutures, 1979, p. 84). Trade links between the two groups were similarly limited. In 1979, only 2 per cent of the manufactures exported by LDCs went to socialist countries. Conversely, the LDCs were marginal markets for the manufactures exported by producers in socialist countries, accounting for 16 per cent of this trade flow (UNIDO, 1982a, p. 10).

In the immediate post-war period, the governments of many LDCs shared a variety of economic and political goals. Economically, their position relative to the advanced countries gave them certain common perspectives. Politically, their rejection of colonialism and their wish for independence gave rise to a feeling of solidarity on certain issues. Similarly, the desire to stay free of the Cold War conflict added further impetus to what became a non-aligned group. Originally composed of 77 countries (now 122), the non-aligned movement came to serve as the political body through which the LDCs negotiated with the advanced countries. This arrangement assumed that there was sufficient common interests among the LDCs to enable them to arrive at common positions through internal negotiation. The 'Group of 77' addressed a range of issues; they not only pressed for increased foreign aid to be delivered on more generous terms, but they also called for an improvement in the conditions under which they traded with advanced economies. At first, negotiations focused on the prices of raw materials exported by various LDCs and the manufactures that they imported. Later, the debate centred on issues of improved market access, notably the relaxation of the import restraints imposed by advanced countries on their exports, including manufactures.

The appeals for more generous treatment met only a limited response. The American view came to be symbolised by the slogan 'trade, not aid', taken from a foreign policy study which argued that, through tariff reductions and increased trade, the costly burden of foreign aid could be reduced. However, there were reasons why the 'trade not aid' solution proved unsatisfactory to industrialists in the LDCs. For instance, the West's preoccupation with Cold War considerations led policy-makers to encourage intra-West trade. This worked to the detriment of the LDCs, undercutting their hopes of expanding exports to advanced countries. Negotiators were interested primarily in reducing those tariffs that hampered their own exporters' efforts in important foreign markets which, overwhelmingly, were those of other Western countries. Moreover, when countries did agree to reduce trade barriers, this was usually in response to some *quid pro quo* from the negotiating partner and the LDCs had very little to offer in this respect.

Unlike the advanced countries, the post-war trading patterns of many LDCs diverged from their pre-war experiences. Throughout the period 1876—1953, the growth of manufactured exports from LDCs had exceeded corresponding gains in the West, but the reverse was true for 1953–66 (Kravis, 1970, p. 862). Thus, the share of the LDCs in world trade in manufactures declined slightly in later years. This result was not only due to an inability to influence trade negotiations. Domestic policies in certain LDCs were also relevant (see Chapter 3) and both factors led to a break in the long-term pattern. Under these circumstances, the West's desire to reduce its foreign aid burden by expanding trade with the LDCs did not suit the policies of either group.

To conclude, this account of the post-war period has stressed the extent to which political goals, in both the advanced countries and the LDCs, shaped industrial strategies and, thus, the global pattern of world production, trade and investment. That picture, however, is neither as complete nor as simple as the foregoing discussion might imply. Causation is not just a one-way affair where political considerations will influence economic realities. Basic changes in the configuration of world industry also circumscribe policy-makers' alternatives and, eventually, alter national and supranational political goals. The following section considers some consequences of these changes for the formulation of international policy and industrial strategies.

Industrial growth and policy consequences

A number of changes, in both the economic structure of countries and in the institutional framework, whose evolution has just been summarised, have become apparent in recent years. Later in this book some of the consequences of these changes will be explored at length. For the present, however, an overview will suffice. Table 2.1 documents various trends which were already apparent in the 1950s and continued during the 1970s. The recently industrialised countries gained steadily. The relative importance of the industrial centre was eroded. As countries like Italy, Japan and West Germany rose in international stature, they acquired greater influence in discussions over industrial production, investment and finance, trade, technology and employment policy. Conversely, the ability of other countries to influence or sway international industrial policy waned as their shares in world MVA declined. The erosion of the industrial leadership of the USA in the non-communist world is shown in Table 2.2. Although the country's decline is exaggerated somewhat by the depreciation of the US dollar during the 1970s, the downward trend was pronounced.

One consequence of waning American leadership in the industrial field is that international policy must now be fashioned from a consensus between several coalitions including, at times, the EEC, Japan, the Scandinavian countries and the socialist bloc, as well as the USA. With this rise in the number of large and relatively equal industrial powers, a collegial pattern of management has evolved. A corollary is that the degree of divisiveness between western countries has increased. Although relations between the USA and the USSR remain an overriding issue, economic differences between Western countries have increased. As later chapters will show, these often pit the interests of producers or other groups in the USA against their counterparts in the EEC, or in other smaller countries.

A trend towards greater decentralisation of power and policy-making influence can also be noted among socialist countries. Various governments have increasingly asserted their independence from the USSR. This is obvious in the different ways that governments choose to manage their economies and in the growing number of confrontations on issues of trade, finance, energy and technology.

In the face of such fundamental changes, most governments have become tentative in their approach to industrial issues of international scope. Their attitude may be partially attributed to inexperience in the present collegial system; however, there are other equally important reasons for the change in Western attitudes. First, greater economic interdependence has enlarged the influence of external forces on a country's industrialisation process. The increasing magnitude of foreign demand relative to domestic demand is one direct consequence of the steady expansion of trade in manufactures which has served to reduce the effectiveness of national macroeconomic policies. As a result, policy-makers are faced with a new element of uncertainty – due to international conditions beyond their control – and have often responded by attempting to shield or isolate their industrial sector from international developments. Efforts to do this for particular industries are documented later in this book.

Second, the pace of post-war growth (in manufacturing and other sectors) had, by the 1970s, significantly altered basic patterns of economic activity in advanced economies. The manufacturing sector's importance as a producer of income, as a provider of employment, as a supplier of exports and as a recipient of capital, had changed significantly. New patterns of economic activity created new types of problems which the West's post-war approaches did not anticipate. The simultaneous occurrence of stagnation and inflation, now dubbed 'stagflation', is one instance; unexpected difficulties due to employment rigidities and labour immobilities are another example. Thus, governments began to re-evaluate their international and domestic priorities for manufacturing in the light of new economic circumstances.

Finally, the slowdown in industrial growth during the 1970s led governments to question the desirability of greater interdependence. When economic growth was a general phenomenon shared by most countries (albeit at widely disparate rates) the costs of increased interdependence were minimal. As the pace of growth slackened, however, interdependence revealed competitive or negative side effects as well as offering positive benefits. The widening range of trade disputes and the spread of public assistance schemes for declining industries are only two examples of ways in which governments have responded to the pressure of foreign competition during the transition from fast to slow growth in the 1970s. All of this suggests that recent years have been a transitional period for industry and industrial policy in most advanced countries.

Turning to the LDCs, different patterns of industrial and political development have led to other types of policy considerations. The period since 1960 may be conveniently divided into two time periods, 1960–8 and 1969–80. The first was one of rapid industrial growth throughout the world, with the growth performance of the LDCs roughly matching that of the advanced countries. After 1968, the LDCs recorded steady, although minor, gains. This trend was partly due to the fact that the LDCs' rates of growth were somewhat more stable than those of the advanced countries – particularly the Western economies where manufacturing output showed an absolute fall in 1974–5. However, these limited gains did little in the way of contributing to a more equitable distribution of industrial activity between advanced countries and the LDCs. In 1960, for example, the LDCs accounted for 57 per cent of world population while they produced only 8 per cent of world MVA. By 1980, their corresponding shares of world population and MVA were 65 per cent and 10 per cent, respectively (UNIDO, 1981a, p. 2). Indeed, demographic gains were, themselves, one probable cause for the LDCs' modest industrial strides. Clearly, such marginal progress was ineffectual in reducing the industrial gap between the two sets of countries.

At least one characteristic of the industrialisation process – the uneven distribution of capacity – was, however, shared by both the LDCs and the advanced countries. This fact is suggested by the data in Table 2.1 which shows that a subgroup of LDCs – the newly industrialising countries (NICs), numbering only 13 – accounted for over 75 per cent of the LDCs' share of the world MVA in 1975. Similarly, data concerning some of the world's poorest countries – the UN category of 31 countries known as the 'least developed' – show another aspect of this divergence. For example, the latter subgroup's contribution to manufacturing activity has steadily declined since the 1960s and amounted to only 1.8 per cent of all the LDCs' MVA in 1980 (UNIDO, 1982a). *Per capita* indicators of manufacturing activity in the poorer LDCs changed very little during these years despite an increase in the corresponding averages of all LDCs. Although the rhetoric of many international fora tended to focus on the gap between the advanced countries and the LDCs, a second gap, which divided the richer LDCs from the poorer ones, was thus emerging over time.

By the 1970s various trends among the LDCs had accentuated the economic diversity between countries and threatened to undermine the unity of the non-aligned movement. Different sets of countries found that they had conflicting economic interests. For instance, members of the Organisation of Petroleum Exporting Countries (OPEC) benefited from high oil prices while the LDCs that imported oil naturally sought to restrain prices; the economic interests of several of the NICs were best served by limiting the prices of raw materials although the exporters of these materials – in other LDCs – hoped for higher commodity prices. Some of the poorer LDCs with heavy debts argued that their obligations should be written off but those that financed debts commercially opposed this idea, fearing that it would jeopardise their future credit worthiness. Finally, the composition of output in the manufacturing sector in the LDCs grew more dissimilar (UNIDO, 1979, p. 71), meaning that industrialists in various countries faced distinctly different sets of problems.

Political divisions and regional affiliations followed from this economic diversity. A subgroup of socialist LDCs (Afghanistan, Angola, Cuba, Kampuchea, Laos, Mozambique and Vietnam) advocated economic policies that were substantially different from those of the non-socialist LDCs. The Lomé Convention linking the EEC with some African, Caribbean and Pacific (ACP) countries and the Association of South East Asian Nations (ASEAN) are other groups with objectives that are not always in conformity with those of the LDCs as a whole. This growing economic and political divergence led one economist to remark that 'outside the diplomatic conveniences of international agencies and other aid donors, there is a real sense in which the Third World no longer exists. Its more advanced members have a good deal less in common with most African states than with the industrialised North' (Killick, 1980, p. 369).

Despite its relatively modest contribution to growth, the development of industry was instrumental in redefining the self-interest of many LDCs. The creation of a modest industrial base in Latin American and East Asian countries provided them with the opportunity to begin exporting manufactures but, at the same time, pitted their interest against countries that continued to specialise in commodity exports. Industrial growth in the advanced countries did much to create the necessary pre-conditions for OPEC's success, while industry's large capital requirements contributed to the division of opinion on financial issues. Finally, trade in manufactures and in the raw materials destined for industry thrived when growth was rapid in the advanced countries and proved to be instrumental in shaping the various regional and political alignments of the subgroups that were later to become formalised.

The post-war industrial experiences of many LDCs had an impact on development theory, industrial policy and international politics. The earlier consensus on the importance of growth through industrialisation was refuted by the disappointing results obtained in a large number of LDCs. Industrial growth, even when it did occur, was often short-lived and was not necessarily any assurance of greater internal political stability. Moreover, general theories of development that purported to fit all LDCs were largely swept aside with the growing recognition of the increasing disparities between these countries.

Having examined how changes in the world industrial map have been reflected in the formulation of international policies in this field, the following chapter looks at these issues in more depth, examining ways in which policies designed to shape industry were conceived and implemented.

3

The Evolution of Industrial Policies – A Sectoral Discussion

The discussion in Chapter 2 stressed the fact that the industrial policy mix adopted in most advanced countries differed from that in LDCs for ideological reasons as well as economic ones. In socialist countries the free market philosophy tended to be rejected. An extensive planning system was created with priority given to the development of heavy industry. The approach of Western countries was more ambiguous; they strongly endorsed market principles as a basis for allocation processes, and seldom advocated any set of industrial policies that entailed a systematic pattern of market intervention. In a practical sense, however, the political objectives discussed in Chapter 2 influenced the policy decisions of Western governments and tempered the role of market forces. In the LDCs, policy choices began from the explicit assumption that market dicta were an inferior means of arriving at decisions on such issues as investment, trade and technological development. The market was thought to be a poor guide for these decisions because it led to avoidable miscalculations and ignored the impact of externalities. The danger of relying on market mechanisms was highlighted by numerous writers (W. A. Lewis, 1951, ch. 1; Scitovsky, 1954; Rosenstein-Rodan, 1961; Griffin and Enos, 1970).

In the West, continued growth was accompanied by a growing range of conflicts between the two major institutions for the distribution of goods and services – the market and the Welfare State (Interfutures, 1979, p. 188). Three aspects of the state's enlarged role emerged as important determinants of the ability of Western countries to adjust to change: 'regulatory policies, increased public expenditure and *government participation in industrial activities*', (p. 171; my italics). Among the LDCs, the already extensive role of market intervention was thought to create a 'vicious circle'. As Krueger (1974, p. 302) has argued, the growing practice of rent-seeking (corruption and bribery as well as more acceptable forms) confirmed the impression that the market mechanism was not compatible with socially approved goals. This re-enforced the tendency to intervene and led to new attempts to extract rents.

In general, the years 1950–83 were characterised by a slow drift away from the market as an institutional mechanism for the allocation of goods and services. Furthermore, this tendency was closely related to the industrial experiences of the advanced countries and the LDCs during this period. This chapter begins with an overview of the broad trends in the industrial progress and policies of the advanced countries and then provides a similar examination for the LDCs.

The drift of Western policy

Given their underlying political motives, it is not surprising that the major policy initiatives of Western countries had an international orientation. Thus, fields like trade, investment and finance were the dominant concern of Western economic policy. Industrial matters – and particularly those having a purely domestic impact – were not among the salient issues of the day. Because the industrial field was overshadowed by other aspects that were thought to have a more immediate political impact, no clearly defined strategies for the manufacturing sector emerged. Instead, policies were fashioned in a pragmatic manner, originally as part of more wide-ranging programmes designed to serve other objectives or, more recently, in response to mounting pressures for adjustment.

The Marshall Plan was the first of these international programmes. Although its main purpose was to rebuild industrial capacity destroyed in the war, its motive was also political – to restore European production capabilities as quickly as possible as a means of discouraging a strong communist presence in those countries. Similar desires gave rise to new organisational alignments and fora for co-operation, notably the Organization for Economic Co-operation and Development (OECD), the EEC and, in the socialist countries, the Council for Mutual Economic Assistance (CMEA).

The institutional initiatives that were concluded with the Bretton Woods Agreement reflected the same pragmatic approach. Significantly, many of the economists' proposals made at Bretton Woods were never fully implemented. Keynes, for example, appealed for the creation of an international trade organisation to stabilise commodity prices, the establishment of a world central bank and a big world development authority. The first of these, the International Trade Organisation, was never implemented owing to disagreement over the extent of its regulatory powers, while the IMF only partially fulfils the second intention. Similarly, the World Bank has a much smaller mandate than Keynes intended. Significantly, it was originally known as the International Bank for Reconstruction and Development (IBRD), a title which reflected the institution's early emphasis on the reconstruction and development of war-torn Europe.

Although these institutional arrangements fell short of the world economic order which some advocates had hoped for, they were to have a significant impact on the way Western policy was handled. A two-track system evolved which distinguished between 'high foreign policy' and 'low foreign policy' (Cooper, 1973, p. 46). The former set of issues concerned national security, transatlantic relations and similar matters, while problems of foreign trade, investment, monetary and financial relations and the international consequences of national policy decisions were relegated to the lower track and tended not to impinge on high policy. The agreements and institutions governing economic relations between western countries, such as the Bretton Woods Agreement, GATT, the IMF and the IBRD, provided the framework that was essential for most economic issues to be resolved in this fashion. Economic matters were not completely depoliticised but generally did not intrude into the realm of higher policy. However as the discussion in Chapter 2 has indicated, high policy did intrude, often in important ways, on lower-track decisions.

The new legitimacy of state intervention

Initially, then, policy-makers had little interest in fashioning any overall strategy for the manufacturing sector. The policies that were initiated were part of a much grander plan where developments in the fields of trade, investment and finance were to serve political ends. This ambivalence towards industrial policy was nothing new, however. As Kemp (1978, p. 90) has noted, 'even in the late developing countries such as Germany, Italy or even Russia, it is difficult to argue that industrialization followed a deliberate course mapped out by the state'. For the most part, there were very few national agencies charged with that responsibility and that fact, in turn, reflected the lack of a well articulated case for bringing such agencies into existence.

The distinction between high and low policy began to erode in the mid-1960s. From the American side, major sources of friction were the Common Agricultural Policy (CAP) and other preferential trading relations established by the EEC and the import restraints imposed by the Japanese. The coalition of American interests that supported free trade broke down as the erosion of international trading rules became apparent. In Europe, dissatisfaction centred mainly on monetary issues. Many were concerned that, under the dollar standard, the US government and American banks were producing too many dollars. By the early 1960s dollar loans were being used widely in international markets, and US firms were using these funds to enlarge their share of European industries. American policymakers, albeit for different reasons, gradually became uneasy at the prospect that Europeans might create a distinct currency zone of their own. At the same time, a large segment of the American public was persuaded, perhaps belatedly, that the external value of the dollar had a great deal to do with their internal well-being (Vernon, 1981, p. 20). These considerations thrust the issue of the international value of the dollar into the realm of high policy, culminating in the abandonment of the link between the dollar and gold in 1971 and the subsequent devaluations. Thus the division between high policy and low policy was breached in several fields. The real danger of this breakdown was clearly set out by Cooper when he noted that once 'the rules break down or cease to be regarded as fair, they cannot be used effectively by governments to block particularistic pressures within their own countries' (1973, p. 55).

The discussion in Chapter 2 stressed the fact that, in the period 1950–73, Western countries enjoyed rates of growth that significantly exceeded the levels achieved during the previous fifty years. Concomitants of this new-found prosperity included educational advances, improvements in standards of health, a relaxation of tangible external threats and a variety of changes in the economic, social and cultural values of Western countries. A description of the political and sociological effects of economic growth are beyond the scope of this book. However, they are relevant to the ways in which industrial policies are formulated and priorities are set. The most notable effects in this field are the emergence of a favourable attitude towards ecological movements such as those emphasising pollution control, a new emphasis on the non-monetary aspects of life and a growing scepticism about the benefits of technological advances.

These shifts in opinion were only part of a more general drift towards greater public acceptance of the legitimacy of state intervention. Western governments had several choices available to them when responding to this shift in public opinion, including direct intervention such as regulatory action, or increased public spending, direct participation in industrial activities, or, alternatively, a decentralised form of intervention by 'sending out the suitable signals to the market'. As the ideological backdrop changed, so too did the willingness of hitherto sceptical governments to adopt rather more *dirigiste* policies towards industry. Indeed, across a wide range of issues, one of the most notable characteristics of post-war development in the advanced countries has been greater public intervention.

A new breed of policy-makers

The growing involvement of the state naturally created correspondingly greater scope for influencing decisions. There were simply more decisions to influence. This process of influencing policy has, perhaps, gone furthest in the USA where the proliferation of lobbies, notably in and around Washington, has proceeded unchecked for many years. Once Americans came to accept an enlarged mission for government, various interest groups actually found the traditional dispersion of authority much to their liking. 'While the whole of government was certainly impervious to control by any group, the many separate parts proved to be uniquely susceptible to special-interest pressures' (Ladd, 1980, p. 66). The growth of what one writer has referred to as 'this fourth branch of government' is reflected by the fact that the number of lobbying groups, is said to have grown from 600 in 1974 to almost 2,000 in 1980 while their 'contributions' to members of Congress rose from $13 million to $60 million (*IHT*, 5 Apr. 1982).

In view of the considerable influence which such unofficial groups appear to wield, it is surprising to find that only recently have they been subject to much academic scrutiny. Among the earliest contributors to the field was Olson (1965), who pointed out that eventually the growth of lobbying activity was likely to lead to substantial, although virtually unquantifiable, welfare losses for the economy. More recently, the same author has also proposed that at least a part of the observed slowdown in American productivity growth, a phenomenon by no means explained even by the most careful econometric work, may be due to this extra institutional baggage which the economy is carrying. The basis for his argument is that the members of associations or collusions formed to affect resource allocation may gain very little from efforts to make their societies more efficient. However, the groups 'do gain from obtaining a larger share of the social output for their members, even if the social loss from the redistribution is a substantial multiple of the amount distributed to them' (Olson, 1982, p. 145).

Others have attempted to locate the causes of this growth in non-official influence over decision-making in more strictly economic factors, rather than in political or sociological trends. The growing importance of international trade in the US economy (in 1980 and

1981 it accounted for some 15 per cent of GNP, or double the level prevailing in 1970) is a significant factor. For government policies in that area can have a major impact upon the volume and pattern of imports and exports, such as through amendments to quotas and other import restrictions or through changes in subsidies offered to exporters by agencies such as the export-import bank. A recent illustration of the stimulus which growing international trade flows have had upon lobbying comes from the US machine tool industry. In 1982 the machine tool producers, through the Electronic Industries Association, were pressing the Reagan administration to deny investment tax credits (worth around 15 per cent off the price of new tools) to those buying Japanese equipment. Arguing simply that net import penetration of numerically-controlled machines had risen from 3.7 per cent in 1976 to 50.1 per cent in the first three quarters of 1981, the US interest group was concerned to alleviate its members' poor order-book outlook (*Financial Times*, Apr. 1982). Since the manipulation of tax credits so as to discriminate between sources of supply is contrary to the spirit of all the multilateral provisions of the GATT, the request could not, however, be accepted.

Another instance is that of the larger steel users in Britain, who banded together during 1981 and 1982 to combat the effects of the increasingly close relationship developing between steel producers and the European Commission. As the Commission pushed up steel prices in Europe as part of its rescue plan, producers of auto components, office furniture and structural steelworks, among others, objected through their British Iron and Steel Consumers Council (BRISCC). Although Viscount Davignon, the European Industry Commissioner, gave assurances that steel consumers would, after 1983, receive more priority than they had hitherto, BRISCC were unsatisfied. In a position paper they argued that, 'before there are any more steel price increases, users need time to rebuild their profit margins' (*The Times*, 8 Sept. 1982).

The Japanese experience has been rather different, chiefly since the *ad hoc*, indeed almost chaotic, bargaining which takes place between government, industry and myriad special interest groups is more formalised and works towards widely accepted objectives. As Allen (1981, pp. 72–3), a long-time observer of Japan, has put it,

In Britain (and in some other western countries) government intervention in the last century or so usually occurred as part of an effort to redress the deficiencies of the market economy. In general, the interests and purposes of government and of private enterprise were different. Politicians and civil servants occupied different camps from the industrialists. The latter might call on the government at times to defend their interests, but in general they regarded government as a power that curbed and frustrated their activities. In Japan this dichotomy was absent from the beginning of the modern era. Indeed, it was alien to the Confucian tradition, inherited from times long past . . . in general, and certainly since the war, policy-making has been regarded as a combined operation in which both government and industry were aiming at the same target – rapid industrial growth.

This approach appears to have been successful in helping to bring about the agreed objectives – in circumstances both of running down old industries and of nurturing new ones. In 1978, for instance, the responsible agency, MITI (the Ministry of Trade and Industry) sponsored a law to rationalise four industries with chronic excess capacity. One result was that the shipbuilding industry's capacity and employment were more than halved (Heathcoat Amory, 1981). Chapter 6 describes how MITI sponsored the development of a Japanese automobile industry. In automobiles and other industries, MITI typically selects a number of existing firms to be future growth poles. Performance is carefully monitored. Technologies are devised or bought in under the auspices of MITI. In drawing an analogy with US policy, particularly with reference to the aircraft industry, Newhouse (1982) has noted that a government agency, like the Department of Commerce, would have to put together a coalition of Boeing, McDonnell Douglas, Lockheed, General Electric and Pratt and Whitney, to develop airframes and engines. Moreover, the agency would already be knowledgeable about the aircraft business and would have acquired a sense of the opportunities. Such an approach is simply not encountered in the USA.

What is important, however, is that MITI and its ancillary agencies are part of a wider social and economic fabric. Such an organisation would be unlikely, if replicated elsewhere, to be successful unless it was firmly rooted in a culture where competing claims on the proceeds of economic growth are resolved. Japanese politicians provide bureaucrats with the freedom to rule by holding off special-interest claimants who might deflect the state from its main development priorities (C. Johnson, 1982).

Industrial policies in socialist countries – an overview

In socialist countries, decisions regarding industrial policies take place in an entirely different environment from that in the West and cannot be exhaustively explored here. It is, nevertheless, helpful to note several of the major characteristics in the approaches of socialist countries (mainly the USSR) for purposes of comparison with other blocs of countries. First, ever since Lenin wrote the first 'draft plan for scientific and technical work', the role of science has been unchallenged. A top priority has been to train technocrats and to provide them with ample support to fulfil Lenin's goal. Second, like Japan and West Germany, the USSR adopted a technology policy to 'import and adapt' after the Second World War. In doing so the country eschewed a weakness of Western countries that often led to the pursuit of technological novelties. In accordance with communist principles, foreign technologies were usually enlarged in order to benefit from economies of scale and, as in other policy areas, heavy industry received the highest priority. Finally, within heavy industry a pragmatic approach has been applied in determining the precise fields – energy, steel, materials science or aerospace – for scientific endeavour.

In several cases, the choices reflected economic conditions in the USSR or the political considerations of that country. For instance, geography dictates that three-quarters of the country's energy output is consumed in the European part of the USSR where only a fifth of its energy is produced. Thus, energy receives a high priority in industrial planning and the country is among the world's technological leaders in the fields of high-voltage transmission, thermonuclear fusion and fast-breeder technology. Despite the pragmatic nature of its programme, the USSR has devoted a large and increasing share of its national income to spending on R & D – approximately 3.4 per cent in 1980 compared with 1.6 per cent in 1960. The Russian Academy of Sciences oversees the entire programme and is answerable only to the Kremlin, while the State Committee of Science and Technology works closely with the Academy to co-ordinate the research of academic and sectoral institutes.

Socialist countries have not managed to avoid the effects of the worldwide slowdown and this has given rise to a number of reforms. In the case of industry, socialist planners are experimenting with 'normless teams' of workers who are paid on a piecework bonus basis. This approach, which is an attempt to raise productivity, faces the opposition of a powerful lobby which argues that larger-scale industrial complexes – with egalitarian principles of payment – are the appropriate way to raise productivity. The emphasis on larger-scale industrial complexes has also given rise to other problems for planners. Examples are the Russian Kama truck complex and the Atommash engineering works where serious bottlenecks in the construction, managerial and production phases have resulted from the large size of the projects. Probably, the productivity of capital has declined despite the large share of income channelled into R & D. For instance, the investment needed to achieve an increase of one tonne in the output of oil is thought to have risen 800 per cent in the 1981–5 Soviet Plan compared with the previous one (*The Economist*, 20 May 1982). In general, after 1978 actual rates of industrial growth have fallen short of the planned rates in most socialist countries – Bulgaria, Czechoslovakia, East Germany, Hungary, Poland and the USSR (ECE, 1981, p. 73–4).

As the followng discussion will show, the industrial policies of the LDCs have evolved along entirely different lines from those observed in the advanced countries in the socialist and Western blocs.

Import substitution in the LDCs: objectives and realities

In addition to other distinctions between the advanced countries and the LDCs, differences in ideology led policy-makers to adopt various approaches in the case of the manufacturing sector. European economies had a long tradition of government intervention, including cartelisation, and many were prone to tackle their problems in terms of specific industries rather than taking a sector-wide approach. The American preoccupation with issues such as anti-trust law had a similar effect, while Japanese planners took a piecemeal approach, focusing first on the development of industries like textiles, steel and consumer electronics, and only later on automobiles and advanced electronic machinery. This line of thinking contrasts somewhat with the approach in LDCs where the attention of policy-makers was often centred on sector-wide issues such as the proper balance between industry and agriculture, balanced versus unbalanced growth or development in labour surplus conditions. As argued in Chapter 2, most governments of LDCs sought to industrialise for political as well as economic reasons and, given this orientation, a sector-wide approach to policy decisions was common.

In its simplest form, import substitution refers to the domestic production of goods that were previously imported. The observed pattern of imports provides a guide to planners in identifying activities where the scope of manufacturing sector can be expanded. Accordingly, the precise industries chosen in this manner will be a function of the country's process of domestic demand. Parallel to this policy exercise, a 'natural' process of import substitution occurs as any growing economy expands and diversifies; new industries are developed to supply domestic needs that were previously met through imports. A conscious effort to foster import substitution, however, calls for policy measures to accelerate the natural replacement process. Tariffs are the traditional form of policy measure that governments employ in order to hasten the natural process of import substitution. Their imposition has the effect of protecting domestic industry from foreign competition by making imports more expensive. Other policies with similar effects include import licenses, import quotas, advanced deposits on imports, outright prohibition of certain imports and complex multiple rate categories for foreign exchange. In this way, policy-makers in LDCs have attempted to alleviate the pressure of foreign competition and to encourage domestic production of the newly protected products.

Although exceptions can be noted, most advocates conceded that import substitution should begin with the domestic production of consumer goods. Over the longer term, the approach was pictured as a sequential process working its way from light consumer goods into the production of intermediate products and industrial supplies and culminating in the domestic production of capital goods. Thus, protective measures were expected to favour different types of industries during different phases in the development process. Producers of consumer goods would be the first to receive encouragement through tariffs and other protective measures. Later, other types of industries would become the major beneficiaries of these policies, according to the sequential process implied by this line of reasoning.

Before examining import substitution policies in practice, the reader should be forewarned that this description leaves several questions open. First, uncertainties arise when economists compare actual results with some hypothetical notion of 'optimal' substitution. For example, if the policies to encourage import substitution (tariffs or quotas) result in a substantial misallocation of the country's resources, the difference between the pattern of resource allocation with actual policies and another, more optimal, combination of policies could be great. This gap may prevail in the initial year of the evaluation, or in the terminal year, or both. An arbitary decision is required as to which combination of actual and/or optimal measures is to be used in each period and the results of evaluation will be altered accordingly (Fane, 1973).

Second, questions of a purely statistical nature may introduce ambiguities. A direct means of measuring import substitution is by comparing the ratio of imports to total supplies at two points in time (Desai, 1969, p. 318). An alternative, or indirect, approach is to identify the additional domestic output that results exclusively from a change in the ratio of imports to total supply after accounting for other sources of growth (Chenery, 1960). When directly observable ratios of imports to total supplies are used, the results differ from indirect measures that employ a hypothetical norm (for example, the growth in output with no change in the import/supply ratio) in the comparison.

Finally, the direction of causation between import substitution and growth is not clearly discernible. Some economists have regarded import substitution as a cause of growth. Others, however, have concluded that the import content of total supplies will decline as industrialisation progresses. The latter interpretation implies that substitution is a consequence of growth and that measurement confuses natural import substitution with the conscious efforts of policy-makers. It is sufficient here simply to note that the measurement and interpretation of import substitution poses many difficult questions not all of which can be answered given present knowledge of the process.

As noted in Chapter 2, the appeal of import substitution was largely a result of the experiences of LDCs during the period 1913–50. By reducing their dependence on outside suppliers, they hoped to mitigate the effects of subsequent disruption. Furthermore, given the tenuous position of many regimes in the post-war era, a desire to maintain existing levels of income in the country was paramount. New industries in the LDCs had flourished during the war by supplying both domestic and foreign consumers with goods that had previously been provided by Western industries. Afterwards, traditional suppliers re-emerged and the consequent growth of imports into LDCs threatened to destroy many of the newly-founded industries. Import substitution was thought to be the quickest way of simultaneously stemming this flow while satisfying the related political and economic objectives.

In practice, import substitution did not conform to the sequential pattern implied by theorists. To be sure, producers of consumer goods were usually the first to benefit. However, the extent of protection granted to consumer goods (indicated by the *ad valorem* value or the 'height' of the tariff) was not always reduced once the industrial base broadened. Favoured producers continued to enjoy more generous levels of protection than those provided to other industries producing industrial supplies and capital goods. This pattern of tariff setting had several undesirable consequences. First, because protective policies entail a bias in favour of the recipient industries, the producers of consumer goods retained a privileged position for a much longer period than was originally anticipated. The relative bias in favour of these firms was reduced but not eliminated as additional protection was granted to producers of industrial supplies and capital goods. Second, the governments' widespread use of protective measures throughout manufacturing discriminated in favour of that sector relative to agriculture. The domestic terms of trade linking the two sectors was altered to the detriment of agriculture while the profits

THE EVOLUTION OF INDUSTRIAL POLICIES 39

earned in manufacturing were sometimes excessive (Little *et al.* 1970, ch. 2 and 3). Finally, protection resulted in a 'home market bias' because domestic prices (and, hence, profits) were maintained at artificially high levels while exports were sold at internationally competitive prices (Corden, 1974, pp. 24–8).

Table 3.1 shows prevailing levels of protection for the EEC and several Latin American countries in 1962. The estimates take account of special import surcharges, multiple exchange rates and advance deposits required for imports as well as tariffs. A comparison between the two groups of countries confirms the results of the tariff-setting practices that were common to the LDCs during the late 1950s and 1960s. For example, irrespective of the product category considered, the rates levied by Latin American countries were generally much greater than those applied to the imports of the EEC. Differences between the various product categories were largest for consumer goods; average rates of protection in the EEC were typically less than 10 per cent of those estimated for Latin American countries. In contrast, the EEC rates on intermediate products (including

Table 3.1 *The pattern of protection in selected Latin American countries and the EEC, 1962 (percentages)*

Import category	Argentina	Brazil	Chile	Colombia	Mexico	EEC
Nonprocessed foodstuffs (13 products)	123	264	46	185	65	21
Durable consumer goods (11 products)	266	328	90	108	147	19
Current consumer manufactures (31 products)	176	260	328	247	114	17
Consumer goods, average (55 products)	181	275	214	205	109	18
Industrial raw materials (10 products)	55	106	111	57	38	1
Semimanufactures, including fuels (32 products)	95	30	98	28	28	7
Capital goods (28 products)	98	84	45	18	14	13
Intermediate products, average (70 products)	90	85	79	28	24	9
Overall average, consumer goods and intermediate products (125 products)	131	169	138	106	61	13

Source: UN, 1964, p. 75

capital goods) were generally much closer to the Latin American levels.

These results are indicative of the general pattern in those LDCs that continued their efforts to replace imports over an extended period of time. In Pakistan, for example, consumer goods were much more heavily protected than other manufactures. Curiously, textiles secured the most generous protection, although Pakistan might have been expected to enjoy a comparative advantage in that industry. On average, over two-thirds of value added by industry was 'due to' protection in various forms (Lewis and Guisinger, 1968, p. 1191). Other studies uncovered similar evidence for Egypt (Mabro and Radwan, 1976, pp. 56–7) and the Philippines (Little et al., 1970, p. 174). The same pattern was found in advanced western countries including Japan, Sweden, the UK and the USA (Balassa, 1968, p. 601). However, because rates of protection in LDCs were generally much higher than those in advanced countries, the distorting effects were greater and contributed to overinvestment in consumer goods as well as to excessive profits (Soligo and Stern, 1965).

Results such as these prompted economists to examine patterns of protection in more detail by attempting to measure the extent by which payments to producers and to factors of production may exceed the corresponding levels if no protection were provided. This concept, known as the rate of 'effective protection', showed that the margin of discrimination in favour of industries producing consumer goods was often much larger than the actual values of the nominal tariffs would suggest (Balassa, 1968, p. 601). Thus, it was probably well worth the efforts of interest groups in particular industries to go to considerable lengths in the way of lobbying, bribery or political persuasion in order to realise these levels of protection.

Assessments of the practical results of import substitution and protective policies in LDCs are numerous (Hirschman, 1968; Little et al., 1970; Sutcliffe, 1971; Baer, 1972; Helleiner, 1972) and it is sufficient merely to note the highlights of previous work. There is general agreement that the results of import substitution fell short of its original objectives. Attempts to replace imports often failed to proceed beyond the consumer goods stage. The composition of imports did change; consumer goods became less important while imports of intermediate goods, fuels and capital equipment took on a greater significance. However, the ratio of imports to total income seldom declined and often increased as industrialisation boosted the demand for various types of industrial supplies and capital goods which were seldom available locally. Consequently, balance of payments constraints were not alleviated, countries' dependence on foreign trade was accentuated and their vulnerability to fluctuations in foreign exchange receipts continued. Other consequences attributed to import substitution policies included an inefficient allocation of resources, a rising dependence on foreign technology, and a wide range of protected industries operating according to oligopolistic or monopolistic principles.

This description of the substitution process in the 1950s and 1960s clearly suggests that protectionism was of much greater significance for manufacturers in the LDCs than it was for those in advanced countries. Protective policies affect manufacturing activities by changing the prices of products or the prices of factors of production. In many LDCs a wide variety of tariffs was employed along with other forms of trade restrictions, and protective rates on different products differed greatly. Under these conditions product prices were likely to be more significantly affected than factor prices (Balassa, 1971a, pp. 254–5). Perhaps an even more important reason for the policy impact on product prices was the relative political strength of different interest groups. In rural areas, the overwhelming number of unemployed and unskilled workers meant that labour's strength as a pressure group was largely ineffectual. Similarly, rural producers' interests were frequently subservient to those of urban inhabitants. Lipton (1976) has characterised the tensions between town and country in LDCs as 'urban bias', a term which refers to the tendency for public expenditure, among other factors, to be concentrated in cities. The relative strength of organised urban labour, and the urban predisposition of expatriate experts (at least until recently) were among the factors explaining this skewed allocation of resources.

Given the protective impact on prices, profits and investment, industrialists were often prepared to go to considerable lengths in the way of political persuasion, lobbying and even bribery, in order to obtain such benefits. The limited and sometimes inexperienced personnel available to the public sector for industrial planning probably facilitated this practice. In the case of Brazil, for instance, industrial priorities have long been shaped by an interplay of public officials and private-sector investors. Although the view of public officials was an important determinant of the priorities accorded to individual industrial branches, the more specific decisions concerning such matters as tariffs, exemptions from tariffs for certain importers and lines of credit, 'owed their design at least as much to the entrepreneurs who stood to gain or lose from them as to the public officials' view of what was best. . .' (Bergsman, 1979, p. 18). The Indian practice of formulating industrial targets through 'close contact' by the Ministry of Commerce and Industry with employers and their associations (Lal, 1979, p. 24) served a similar purpose for industrial interests in that country.

The desire of industrialists to influence policy often had unexpected consequences. For example, the extreme concentration of Pakistani industry and Mexican industry around the capital cities was partially due to the manufacturers' wish to be within easy reach of government offices. The ease of obtaining import licensing was a primary motive for industrialists' choice of location. In the case of Pakistan, Karachi's share of import licenses ranged from 57 to 89 per cent of all those issued in the years 1953–6, although the city's share of value added in large-scale manufacturing was only 30 per cent of the national total (Little *et al.*, 1970, p. 213). In Malaysia, one reason why import substitution was never widely accepted was, apparently, that protection would have benefited the Chinese who form the bulk of the industrialists, while the Malays predominate in the countryside and the government (Reynolds, 1977, pp. 367–8).

The fact that import substitution was often 'stuck' at the consumer goods stage suggests the need for a closer look at the influence of industrialists on national decision-making. Certainly, production of consumer goods was the preponderant form of manufacturing activity in the LDCs during the 1950s and early 1960s. At that time, consumer goods accounted, on average, for 54 per cent of MVA in nine of the largest LDCs (Ballance *et al.*, 1982, p. 47). The ability to influence policy varied with industrial prominence; small, isolated manufacturers had little influence on political, financial and industrial decisions.

Also relevant is the fact that the profits of import-substituting establishments are higher when there is a substantial difference between the levels of protection accorded to their final products and to their imported inputs. These high profit margins would have been jeopardised if domestic production of the inputs had been started and if the producers of these inputs had been granted protection at levels comparable to those received by their domestic buyers. Thus the producers of consumer goods had very good reasons for resisting the type of sequential process originally envisaged for import substitution. Consequently, they used their influence to oppose the sequential process envisaged by the advocates of import substitution.

Other strategic reasons reinforced the reluctance of consumer goods producers to establish domestic capacity to supply industrial inputs and capital goods. First, industrialists who had hitherto relied on imported inputs may have feared that the domestically produced inputs would be of inferior quality. Second, there was a danger of becoming dependent on a single domestic supplier where, previously, the industrialist could shop around the world. Third, once the basic materials were available locally, domestic competition in consumer goods might have increased. For these reasons, the interests of producers in the consumer goods subsector were frequently opposed to the establishment of domestic materials and equipment suppliers (Hirschman, 1968, p. 118).

A final point with relevance to both this section and the following one concerns some of the costs of government involvement in manufacturing. The pervasiveness of government intervention gave rise to the existence of economic rents, including bribery, corruption, smuggling and black markets, as well as the normal, competitive forms of rent-seeking. Thus there were good reasons why the involvement of industrialists in the policy-making apparatus was also widespread. In the case of India, Krueger's estimates put the value of rents at 7.3 per cent of national income in 1964, while her calculation for Turkey was 15 per cent of GNP for 1968 (1974, p. 294). In both countries, the bulk of these rents depended on the ownership of import licences. The estimates suggest that the returns from rent-seeking were extensive, particularly in comparison with the countries' rates of saving.

The following section traces the move away from import substitution to other types of industrial policies. The transition was a change in emphasis, however, and did not mean that the extent of government intervention, or the scope for competitive rent seeking, was necessarily lessened.

The transition to export promotion

Disillusionment with import substitution spread once it became apparent that the objectives were not to be quickly realised and that its pursuance entailed a variety of undesirable side effects. Parallel to this growing scepticism, a number of changes were occurring – both at the national and at the international level. These changes led to a reappraisal of the strategy and to its replacement or, in some cases, its supplementation by others.

The rapid growth in world income was steadily improving the export prospects of producers in LDCs. Realisation of this was slow; export opportunities were not always apparent, partly because an overvalued exchange rate sometimes made domestic prices appear to be uncompetitive. Other forces favouring the expansion of world trade were also at work. They included greater standardisation in patterns of national consumption, a more liberal trade environment, the falling cost of international transport, the emergence of the transnational corporation (TNC) as a prominent form of industrial organisation and the development of a semi-skilled and skilled labour force in certain LDCs. Political considerations arising from the West's fear of a growing communist threat were probably also relevant. Thus, the USA maintained close trading relations with the

Philippines, South Korea and Taiwan, while the UK provided for a preferential trading status with Hong Kong, Malaysia and Singapore. For all these reasons, world trade was expanding at a pace far exceeding previous expectations; at 8 per cent per annum in the period 1953–73 (W. A. Lewis, 1981, p. 11). This phenomenon cast doubt on a whole subset of development themes – import substitution, balanced growth and regional integration – which assumed that industrialisation would occur in an environment of relatively stagnating world trade.

Changes in the structure of domestic production in some LDCs made it easier to discard import substitution as a favoured approach. The emergence of a growing coalition of industrial exporters eventually led to policy modifications that indirectly improved the trading prospects of this group. Policy-makers in LDCs had traditionally sought to foster industrialisation by maintaining an overvalued rate of exchange. Overvaluation meant that agriculturalists – typically the country's main exporters – often received a smaller real income than would have been provided by an equilibrium or undervalued exchange rate. Industrialists benefited since they could import supplies and capital goods at favourable prices (in domestic currency). Thus the policy provided a means of transferring income from primary exporters to the owners of new industries. Simultaneously, the overvalued exchange rate made exports uncompetitive and discouraged these initiatives by new industries. Hirschman (1968, p. 27) ascribes the appeal of overvaluation to the fact that it was an 'indirect rather than a direct squeeze of the politically socially powerful groups' in the primary export sector. For a long time this squeeze was an unnoticed by-product of efforts to 'defend' the currency against depreciation. As the manufacturing sector grew, however, overvaluation came to be regarded as pernicious by the newly influential industrial groups. Not surprisingly, exchange rate devaluations became more frequent in later years, although sometimes too little and too late. This step was made easier by the fact that the expansion of the domestic market had enlarged the state's tax base and its ability to borrow from an incipient capital market.

While such changes paved the way for a new set of industrial policies, the opinions of development economists also began to change. Import substitution came under severe criticism from a number of economists and institutions including the World Bank (Balassa, 1971b), the Organization for Economic Co-operation and Development (Little *et al.*, 1970) and the Brookings Institution (Johnson, 1967). Exporters were thought to be better able to realise economies of scale since output levels were not constrained by a small domestic market. Learning-by-doing effects were also expected to bring improvements in managerial and marketing performances as well as gains in labour productivity. Exporting firms would be most likely to introduce the latest technological developments occurring in advanced countries.

Other, broader types of benefits were foreseen by the advocates of export promotion. For example, the exporters' requirements for additional primary imports, industrial supplies and capital equipment would boost aggregate demand and thereby enlarge the size of the domestic market. A successful export programme would alleviate balance of payments problems that handicapped many LDCs. In general, a relatively open market would enable an LDC to find its fields of comparative advantage and to avoid high-cost, inefficient projects. Various empirical studies (Emery, 1967; Maizels, 1968, pp. 41–9; Michaely, 1977; Balassa, 1978b; Tyler, 1981) lent support to this line of argument by concluding that the rapid growth of exports accelerated the growth of the economy. The renewed emphasis on exports following the hiatus in 1913–50 went a long way towards reviving the earlier opinion of some economists that trade could serve as an 'engine of growth'.

The policies introduced in LDCs when shifting from import substitution to export promotion were generally similar in nature, if not in scope. The most prominent feature was the attempt to cut levels of protection and to reduce the range of the protective rates for different industries. This step was prompted by a desire to lessen the home market bias that made exporting relatively unprofitable. Governments also offered to remit the tariffs paid on imported inputs if these were used in the production of goods for export. Exemptions or reductions in indirect taxes were allowed for exporters. Vouchers for import replenishment and the priority allocation of foreign exchange to exporters became common practices along with income tax concessions on the earnings from exports. Other incentives included preferential credits to exporters, the gradual devaluation of exchange rates and government assistance to marketing abroad.

There is only scanty information concerning the impact of these policies and the extent to which they rectified the earlier policy bias against exporting. In the late 1960s, South Korea's programme of export incentives was thought to be equivalent to a subsidy of about 12 per cent of the value added in exports of manufactures. Brazilian export incentives carried a subsidy element varying from 6 to 38 per cent of the exports' value. In Argentina a roughly comparable figure for 'non-traditional exports' was 20 per cent. Corresponding estimates for Colombia and Mexico were lower and applied only to specific products (Balassa, 1978b).

Typically, when policy makers in an LDC opted for export promotion after an extended period of import substitution, export subsidies and incentives were simply grafted onto the existing policy framework. One result of this practice was that, in the opinion of most observers, the net effects were probably not sufficient to equate the benefits from exporting with those derived from selling in the home market (Donges, 1976, p. 655; for the Philippines see the World Bank, 1976, pp. 216–18; for Chile and Mexico, see Balassa, 1977, pp. 34 and 75–7). Since export promotion policies were supplementary to the existing protectionist framework, the latter continued to be the most attractive, or profitable, policy alternative for industrial interest groups.

Despite the desire of many governments to create a favourable policy environment, industrialists were hesitant to mount an export drive. Although lower levels of protection and occasional depreciation served to reduce the bias favouring domestic sales, they did nothing to promote sales to foreign markets. Exporting entailed special risks and additional overhead costs such as investments in research, design and packaging, advertising outlays, the painstaking establishment of relations with foreign buyers, improved production processes and quality control. Many firms were reluctant to undertake these expenditures without government assistance. Ultimately, the business community wanted to be reasonably sure that it could control a variety of crucial fiscal and monetary policies before launching an export campaign (Hirschman, 1968, p. 28).

The recent experience of Colombian clothing firms shows how an export drive can be stifled when exporters have no long-term influence over policy. After 1967 the government introduced export incentives and a policy of frequent, small devaluations, with the result that exports of clothing rose more than three-fold between 1969 and 1973. Without any official announcement (and contrary to the government's public statements) these policies were abruptly reversed in 1973. By 1978, firms producing jeans, blouses or shirts from domestic fabric received a subsidy of 30–100 per cent if the garments were sold in Colombia, but suffered a penalty of 32–62 per cent if it exported them. Both effects were due to the post-1973 policies (Morawetz, 1980).

Table 3.2 indicates the major exporting 'industries' in the LDCs in 1977. Because of significant differences in production techniques, factor requirements, forms of ownership and exporting practices, the industries have been divided into those that are resource-based and those that are not. The data show a surprising concentration of exports. Twenty-six industries provide over three-quarters of all exports of non-resource-based manufactures. Eleven industries accounted for the same proportion among the resource-based exporters and only three of these industries supplied over one-half the latter total.

Several of the exports listed in Table 3.2 share certain common features. Among non-resource-based industries, a reliance on unskilled labour is prevalent. Precise statements about the extent to which different production processes are intensive in their use of labour are difficult for several reasons. First, almost any industry operating in an LDC would bu apt to use more labour than would be the case if the same establishment were located in an advanced economy. At the very least, labour is likely to be substituted for capital in the performance of auxiliary services (maintenance, storage and the movement of materials) if not in production processes themselves. Second, the identification of labour-intensive activities is hampered by the fact that production technologies in some industries are more readily adjusted to changing shares of labour and capital inputs than those in other industries. Third, differing levels of natural resource endowment may influence the amounts of labour employed.

Within the manufacturing sector there are some grounds for believing that the opportunities for factor substitution are limited and that production technologies are not easily adaptable to differing patterns of factor endowment. Discussions of factor intensity led to several studies that attempted to classify industries according to their labour requirements. Although such work necessarily involves some degree of subjectivity, independent investigations (Lary, 1968; Hufbauer, 1970; Rahman, 1973; Hirsch, 1975) revealed a substantial area of agreement on the types of industries regarded as labour intensive. A majority (15 of 26) of the non-resource-based industries shown in Table 3.2 apparently owe their export success, at least partly, to the availability of cheap unskilled labour. In addition, other industries producing non-electrical machines, motor vehicles, office machines and scientific instruments have moved the labour-intensive parts of their operations, such as assembly and packaging, to LDCs from where the final product is then exported (Helleiner, 1973).

A second characteristic of the industries shown in Table 3.2 concerns the extent of transnational ownership and control. Evidence on the TNCs' penetration of specific industries in LDCs is fragmented and incomplete. As early as 1970, they accounted for perhaps 50 per cent of the exports of manufactures by advanced market economies (Batchelor et al., 1980, p. 91). No corresponding estimate is available for the LDCs although it is likely that the TNCs' share is a significant one. The list of products and processes in which TNCs are involved is a long one. They include (by SITC) the sewing of garments, gloves and leather luggage (841, 611 and 681), the assembly of television and radio sets and components (724), the production of automobile parts such as antennae, piston rings, batteries and brake linings (732), typewriters, calculators and other office machines (714), electrical lighting and simple hand tools (729), and a number of other non-resource-based products exported by the industries listed in Table 3.2. Traditionally, the TNCs' control over the production and export of resource-based products surpassed their influence in other types of industry. Petroleum, copper and tin are examples which are well-known as a result of expropriation disputes with LDCs. The TNCs' predominance in various food categories, including sugar, animal-feed, frozen meat and poultry has also been noted (UNCTC, 1980; UNIDO, 1981a, pp. 164–7).

A third development with an indirect effect on the composition and behaviour of industrial interests with export ambitions is the emergence of public-owned or -operated manufacturing enterprises. This trend, discussed in detail in later chapters, has led to a gradual over-lapping of the 'public' and 'private' character of many industrial enterprises in both the LDCs and the advanced economies. Information about public manufacturing enterprises (PMEs) is not available in a form that would permit an assessment of their significance among the industries shown in Table 3.2. It is clear, however, that such firms are mainly found in heavy manufacturing. Few of these industries are important exporters, the major exceptions being road motor vehicles and resource-based industries like petroleum, copper and tin, where nationalisation has led to public ownership. Thus, the PMEs' direct affiliation with export-oriented strategies is not significant, although

Table 3.2 *The LDCs'[1] major exports of manufactures as a percentage of total manufactured exports, 1977*

Non-resource based exports (SITC)[2]	Cumulative percentage	Resource-based exports (SITC)	Cumulative percentage
Clothing, except fur (841)*	20.37	Petroleum products (332)	37.21
Electrical machinery and apparatus (729)*	26.18	Sugar, refined or raw (061)	44.20
Telecommunications apparatus (724)	30.83	Feed stuff for animals (081)	50.50
Cotton fabrics, woven (652)*	34.92	Copper (682)	56.16
Textile yarn and thread (651)*	38.76	Vegetable oils (422)	60.71
Woven textiles, fabrics, not cotton (653)*	42.01	Tea, maté (074)	64.29
Road motor vehicles (732)	45.17	Tin (687)	67.29
		Rice, glazed or polished (0422)	69.95
		Meat and poultry, chilled, frozen (011)	72.48

Non-resource based exports (SITC)[2]	Cumulative percentage	Resource-based exports (SITC)	Cumulative percentage
Toys, games, sporting goods (894)*	48.20	Wood, shaped or worked (243)	74.94
Footwear (851)*	51.15	Veneers, plywood boards (631)	77.09
Non-electrical machines, parts (719)	53.06		
Leather (611)*	55.15		
Made-up textile articles (656)*	57.21		
Watches, clocks (864)	58.98		
Electrical power machinery, switchgear (722)*	60.63		
Floor covering, tapestries (657)*	62.27		
Non-electrical power generating machinery (711)	63.71		
Travel goods, handbags (831)*	65.10		
Lime, cement, building materials (661)	66.47		
Office machines (714)	67.75		
Finished structures and parts (691)	68.97		
Scientific, measuring, optical instruments (861)	70.17		
Pig iron, spiegeleisen (671)	71.35		
Tubes, pipes of iron, steel (678)	72.53		
Printed matter (892)*	73.65		
Medicinal, pharmaceutical products (541)	74.73		
Medical instruments, sound recorders (891)*	75.76		

Source: UNIDO, 1982b, pp. 9–13.
Notes:
1. LDCs exclude Yugoslavia.
2. Products are ranked according to their share in the total of resource-based or non-resource-based exports of 60 developing countries. For a definition of the two export categories, see UNIDO, 1981a, annex to chapter II.
An asterisk (*) indicates a labour-intensive industry. For definitions and sources used for the measurement of labour intensity, see UNIDO, 1981a.

public participation in heavy manufacturing sometimes has an indirect negative effect on the exports of light industries. The experiences of two important exporters – South Korea and Taiwan – are illustrative. In South Korea, the passage of more than a dozen special loans during the 1970s assured that preferred heavy industries received virtually unlimited credit from government-controlled banks so that, by 1977–9, approximately 80 per cent of fixed industrial investment was in heavy industry (*The Economist*, 12 Sept. 1981). The result was that light industries such as textiles and small firms making industrial parts had inadequate funds for modernisation and equipment replacement. Taiwan has resorted to government investment rather than following the Korean approach of providing cheap finance to private firms. During the 1970s the Taiwanese public sector accounted for more than one-half of all fixed capital formation. Most of these funds went to heavy industries like chemicals, shipbuilding, steel and automobiles, while the exporters of light manufactures found that their access to capital was limited.

The contradictory positions of various industrial interests initially often led to overt tests of strength between various groups. The issue of expropriation, for example, ostensibly pitted the interests of governments against those of TNCs. When the governments of LDCs began to stress their right to sovereignty over national resources, financial and industrial elites in these countries found good reasons to support a policy of expropriation. These groups had been faced with increased competition as TNCs set up domestic production facilities in order not to lose local markets that were shut off by protection. Expropriation was an appealing way to eliminate this competitive threat (Bennett *et al.*, 1978, p. 275). Although a case may be made for expropriation on other grounds, it did not complement a sector-wide attempt at export promotion since local firms could not match the international channels for finance, marketing and distribution available to the TNC.

With regard to the government's participation in the industrialisation process, the most direct route – nationalisation of industrial enterprises – has been a commonplace in many LDCs (UNIDO, 1979, ch. X). The practice sometimes divided the government and the business community, with industrialists seeing widespread nationalisation as a threat and an unwarranted government intervention in the proper functioning of the economy. Nationalisation has become increasingly problematic, however, owing to fiscal limitations. These limitations were partially due to the growth of welfare expenses but equally important was the shortage of domestic sources of finance as a result of the banking and industrial community's resistance to the policy.

More recently, relationships between diverse interest groups have reached a more sophisticated or subtle state in many LDCs. Decisions on pricing, production or finance are often the subject of protracted negotiations between the various groups. Elaborate networks for institutionalising the relationships between TNC strategists, local industrialists, government planners and managers of public enterprises have evolved, and negotiations have increasingly focused on ways of modifying behaviour (or proposed behaviour). This approach has partially replaced more direct means of controlling industrial activity such as expropriation or nationalisation once it became apparent that ownership itself was not sufficient to ensure the successful pursuit of an industrial strategy such as export promotion.

In conclusion, the export ambitions of various LDCs and advanced countries have led to policy revisions that are far more basic than the simple introduction of export incentives. Governments have taken steps to reinforce the impact of export incentives by extending the role of the state in a variety of ways. An important determinant of the state's ability to introduce these changes successfully is the underlying conflict between vested interests geared to serve the home market and those interests whose prospects are best served by more outward-looking policies. The necessary political support for any basic shift in policy approach will depend, at least in part, upon the country's prevailing patterns of growth and structural change. The following chapter examines these aspects in some detail and considers their implications for policy-makers in the advanced countries and the LDCs.

4

Structural Change at the Sectoral Level

In preceding chapters the motives for industrialisation were discussed in an international context. But interrelationships between policy and industrial growth become more apparent when studying an individual economy. Before addressing this subject some framework is needed for analysing the pattern of growth in manufacturing relative to other sectors – agriculture, mining and services. In the first section of this chapter a typology is developed, while the following section examines growth patterns in terms of this framework. The concluding section provides a comparison of agriculture and manufacturing in terms of the adjustment pressures experienced by the two sectors and the types of policy responses that have emerged.

A typology of countries

Although the growth experiences of advanced countries lend themselves to certain generalisations, the discussion in Chapter 2 concluded by pointing to the growing danger of lumping LDCs together in a mythological Third World. The conditions governing patterns of structural change can be diverse, complex in their interaction, and varying in influence over time. For these reasons, generalisations are best limited to subsets of countries that share one or more salient characteristics. Thus a discussion of sectoral patterns of structural change best proceeds by distinguishing between categories of countries in a typology that uses the following criteria.

(i) The endowment of natural resources. Resource endowment has both a direct and an indirect effect on countries' economic structure. A direct effect may be observed in the extent to which the availability of natural resources constrains or facilitates the expansion of certain sectors such as mining or manufacturing. The significance of this effect, of course, depends upon the resources at hand. The existence of precious resources (such as oil or certain metals) may have a significant impact on the economic structure, while the common ones (the raw materials for brick, cement or certain synthetics) are of minimal consequence. Thus resource endowment has an indirect effect on economic structure by circumscribing a country's choice of development policies. In exceptional cases where there is an abundant natural resource base (Australia, Canada, Saudi Arabia or Zaire), or a total lack thereof (Hong Kong), endowment dictates policy choices to a large extent.

Virtually all countries with ample resources have used them as an export base. A relative abundance of natural resources tends to shift the emphasis away from manufacturing to agriculture or mining since the resource costs of exporting unprocessed products is less. In such countries the manufacturing sector's share of GDP is often decidedly less than that of agriculture or mining and, over time, it generally increases more slowly than is the case in countries with a narrower range of development alternatives (UNIDO, 1979, pp. 45–50).

(ii) Size of the domestic market. Market size is a clear indication of the extent to which domestic demand can influence the economic structure. The most obvious effect of market size is on the volume of trade. In large countries imports and exports tend to account for a much lower proportion of GDP than in small countries. A corollary is that large countries often favour inward-looking policies that are dependent on the domestic market while small countries are more prone to adopt outward-looking policies that assign an important role to exports. The policies of Brazil, Germany, India, Pakistan and the USA have all followed the former course at various times while city-states like Hong Kong and Singapore represent the other extreme. The basis for this distinction is simply that the size of domestic demand in large countries affords them a greater latitude in their policy choices and in the pattern of their economic development.

There are two reasons why the options of an inward or an outward orientation are more accessible to manufacturers than to producers in other sectors. First, certain activities carried out in the construction, agricultural and service sectors do not result in tradeable goods, while most manufactures can readily be exchanged internationally. Second, when governments choose to pursue an inward-oriented approach, they may find it easier to divert resources away from other sectors to new industries. Agriculture was typically the largest sector when LDCs began to industrialise and the burden of these resource transfers could be spread over a large number of farmers (Little *et al.*, 1970, pp. 41–2). Thus it is no accident that most countries which have opted for an inward-oriented pattern of industrialisation have large domestic markets and a sizeable agricultural sector. By contrast, small countries like Israel, the Netherlands or Taiwan, with relatively small agricultural sectors, have found that inward-oriented policies are not compatible with their domestic structure.

(iii) Stage of development. In the course of development, both demand and supply patterns change substantially and, as *per capita* income rises, the composition of domestic demand is altered. An overriding feature is the declining proportion of total expenditures on necessities like foodstuffs and clothing, balanced by an increase in the share spent on luxuries, household appliances, industrial supplies and equipment. These types of changes may be explained in terms of Engel's Law which specifies that the income elasticity of demand for necessities is typically less than unity, implying that their share in total consumption will fall as the level of income rises.

On the supply side, a country's available stock of capital will increase as development continues. The share of savings in income is generally thought to rise due to rapid growth in the modern, capitalistic sector with its potential for saving. Over time there is also an increase in the proportion of the labour force which is skilled or semi-skilled, due to rising investment in education and training. Both accumulation processes will boost labour productivity, since a growing number of skilled workers are provided with additional capital equipment. Historically these processes, as well as the political and policy motives described in Chapter 2, may have tended to favour the manufacturing sector, for several reasons. First, technological advances have probably concentrated on this sector relative to services or agriculture. Second, most of the modern capitalistic activities in LDCs that have a high savings potential are found in manufacturing and, thus, are prone to reinvest in that sector. Finally, the bulk of skilled labour (but not necessarily unskilled labour) is absorbed by manufacturing where wages are relatively high, owing partly to high levels of labour productivity.

In advanced countries, demand and supply characteristics exhibit a somewhat different pattern. At comparatively high levels of income the demand for social services, entertainment and recreation tends to absorb a larger proportion of income gains than manufacturing, and the composition of demand once again changes accordingly. The age structure of the population in these countries differs from that in LDCs owing to a faster decline in fertility rates and greater longevity. This serves to increase further the demand for specialised services like medical treatment and welfare programmes. As far as the manufacturing sector is concerned, a rising portion of investment funds may be required for pollution abatement or for the acquisition of increasingly scarce raw materials and energy. Both may reduce the output per unit of investment, making industrial expansion a more expensive proposition. Certain characteristics of the labour force, such as the demand for greater leisure and part-time employment, the rising educational level and the decrease in geographical mobility, may make manufacturing a less attractive source of employment than services.

Thus, in addition to political considerations, economic factors – resource endowment, market size and stage of development – are important determinants of economic structure. A unique economic structure, however, does not mean that the long-term pattern of change is uniquely determined. In fact, the foregoing typology implies the opposite. Similar variations in the patterns of consumer demand, the accumulation of human and physical capital, private savings, government revenue and expenditure, may lead to similarities in structural patterns, at least among homogeneous subsets of countries.

Sectoral patterns of growth

Changes in the sectoral composition of GDP are a frequently used measure of structural change. Because rates of growth can diverge widely, sectoral shares in GDP will naturally change during the course of economic advancement. These relative shifts, or structural changes, can also arise from the contraction of one sector and the simultaneous expansion of others. The sectoral composition of GDP is used here as a means of comparing the structure of various subsets of countries. Alternative indicators, such as a sector's share in total employment or exports, could be employed for similar purposes and are considered elsewhere in this book.

The figures in Table 4.1 indicate the composition of GDP in groups of countries arranged to approximate this typology. When economic structure is related to level of income the heterogeneity of the LDCs is apparent. Agriculture shows the greatest variability across the country groups, ranging from 6 per cent to 40 per cent of GDP in 1978. The long-term decline of agriculture is also obvious; and the sector's share of GDP is shown to be universally related to the level of income. The effects of resource endowment can be seen from the figures for high-income LDCs and OPEC countries. There the mining sector (including petroleum) is of considerable importance, while manufacturing accounts for a lesser share of GDP and agriculture is

Table 4.1 Sectoral composition of GDP, selected years (percentage)

Country group (number of countries)	Agriculture			Mining			Manufacturing[a]			Services[a]			Others[b]		
	1960	1970	1978	1960	1970	1978	1960	1970	1978	1960	1970	1978	1960	1970	1978
A. LDCs by income group:[c]															
low (28)	51.5	43.3	39.6	2.6	3.0	3.4	5.7	8.6	9.9	35.5	39.2	40.9	4.7	5.9	6.2
lower middle (23)	39.2	32.9	31.5	5.0	6.7	5.4	9.9	11.9	12.9	39.9	42.8	43.7	6.0	5.8	6.5
intermediate (20)	30.2	25.0	22.0	3.5	4.4	6.6	13.4	16.0	16.6	46.7	48.1	47.4	6.2	6.5	7.4
upper middle (10)	17.3	12.5	10.0	7.8	7.5	10.5	15.6	17.9	18.5	51.5	54.1	52.6	7.8	7.9	8.4
high (8)	13.4	7.5	5.5	7.6	15.5	18.6	14.2	15.5	16.4	56.7	52.5	49.7	8.0	9.0	9.8
B. All countries by size and resource endowment[d]															
large countries (24)	25.7	20.8	19.9	3.1	2.8	2.4	20.8	22.1	22.0	44.4	46.9	48.2	6.0	7.4	7.5
small countries with modest resources (38)	44.1	36.4	33.1	2.1	2.7	4.1	7.7	10.6	11.4	40.3	44.7	45.4	5.9	5.6	6.0
small countries with ample resources (40)	23.3	18.6	18.0	4.9	5.4	4.8	17.4	19.5	19.3	47.0	48.5	49.7	7.4	8.0	8.2
OPEC (9)	29.7	22.1	12.7	12.2	21.4	30.4	8.8	10.2	9.6	42.5	39.8	36.6	6.8	6.5	10.6
C. Totals															
all LDCs (89)	36.3	29.8	27.2	4.4	5.9	6.8	10.3	12.8	13.7	42.9	45.0	45.2	6.0	6.5	7.1
advanced market economies[e] (22)	12.3	7.7	6.5	2.3	1.7	2.3	28.6	28.8	25.8	47.8	51.5	55.3	9.1	10.2	10.2

Source : UNIDO, 1982c, Table, p. 14.
Notes:
a Including wholesale and retail trade, transport and communication, financing, insurance and real estate, community, social and personal services.
b Including construction, electricity, gas and water.
c LDCs were grouped according to the following levels of per capita GNP in 1975: < $265; $265–$520; $521–$1075; $1076–$2000; > $2000. Where GNP was not available, GDP was used.
d The demarcation between large and small countries was a population of 15 million in 1970. A cluster analysis was used to distinguish between small countries having modest and ample resource endowment. For a description, see UNIDO, 1979, annex I.
e Figures exclude socialist countries.

of little significance. The influence of market size is not so obvious. That characteristic is found to be a more important determinant of the composition of output within the manufacturing sector (see Chapter 5).

Western economies experienced a continuous decline in the share of agriculture, although the rate of contraction apparently fell after 1970. A less obvious reduction occurred in the share of manufacturing, equivalent to 3 per cent of GDP in 1970–8. Nevertheless, this was the largest percentage change recorded for that sector throughout the period 1960–78. In view of the fact that the GDP of advanced market economies (in US dollars) was 4.5 times greater than that of the LDCs in 1978, the absolute magnitude of the decline in manufacturing was also substantial. Comparable figures (in current prices) are not available for socialist countries, although evidence from other sources suggests a somewhat different pattern of structural change. Since 1960, their development has been characterised by rapid growth of MVA and a persistently high proportion of GDP in manufacturing (UNIDO, 1979, p. 44). Nevertheless, recent studies have found that the expansion of manufacturing has moderated (UNIDO, 1979, p. 52) as the rising costs of natural resource extraction, higher investment outlays and technological innovation take their toll.

The role of the service sector deserves specific comment. By 1978 that sector accounted for the largest share of GDP in each group of countries. As expected, the service sector's contribution to GDP has risen substantially in advanced Western economies. Curiously, its share also followed an upward trend in the poorer LDCs. No clear pattern can be found from the figures for LDCs in the *per capita* income range of $521–$2,000, although a definite decline occurred in the richest LDCs. Only this last shift is readily explainable, owing mainly to the growing importance of the mining sector, particularly in OPEC. No significant departure from the upward trend is observed when countries are arranged according to criteria of market size or resource endowment.

The sector's development is not subject to the same types of political considerations and economic forces that influence other sectors. Although the demand for services is known to be income-elastic (Baer and Samuelson, 1981, p. 511), its steady growth in countries with a low *per capita* income and a large poverty group can hardly be attributed to an increase in demand. Nor are the usual notions regarding savings and investment behaviour applicable, since many service activities are outside the modern sector and seldom require large injections of capital.

Reynolds (1977, p. 274) offers two possible explanations for the sector's predominance. First, the earnings differential between white-collar workers and manual workers is much larger in LDCs than in advanced economies. Since most white-collar workers are employed in services, their higher wages swell the value of the sector's output. Second, high rates of population growth and rural-to-urban migration increase the proportion of the labour force available for porterage, petty trade and personal services. Many of these workers earn a minimum wage and their output is priced accordingly, thus inflating services' share of GDP. Apparently the part which services play in the growth process in some LDCs is often passive in response to pressure arising from growth and contraction elsewhere in the economy; the active forces leading to changes in the structure of output are largely associated with agricultural and manufacturing activities. Casual observation supports this interpretation. In agriculture, for example, land reform, the introduction of irrigation facilities, the replacement of subsistence products by cash crops or new hybrids can all have a dramatic impact on the sector's share of output and employment. Similar comments apply to manufacturing where rapid technological change, and large-scale investment in the infrastructure or in manufacturing itself, can lead to abrupt shifts in the country's economic structure. The service sector affords relatively few opportunities to substitute capital for labour (Sabolo, 1975, ch. 3) and has benefited very little from technological advances (Berry, 1978).

The adjustment processes in agriculture and manufacturing

The foregoing discussion suggests that at least some similarities in the sectoral growth patterns of different countries can be expected. These similarities become more apparent once the effects of structural determinants like resource endowment, market size and stage of development are taken into account. This line of reasoning provides some basis for generalisations about the adjustment pressures experienced by various sectoral interests.

Changes in the sectoral composition of a country's GDP will alter the present and future income of producers, workers, investors, or others who are associated with a given sector. However, the effects of any sectoral contraction, relative or absolute, are not equally distributed across all the activities in a given sector. Some groups may find that their existing claims on the country's income and resources will be reduced because of the prevailing pattern of structural change, and they will usually search for means of averting this unpleasant prospect. When this viewpoint is generally accepted, or is accepted by the more influential interest groups in the sector, considerable pressure may be mounted to change the country's policy priorities for the given sector. In such cases, interest groups will usually reject market principles as a basis for distributing income and for allocating resources. They resort, instead, to political pressure for new policies that will postpone or reverse the existing pattern of structural change.

In view of agriculture's long history of structural decline, the range of policies applied to that sector provides evidence of the results of interest group pressure. The relative contraction of agriculture occurred as resources were shifted to manufacturing and labourers moved into services and, to a lesser extent, manufacturing. These transfers, and the implicit costs which they entailed, have given rise to intense pressure on governments for new policies that would reverse or delay the otherwise natural process of structural change.

The responses of most Western governments to appeals of agricultural interest groups are guided by a similar set of considerations. First, the attitudes of politicians and bureaucracies have not yet adjusted to the sheer drop in farm population and, thus, voting strength. Second, agricultural interest groups are strong and are well organised to exert political pressure. Third, many governments fear that a rapidly declining agriculture sector will make them too dependent on foreign supplies and could eventually lead to some form of economic blackmail. Fourth, agricultural issues evoke an emotional response from many segments of society. The recent emergence of European 'green politics', coupled with ecological movements, have reinforced this thinking. Finally, the rise in general unemployment since the late 1970s added a new argument; supporters argued that reductions in the farm population should be avoided since there was little likelihood that labour would find employment in other sectors.

A general trend in advanced countries has been to create a network of national policies that isolate agriculture from the market forces which would otherwise govern the allocation of resources. Nowadays, there is no more impressive example of the influence exerted by agricultural interests than the Common Agricultural Policy (CAP) of the EEC. The main pillar of the CAP is its price policy which is designed to maintain farm prices at politically determined levels. In 1980 about 90 per cent of EEC farm production was covered by various types of 'guaranteed' funds which took the form of support prices, supplementary aid and variable tariffs on agricultural imports (*The Economist*, 1 Nov. 1980). The agricultural sector in most advanced countries continues to decline in relative importance, albeit at a reduced pace thanks to the generous range of protective measures and subsidies provided by the state.

For several reasons the experience of LDCs has differed from that in advanced countries. First, as noted in Chapter 2, political considerations led governments to favour the manufacturing sector at the expense of agriculture. Accordingly, policy-makers were reluctant to introduce the types of assistance that agriculturalists might have wanted. Second, the agricultural sector in LDCs was mainly composed of subsistence farmers. In comparison with their counterparts in advanced countries, these individuals have little or no ability to influence national policy. Third, in periods of export expansion the more successful agriculturalists and traders often chose to exit from the agricultural sector. Earlier studies have noted a tendency for these groups to move into the production of consumer goods and other lightly processed manufactures where profit rates are higher, owing to the government's policies for promoting industry (Hirschman, 1968, p. 10). More recently, a similar pattern has been observed among the newly emerging class of Asian entrepreneurs who, having succeeded in agriculture or commerce, turned to the production and export of luxury foods (fresh and frozen seafoods, tropical fruits and juices). The effects of this move have been dramatic; luxury food exports now account for about one-quarter of the LDCs' total output of processed foods (*Far Eastern Economic Review*, 11 July 1980). Government policies have encouraged this mobility by providing more generous incentives, subsidies and other forms of support for agro-processing activities than for more mature industries. Thus the tendency for successful entrepreneurs to leave agriculture removes a group with an important political voice in policy debates.

Turning to manufacturing, the patterns of structural change observed in advanced countries and LDCs suggest the basis for a general distinction between the two groups of countries. In LDCs, growth begins with a relatively small share of manufacturing in GDP at low levels of *per capita* income. Changes in the composition of GDP are extensive once the country has reached an intermediate income range ($300 to $1,000 *per capita*). In this phase, manufacturing expands rapidly and provides the impetus for structural change. As income rises the sector's share continues to grow, albeit at a slower pace once the country reaches an advanced or developed state.

The manufacturing sector's growth pattern can be hypothetically represented by an S-shaped curve, known to statisticians as a logistic (see Figure 4.1). The curve exhibits the distinctive structural features described here. When sets of countries are arranged according to the criteria employed in the typology outlined above, the position of the curve shifts or rotates although its distinctive shape remains unchanged (UNIDO, 1979, annex I). The shape of the curve suggests that during some period in the development process industrial growth is the overriding determinant of structural change. Once economies have reached an advanced state, the dynamic role played by manufacturing wanes.

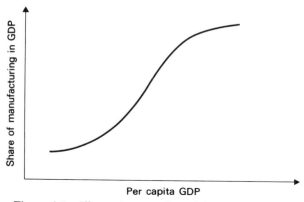

Figure 4.1   *Illustrative growth path for manufacturing*

This stylised growth pattern has certain implications for interest group behaviour and, hence, industrial policy. In comparing the LDCs with the advanced countries, counter-structural policies are more commonly associated with industrial interests in the latter countries once certain manufacturing activities have begun to experience a relative decline. The same types of policies are not evident in the LDCs where manufacturing plays a very limited role or, alternatively, is expanding rapidly.

There are other differences between agriculture and manufacturing that influence the behaviour of various sectoral interests and determine the types of competitive pressures which they may experience. Producers in the manufacturing sector are subject to a range of economic conditions that are far more heterogeneous than those encountered by agriculturalists. Market characteristics, for example, vary widely from one industry to another. The demand for processed food, textiles, clothing or footwear is income-inelastic, although the demand for other manufactured products – automobiles, various consumer electronics, furniture, professional and scientific equipment – often tends to rise dramatically with an increase in disposable income. Many industries respond to a derived demand generated by consumers within the manufacturing sector itself. Thus the market for steel reflects the demand for automobiles, capital goods and other metal products.

The demand for agricultural products is by no means monolithic; different characteristics apply to the markets for staples and luxury foods, to basic consumer items and speciality foods. Nevertheless, the characteristics of demand for agricultural products are more uniform than is the case for manufacturing. Moreover, agricultural output is also intended to meet consumer needs. Few products can be regarded as intermediate supplies and the linkages between different processing operations within the agricultural sector are weak.

Other relevant distinctions between the two sectors can be briefly noted. First, agricultural inputs are primarily renewable raw materials which are found in almost all countries. Many of the inputs in manufacturing are neither renewable nor readily available. This means that industrialists may frequently face factor markets that are oligopolistic in nature although this is less common for agriculturalists. Second, the two sectors have experienced differential rates of technological development. In manufacturing, the pace of development, as well as of its international transfer and diffusion among firms, differs widely between industries like steel, textiles, capital goods and petrochemicals, while the range of existing technologies is not so great in agriculture. Third, the labour and skill requirements of the two sectors are distinct. The agricultural labour force is mainly unskilled while many manufacturers require highly skilled employees. Wage patterns and union tactics in the two sectors differ accordingly.

Although this list could be extended, the distinction between the two sectors should already be clear. Briefly stated, prevailing economic characteristics are largely unique to a given industry or even a subset of firms within an industry. The economic forces that help to shape the path of agricultural development, although certainly not uniform, are not by any means so diverse as those operating in the manufacturing sector. Because agriculturalists are subject to a more homogenous set of economic forces, they have found it relatively easy to forge common policy objectives. Thus they have been comparatively effective in exerting political pressure and in influencing the policies applied to agriculture. The degree to which manufacturers share a common set of economic constraints is along narrower lines that are confined to particular industries rather than sectorwide. This is reflected in their policy objectives as well as in their responses to adjustment pressures. As a consequence, the role of industrial interest groups is somewhat fragmented. The following chapter looks at specific industries in more detail; the changing composition of output within the manufacturing sector is examined, along with various interpretations of these shifts and some of their policy implications.

5

Structural Change within the Manufacturing Sector

This chapter looks at the composition of the manufacturing sector in more detail and considers some of the major determinants of change at the level of individual industries. Earlier chapters have stressed the fact that changes in the existing economic structure often provide the impetus or political pressure for new policy initiatives. This chapter also introduces a discussion, to be elaborated later, of the ways in which political and policy motives may be associated with – and, indeed, sometimes cause – these changes.

Interpretations of structural change

The search for similarities in patterns of structural change has a comparatively short history dating back to the work of Fisher (1939) and Clark (1940). Originally attention focused on sectoral interrelationships; economists observed the progressive movement of labour from agriculture to manufacturing and to services and explained these shifts in terms of the changing pattern of domestic demand. Subsequent work (Kuznets, 1957) showed the need for a more comprehensive treatment of the factors determining patterns of structural change. Simultaneously, the widening industrial base in many countries, coupled with the proliferation of industrial data, allowed economists to extend their investigation to include industrial branches within the manufacturing sector (Hoffman, 1958; UN, 1963b; Chenery and Taylor, 1968; UNCTAD, 1976; UNIDO, 1979, ch. II and annex I). Before examining some alternative explanations for the changing structure within manufacturing, it will be helpful to take a closer look at the actual distribution of net output. The data in Table 5.1 summarise long-term trends in the composition of net output in manufacturing among a large number of countries. The results suggest three general tendencies. First, shifts in the shares of specific

Table 5.1 *The structure of net manufacturing output by country group, 1963, 1970 and 1978[a] (percentage)*

Industry	ISIC	Country group [b] (number of countries)								
		Advanced market economies (23)			Advanced socialist countries (7)			LDCs (47)		
		1963	1970	1978	1963	1970	1978	1963	1970	1978
Food products	311/2	12.9	10.9	10.7	15.2	12.7	10.7	26.3	21.2	18.9
Beverages	313	2.8	2.6	2.6	2.9	2.6	2.2	5.7	4.9	5.7
Tobacco	314	1.5	1.1	1.0	1.9	1.3	0.9	6.3	4.9	4.4
Textiles	321	7.0	6.3	5.4	10.5	9.1	7.7	11.3	11.8	10.8
Wearing apparel	322	4.2	3.6	4.1	4.0	4.0	3.5	3.6	3.9	4.1
Leather and fur products	323	0.9	0.7	0.6	1.0	0.9	0.7	1.0	0.9	0.9
Footwear	324	1.4	1.0	0.9	1.8	1.5	1.3	1.7	1.8	1.6
Wood and cork products	331	3.5	3.1	2.8	3.2	2.4	2.0	3.7	3.2	2.8
Furniture and fixtures excl. metal	332	2.9	2.7	2.5	1.4	1.5	1.6	2.1	1.8	1.3
Paper	341	4.1	4.4	4.3	1.5	1.4	1.3	1.8	2.0	2.3
Printing and publishing	342	5.5	4.9	4.8	0.9	0.9	0.8	2.9	2.6	2.4
Industrial chemicals	351	3.2	4.2	5.0	4.1	6.0	6.7	2.1	2.8	3.2
Other chemicals	352	2.9	3.4	3.7	1.3	1.7	1.9	4.2	4.6	5.3
Petroleum refineries	353	1.0	1.4	1.4	1.7	2.4	2.6	5.6	7.2	7.1

Miscellaneous products of petroleum and coal	354	0.8	0.5	0.4	0.7	0.6	0.4	0.2	1.0	0.8
Rubber products	355	1.3	1.6	1.4	1.3	1.4	1.5	1.9	1.6	1.6
Plastic products	356	1.0	1.7	2.0	0.6	0.8	1.0	0.6	1.1	1.4
Pottery, china and earthenware	361	0.5	0.5	0.5	0.5	0.5	0.5	0.6	0.5	0.5
Glass	362	0.9	0.9	0.9	0.9	1.0	1.0	0.6	0.7	0.7
Other non-metallic mineral products	369	3.8	3.8	3.5	4.0	3.9	3.4	3.5	3.9	4.0
Iron and steel	371	4.5	4.9	4.8	8.7	7.7	6.6	1.6	2.5	2.6
Non-ferrous metals	372	1.6	1.7	1.8	2.4	2.4	2.1	1.5	1.2	1.3
Metal products, excl. machinery	381	7.6	8.1	7.7	⎫	⎫	⎫	3.5	4.2	4.3
Non-electrical machinery	382	7.7	8.2	8.1	⎬ 26.6	⎬ 30.4	⎬ 36.6	1.6	1.9	2.3
Electrical machinery	383	5.4	6.6	7.9	(26.6)	(30.4)	(36.6)	1.5	2.6	3.7
Transport equipment	384	7.8	8.3	8.4	⎭	⎭	⎭	2.7	3.1	3.8
Professional and scientific equipment, photographic and optical goods	385	1.0	0.9	1.1	⎫ 2.9	⎫ 2.9	⎫ 3.0	0.3	0.4	0.5
Other manufactures	390	2.3	2.0	1.7	⎭	⎭	⎭	1.6	1.6	1.6

Source: UNIDO, 1982c, Table 6, p. 19.

Notes:

a All calculations were based on data in US dollars at 1975 prices.

b Percentages for 1970 and 1978 used an identical country sample for each economic grouping. In a few instances data for 1978 were not available and the country's composition of net manufacturing output in 1977 was used. Owing to variations in the country coverage, the composition of the sample in 1963 differed slightly from that in later years.

industries have usually been more pronounced than the expansion or contraction of the manufacturing sector itself. Second, there are few instances where the share of a specific industry revealed no definite trend – upward or downward – during the period shown. Finally, the direction of change was often (but not always) repeated in each of the three country groups. Although these observations on their own provide no real basis for generalising about structural change within the manufacturing sector, they do suggest some similarities in the growth patterns of specific industries.

A rough impression of the magnitude and scope of structural change can be obtained by comparing the shares of expanding and contracting industries in different years. The results, given in Table 5.2, help to distinguish between the pattern of change occurring in the 1960s and that observed during the 1970s. In advanced market economies the magnitude of the contractions and expansions between 1963 and 1970 was equivalent to 6.4 per cent of MVA, compared with shifts of 7.3 per cent in socialist countries and 9.1 per cent in LDCs. The magnitude of structural change during the 1970s was noticeably reduced in both the LDCs and in the advanced market economies. In the former group, redistribution was equivalent to 5.4 per cent of total MVA, while an even smaller shift (3.6 per cent) was observed in the advanced market economies. Socialist countries were the only group that continued to experience a pattern of structural change that was roughly comparable in both the 1960s and 1970s. The scope of industrial contractions – meaning the share of those industries experiencing a relative decline – also differed during the two periods. Again, the distinction was most pronounced in the advanced

Table 5.2   *The shares of manufacturing value added in expanding and contracting industries by country group, 1963–78 (percentage of total MVA)*

	Advanced market economies		Advanced socialist countries		LDCs	
	1963–70	*1970–78*	*1968–70*	*1970–78*	*1963–70*	*1970–78*
Contracting industries	46.7/40.3	64.2/60.6	51.4/44.1	51.4/43.6	52.0/42.9	55.5-50.1
Expanding industries	48.1/54.5	30.4/34.0	37.9/45.2	47.1/54.9	46.4/55.5	39.1/44.5

Source: Table 5.1
Note: Contracting industries were defined to be those whose shares in total MVA declined during the period indicated; expanding industries are defined as those where the share rose in the period shown. Industries that had no change in share are excluded from the total which, therefore, does not add up to 100.

market economies where industries accounting for more than two-thirds of all MVA in 1970 experienced a relative decline in the subsequent decade compared with only 47 per cent in the earlier period. These comparisons suggest the possibility of a definite break in the pattern of structural change in Western economies and, perhaps, in LDCs. The result might be attributable to the general slowdown in economic growth during the 1970s. It is not self-evident, however, that slow growth inevitably leads to a more stable industrial structure; causation might also run in the reverse direction, meaning that only a modest degree of structural change will result in a comparatively low rate of growth. In any case, it is apparent that a search for empirical regularities requires a more thorough investigation of the interrelationships between growth and structural change in manufacturing.

Economists have put forward several different explanations for structural change. An early version focused on long-term changes in demand and distinguished between light and heavy industries (Hoffmann, 1958; UNIDO, 1969). A second, closely related, explanation of structural change stressed the differences between consumer non-durables, capital goods and (sometimes) industrial supplies or intermediates. The definition of consumer goods overlaps with that of light industry, while industrial intermediates and capital goods are mainly supplied by heavy industry. Both these classifications were based on similar lines of reasoning. The share of investment in GDP was expected to grow most rapidly in countries at early stages of development. As income increased, the growth of domestic demand would favour heavy industries producing capital goods and consumer durables. This pattern of structural change was also expected to prevail in advanced countries as well as in LDCs, because specific industries such as machinery and transport equipment would continue to absorb a growing share of investment and because the proportion of capital goods in a total exports would rise as a country became more advanced.

Table 5.3 describes the evolution of the manufacturing sector in terms of these classifications. Two alternative sets of estimates are available for the sectoral breakdown into light and heavy industries. Although differences in country coverage and statistical methods affect the estimates for the two subsectors, the patterns of change are similar. The share of heavy industry has indeed increased everywhere, although the extent of the shift was most evident in the LDCs. Among the advanced countries the shift from light to heavy industry slowed after 1970. The trends suggest that the light–heavy ratio will eventually be stabilised in the advanced economies. Studies of individual countries – Australia, Canada and the USA – have found a tendency for the light–heavy ratio to stabilise at around 0.5 (Batchelor et al., 1980, p. 131). Not surprisingly, when the data is arranged to conform to the second classification, the distribution of net output among industries producing consumer non-durables, industrial intermediates and capital goods reveals a comparable pattern. That portion of value added which is attributable to the production of consumer non-durables has steadily declined. In contrast, the corresponding share of capital goods has risen substantially, while there was a moderate increase in the share of net output (MVA) in those industries producing industrial intermediates.

A more elaborate effort to identify consistent growth patterns in manufacturing was made by Chenery and Taylor (1968, pp. 409–15), who chose to distinguish between industries in terms of the *relative* changes in income elasticities that occurred as income rose. This led them to consider the level of *per capita* income at which each industry makes its main contribution to the growth of the manufacturing sector. Thus 'early industries' supply essential demands in poor countries although their share of manufacturing activity does not rise as income grows. 'Middle industries' are those whose share of net manufacturing output expands rapidly at intermediate levels of *per capita* income but record only modest gains at higher income levels. 'Late industries' take over as the most rapidly expanding form of manufacturing activity once the country reaches an advanced state.

Table 5.3 shows how the pattern of manufacturing activity has changed when industries are arranged according to their income (or growth) elasticities. The results provide a more marked contrast between different country groups than those obtained when using a light–heavy or an end-use demarcation. In the LDCs, early industries continue to predominate, although their share of MVA has steadily declined. At present, this subgroup accounts for less than one-quarter of the MVA in advanced countries, where the bulk of manufacturing activity is carried out by late industries. These trends leave the impression that the expansion of late industries takes place largely at the expense of early industries, while middle industries maintain a roughly constant share. In part, this result may be due to the fact that the available information lumps all LDCs together, thereby preventing a comparison of industrial patterns between countries in the low-to-intermediate range of the income spectrum. Furthermore, the data for advanced countries may overestimate the share of middle industries, because the statistical classification available at that time was not precise. Chenery (1968, p. 421) noted, for example, that a 'large portion' of chemicals would probably be defined as a late rather than a middle industry if the data that was available to him had specified industry shares rather than applying to the entire chemicals division (ISIC 35). Presumably, his comments referred to chemical products (ISIC 352) and plastics (ISIC 356).

Table 5.3 The distribution of manufacturing value added (in constant prices) by industrial sub-groups, 1963, 1970 and 1978 (percentage)

Industrial sub-group[a]	Advanced socialist countries			Advanced market economies			LDCs		
	1963	1970	1978	1963	1970	1978	1963	1970	1978
I Industrial sub-sector (as compiled from country data)									
light industry	47.6	42.0	36.9	47.2	42.2	40.5	68.7	61.3	57.5
heavy industry	52.4	58.0	63.1	52.8	57.8	59.5	31.3	38.6	42.4
II Industrial sub-sector[b] (as compiled from indices for sub-sector)									
light industry	36.0[c]	33.0	33.3	35.2[c]	33.0	32.8	56.8[c]	52.8	43.4
heavy industry	64.0[c]	67.0	66.7	64.8[c]	67.0	67.2	43.2[c]	47.2	56.6
III End use									
consumer non-durables	45.7	39.8	34.4	44.9	38.9	37.1	66.2	58.6	54.4
industrial intermediates	16.6	19.7	20.3	19.5	22.4	23.1	21.1	25.4	27.0
capital goods (including consumer durables)	37.7	40.5	45.3	35.6	38.7	39.8	12.7	15.9	18.5
IV Income elasticity									
early industries	26.5	22.6	21.2	33.3	28.1	23.5	52.3	45.5	42.3
middle industries	21.8	23.8	24.1	19.7	22.2	22.6	25.1	28.4	28.7
late industries	49.4	51.6	53.0	44.1	46.8	50.9	21.0	24.4	27.3

Source: Table 4.1 and, UNIDO, 1982c, Table 5, p. 17.
Notes:
a For the statistical definition of light and heavy industry, see UNIDO, 1974, p. 19.
b Percentages were originally derived from United Nations indices for the two sub-sectors and country coverage was more complete than data compiled from individual country information.
c 1965.

There are several reasons why these approaches are only of limited use for an analysis of interrelationships between industrial policy and structural change. First, they resort to a 'broad brush' technique by classifying a number of industries according to investment, demand or income characteristics that, at any time, may accurately describe some production processes within a given industry but not others. Second, the product range supplied by any set of firms can change dramatically in only a few years, so that an entirely new set of criteria may be needed. Third, generalisations about industrial structure across countries are of only limited applicability, even among countries at comparable levels of development. The effects of national differences in the pattern of domestic demand, the level of resource endowment or the choice of industrial policies, have already been noted. Finally, there is a network of other determinants – the involvement of the TNC and the state, the production technologies used and the degree to which they can be transferred, the structure of firms – all of which can affect the development of a particular industry or even a subset of firms. The impact of these characteristics becomes greater once attention is focused on the composition of net output within the manufacturing sector rather than on a comparison between economic sectors. For these reasons, a more detailed frame of reference is preferred for examining the relationship between industrial structure and policy.

Industrialisation in a global context

The figures in Table 5.4 describe world industry from another viewpoint. Like the domestic conditions noted above, the global dispersion of manufacturing activity (measured by value added) in a particular industry has a bearing on the policies applied to the industry. The global dispersion of industrial activity provides a rough impression of the nature of these external forces in much the same way as the national composition of manufacturing output can be used to gauge the extent and direction of domestic forces. Some economists would choose to explain the industrial configuration in Table 5.4 in terms of the conventional dicta of international economics such as comparative advantage, market size, proximity to buyers and resource endowment. Thus the rising importance of textile producers in LDCs would be interpreted as a reflection of these firms' comparative advantage in lower labour costs. Similarly, the gains recorded by steel producers might be partly due to the growing market for steel in the LDCs, while the global distribution of petroleum refining activities can be attributed to the random distribution of natural resources.

Table 5.4 The distribution of value added (at constant prices) by economic grouping in selected industrial branches and selected years (percentage)

ISIC	Branch	LDCs			Advanced socialist countries			Advanced market economies		
		1970	1975	1979	1970	1975	1979	1970	1975	1979
311/2	Food products	15.2	15.2	15.8	23.7	25.9	25.3	61.1	58.9	58.9
313	Beverages	14.2	15.8	19.2	20.3	22.0	21.4	65.5	62.2	59.3
314	Tobacco	28.8	30.7	32.7	13.8	15.2	15.5	57.4	54.1	51.9
321	Textiles	16.8	18.5	18.6	24.8	29.0	29.6	58.5	52.6	51.8
331	Wood and cork products	9.8	10.8	11.5	17.5	21.1	19.6	72.7	68.1	68.9
341	Paper and products	6.6	8.0	8.5	6.9	9.1	8.0	86.5	82.9	83.5
351	Industrial chemicals	6.1	7.6	7.6	20.7	26.5	24.8	73.2	65.8	67.6
352	Other chemical products	14.3	17.6	18.4	5.8	7.4	6.8	80.0	75.0	74.8
353	Petroleum refineries	37.3	35.8	34.7	10.6	15.3	16.3	52.1	49.0	49.0
354	Miscellaneous products of petroleum and coal	11.3	13.9	16.0	38.1	40.5	40.2	50.6	45.6	43.8
355	Rubber products	11.5	13.3	13.6	15.7	20.2	19.9	72.8	66.5	66.5
361	Pottery, china and earthenware	11.8	12.9	12.8	26.6	34.7	37.3	61.6	52.4	49.8
362	Glass	8.1	10.2	10.1	18.2	24.2	25.3	73.8	65.6	64.6
369	Other non-metallic minerals	8.2	10.2	11.7	28.6	33.7	31.1	63.3	56.1	57.2
371	Iron and steel	6.2	8.2	9.4	18.9	23.2	22.8	74.8	68.5	67.7
382	Machinery, excluding electrical machinery	2.7	4.6	4.7	16.4	22.5	24.7	80.9	72.9	70.6
384	Transport equipment	5.2	7.2	7.0	16.1	22.0	24.2	78.8	70.7	68.8
300	Total manufacturing	8.7	10.2	10.2	18.6	22.8	23.4	72.7	67.0	66.5

Source: UNIDO, 1982a, Table 1.5

Most economists would also consider various characteristics of demand such as those noted in connection with the various classification schemes described above. While these observations are surely pertinent, they may not provide a complete picture, particularly in a world of growing industrial interdependence. For instance, current decisions as to the location of new capacity or the extent of product specialisation in steel, petrochemicals or other industries, will be tempered by the investor's judgement concerning the action of competitors elsewhere in the world and the expected policies in host countries.

The global distribution of manufacturing output shown in Table 5.4 can be regarded to some extent as a consequence of traditional economic determinants, since it provides a rough measure of the extent to which changes in competitive abilities have altered the world industrial map. However, the interpretation offered here would go beyond the traditional confines of economic theory. To the extent that the evolution of industrial policies takes place in an environment that is rife with political implications, the configuration in Table 5.4 reveals more than merely the forces of the 'invisible hand'.

A parallel may be drawn between the present line of argument and the discussion of international policy and industrial leadership in Chapter 2. It was noted there that the post-war concentration of industry in Western countries was important in influencing the choice of development priorities and industrial policies in many LDCs. Similarly, the prevailing industrial map featured in the West's post-war efforts to foster a greater degree of economic interdependence between their countries. Furthermore, an analogy applies at the level of individual industries or subgroups of firms. It should be obvious that many decisions concerning investment programmes, the priorities and expenditures for R & D, the choice of industry-specific policies, the development strategies of firms, wage negotiations and the extent of public or foreign ownership, can all be subject to non-economic considerations.

A closer look at Table 5.4 provides further insights. First, in comparison with sectoral patterns (see Table 4.1) the type of global shifts shown here can occur surprisingly rapidly. These changes usually follow a definite trend and are not simply random fluctuations. However, they affect various industries differently. As a result, adjustment pressures are unequally dispersed among industries and countries, with some industries subjected to intense, even cumulative, contractive pressure while others carry on business as usual. The intensity of interest group responses and the resultant policies vary accordingly. Second, while the redistribution of manufacturing activity generally takes place at the expense of Western producers, the source of external pressure can vary. The impetus for shifts may originate in the LDCs (as has been the case with beverages, textiles or petroleum and coal products); in socialist countries (textiles, industrial chemicals, refining, pottery and glass); or result from advances in both groups (iron and steel, and transport equipment). Alternatively, the source of external pressure often lies within the Western countries. This last possibility is obvious for industries that are largely confined to the West, such as paper, certain chemicals and non-electrical machinery. However, competition from other Western producers is an equally probable source of adjustment pressure in other industries, supplementing or even overshadowing similar forces in the LDCs or socialist countries.

This excursion into some of the international aspects of industrial adjustment and structural change reinforces the opinions expressed in the preceding section. There it was argued that attempts to generalise about the formulation of industrial policies and corporate strategies are handicapped by the heterogeneity of industries. The varying degree to which particular industries are 'sensitive' to external considerations accentuate these differences in the economic milieu. Further, once the influence of external forces is recognised, both political objectives and economic dicta are bound to shape the actions of interest groups and result in appeals for new policies for an industry or subset of firms.

The points made above all suggest the need for a more detailed or industry-specific analysis. This step is necessary in order to clarify the complex and diverse links which are likely to exist between structural change and interest group behaviour on the one hand and industry strategies and policy initiatives on the other. The following two chapters are intended to serve such a need by examining ways in which public policies and corporate strategies have evolved in response to changes in domestic and international economic conditions in five specific industries. The industries chosen for this purpose are automobiles, steel, consumer electronics, advanced electronics and oil refining. However, before embarking on the industry studies, an overview is helpful in gauging how each case relates to the foregoing discussion of world industry.

Table 5.5 documents the pattern of world production for three of these industries – automobiles, steel and oil refining. The figures clearly show that a substantial rearrangement of global production occurred in the period 1950–81. In the automobile industry the gains recorded by producers in the socialist economies and the LDCs have resulted in some loss of export markets for established Western firms. However, a more important source of adjustment pressure and uncertainty has been the emergence of Japanese car-makers as a

major force. In 1960 these firms accounted for only 1.1 per cent of
automobile production in advanced western countries but, by 1980,
they claimed 28.2 per cent of this total (JAMA, 1982, p. 12; *Automotive News*, various issues). Moreover, in recent years much of this
production has been for export. For instance, American imports from
Japan amounted to 21 per cent of all domestic car sales in 1980 and
1981, almost double the corresponding figure for 1978 and 1979
(Gomez-Ibanez and Harrison, 1982, p. 319). Such developments

Table 5.5   *The changing pattern of world production in automobiles,
steel and oil refining, 1950–81*

Year	Advanced market economies	Advanced socialist economies	LDCs
	Automobiles[a]		
1950	10147	394	36
1960	15325	730	322
1965	23058	936	548
1970	27245	1530	912
1975	28810	2851	1604
1980	24972	3110	2275
	Steel[b]		
1950	148.9	35.9	5.2
1960	228.5	86.5	20.0
1965	301.6	119.6	32.8
1970	388.5	155.6	49.9
1975	381.0	192.6	86.1
1980	394.9	209.1	113.4
1981	390.5	207.0	110.1
	Oil refining[c]		
1950	418	49	136
1960	806	164	270
1965	1071	267	397
1980	2358	742	942
1981	2356	796	936[d]

Source: Automobiles: for 1950–75, MVMA, 1977; for 1980, *Automotive News*,
various issues.
Steel: for 1950–70, ECE, 1976, annex Table III.1; for 1975, 1980, IISI, 1981, Table 1;
for 1981, IISI, 1982, p. 2
Oil refining: for 1950–65, Institute of Petroleum; for 1980–1, BP, 1982.
  Notes:
a   in thousands.
b   in millions of metric tonnes.
c   in millions of tonnes.
d   fall due to estimated cut in Iranian capacity.

had important repercussions throughout the manufacturing sector in many advanced countries by virtue of the automobile industry's overall importance, because of its links with suppliers in the steel and machine tools industries, and because of the extensive (and growing) role of sub-contracting or 'buying-in' of components and sub-assemblies.

In the case of steel, the existence of a viable industry has traditionally been regarded as a prerequisite for successful industrialisation. This emphasis contributed to the rapid post-war development of new capacity in the socialist countries, in the LDCs and in some of the more recently industrialised western countries like Italy, Japan and Spain. The high priority accorded to the steel industry also helps to explain the increase in state ownership throughout the LDCs. Governments in Western countries have responded to changes in the world steel market in different ways and although their remedies have usually stopped short of outright state ownership, major steel industries everywhere have become more dependent on public intervention to remain in business. Murrell suggests that in the UK and the USA organisational rigidities have emerged within the steel industry owing to the growing influence of interest groups and, as a result, firms have been particularly slow to adopt new innovations (1982, pp. 986–8). Such observations do not apply to Japanese steelmakers, however, since during the period 1950–80 the production of crude steel in that country rose from 5 million tonnes to 111 million tonnes (ECE, 1976, Table III.1; IISI, 1981, Table 1).

The refining industry represents a somewhat different situation again, since shifts in world leadership are necessarily constrained by countries' resource endowments. Nevertheless, the creation of new refining capacity has led to substantial changes in the pattern of world production since 1950. Drastic changes occurred during the 1970s, among the more significant being the emergence of several members of OPEC as important sites for refining. The spread of state ownership and intervention outside the OPEC countries, as well as the spread of environmental controls further politicised the industry. At the same time as these changes were becoming evident, some of the industry's main clients – the producers of chemicals and petrochemicals – were also undergoing a transition as they entered a new and more mature 'service phase' (UNIDO, 1981, p. 7), and this exacerbated the pressures for adjustment in refining itself. Nevertheless, casual observers can not help but note the degree of turmoil and conflict that divided producers and policy-makers in Western countries as well as the wider-ranging disputes that marked relations between OPEC and the advanced countries.

The growing need to accommodate changes in the existing map of world industry has been complicated in another way. In the advanced countries each of the three industries shown in table 5.5 has experienced stagnating or contracting levels of production since the mid-1970s. Logically, such trends should prompt considerable revisions in modernisation or expansion plans, in the choice of optimal plant sizes and in the development of new technologies. But the results of any such revisions tend to show up only after a considerable lag – it takes four years to plan a new car, for instance, and as many to build a steel plant – even under ideal conditions, when firms and related interest groups agree immediately on the appropriate response.

Turning to the electronics industries, table 5.6 provides a rough impression of the pattern of world production. It is immediately evident that the location of production facilities supplying consumer products such as television sets, radio receivers and sound reproduction equipment has altered drastically since 1966. As in the other industries described above, American and European producers have experienced a long-term decline in the number of units produced, while even Japanese rates of growth have slowed, and in some cases output has begun to fall. Opposite trends may be observed in socialist countries and in other countries (mainly LDCs). In fact, producers in the latter countries have now emerged as the world's major suppliers of many consumer electronics products. However, the relationship between these suppliers and others in advanced countries differs considerably from that found elsewhere, such as in the automobile, steel or refining industries. For many of the suppliers based in the LDCs are subsidiaries or affiliates of TNCs located in Europe, Japan or the USA. Furthermore, the electronics industry also differs from, say, the steel or auto industries, in that the extent of government ownership is modest. Although, as Chapter 7 will demonstrate, public purchasing, particularly of sophisticated electronic capital goods, provides a crucial element of sponsorship for certain firms in the industry, other parts of the business are scarcely touched by state intervention. Consequently, the type of adjustment witnessed among consumer electronics firms rarely owes anything to government plans, but tends instead to reflect the frontiers of new technologies and the rapid shifts in comparative costs between production sites which have made the industry among the most footloose in the world. As noted, government involvement in advanced electronics is rather greater (in the defence area, this is of course necessarily so). It is also noticeable that these goods are produced almost exclusively by Western firms. The only involvement of LDCs is in the assembly of semi-conductors and, even there, 98 per cent of production is carried out under Western firms' control (Dosi, 1981, p. 62).

The next two chapters assess the industry strategies open to firms in

Table 5.6 The changing pattern of world production in selected electronic products

a consumer electronics[a] (in millions of units)

Year	USA A	USA B	USA C	EEC A	EEC B	EEC C	Japan A	Japan B	Japan C	Socialist countries A	Socialist countries B	Socialist countries C	other A	other B	other C
1966	11.7	24.7	5.0	6.7	11.6	4.9	5.1	25.2	4.6	6.1	8.4	0.2	3.8	33.0	1.8
1970	8.3	13.6	4.0	9.3	16.4	7.3	12.4	32.6	7.4	8.9	10.8	0.2	6.3	49.0	2.0
1975	7.5	10.4	1.5	9.7	11.0	5.3	10.6	14.2	6.0	9.9	12.4	0.5	11.0	73.4	2.5
1978	9.3	11.1	2.2	11.9	10.4	4.0	13.1	16.2	10.7	10.1	13.7	0.3	16.3	79.9	2.9
1979	9.5	11.0	1.9	11.2	9.7	3.3	13.6	13.9	9.4	10.3	13.4	0.4	19.7	83.1	3.3

b semiconductors[b] (in millions of US dollars)

	USA	Western Europe	Japan
1973	3640	1100	1280
1976	4470	1250	1500
1978	5800	1700	2500

c industrial robots[c] (number of units)

	USA	Western Europe	Japan
1972	1200	—	[d]
1978	3250	2135	14000

Sources:
for part a., UN, Yearbook of Industrial Statistics, vol. II (various issues); for part b., Dosi, 1981, table 2; for part c., Fortune, 17 Dec. 1979 and The Economist, 19 Dec. 1981.

Notes:
a A = television receivers, B = radio receivers, C = sound reproducers.
b Data is for gross output. Figures include integrated circuits and estimates of US production for in-house consumption.
c Figures excude pick-and-place machines or manipulators.
d Start-up was in 1968.

these five industries. In each case the patterns of adjustment exhibited by the firms involved in the industry are discussed with particular attention paid to the interaction between change and the policy framework. For, as was argued in Chapter 1, while abstract treatments of economies' evolution necessarily overlook the exact processes whereby decisions are reached, these processes can in practice be extremely important in shaping the nature of the outcome itself, the speed at which decisions are made, and the subsequent distribution of the benefits and costs. Illustrating the influence of interest groups in the process of structural change in industries is therefore a primary objective in the following pages.

6

Ageing Poles of Industrial Growth – Automobiles and Steel

Preceding chapters have examined the process of industrial growth and the policy framework which shaped it throughout the post-war period. Particular attention has been paid to changes in inter-sectoral priorities and to the ways in which policies designed to influence the entire range of industrial activities have been implemented. Various interpretations of the changes in patterns of output in the manufacturing sector were also discussed in Chapter 5. It was argued there that the nature of policy-making and the wide disparity of the forces acting upon a given industry make a more parochial and less aggregative approach to structural investigation imperative. Chapters 6 and 7 provide an analysis of five industries in which the forces discussed earlier have been particularly noticeable. The patterns of adjustment exhibited by the firms in each industry are discussed with particular attention to the interaction between structural change and policy. For, as was argued in Chapter 1, abstract treatments of industrial development and change overlook the exact processes whereby decisions are reached; in practice these processes can be extremely important determinants of the outcome itself, as well as the speed at which decisions are made and the subsequent distribution of benefits and costs.

In view of these considerations, the role played by interest groups in the process of structural change is highlighted in the organisation of the following material. In using their new-found ability to influence public policy, producer associations – in combination with representatives of labour, managers and operators of state-owned firms, consumers or others whose interests are associated with an industry's prospects – have added a political dimension to the normal range of economic and corporate issues that are traditionally part of the firm's normal decision-making responsibilities. Interest groups such as these, acting through agreement or compromise, tend to fashion each industry's response to a competitive threat (domestic or foreign), to a shift in demand patterns or relative prices or – more generally – to a relative or absolute shift in the industry's position as a supplier, as an employer or as a user of resources. Together, the actions of interest groups affiliated with a given industry give rise to a range of 'industry strategies'. Such strategies are distinct from sector-wide approaches like import substitution; instead they are industry-specific or apply to subsets of firms or products within an industry. Several may be simultaneously pursued.

Because the prevailing directions of structural changes can be altered through interest group pressure, it is also necessary to look at how different groups voice their preferences between outcomes. For a firm facing a collapse in profits because of foreign competition, for example, the options open to it, such as developing a new product or products, subcontracting, or setting up offshore manufacturing facilities, will tend to be circumscribed by pressure groups whose interests stand to be affected by each outcome.

Within this overall treatment of structural change and policy formulation, a number of other themes will be developed as the industries are investigated. A particular form of interest group behaviour is that involving public ownership. Enough has been said about world industry in the preceding chapters to demonstrate that public ownership is widespread, even outside socialist countries. But public policy also affects manufacturing very obviously, through the apparatus of policies introduced to alter the way resources are used in that sector, and no discussion of structural change is complete without some attention being paid to this aspect. Another aspect, whose importance has been stressed throughout the book, is the unmistakably international character of contemporary industries. This suggests that a look at forms of international organisations such as transnational corporations and joint ventures is necessary.

Finally, following the lines of thought of Olson (1965, 1982) and Murrell (1982), the options for firms to move out of difficulty are thought to be related to the size and age of the industries concerned. From the early work of Clark and others, mentioned at the beginning of Chapter 5, it has been known that in a 'mature' economy the share of manufacturing in GDP tends to decelerate, to cease growing and finally to decline slightly. Moreover, from the nineteenth century onwards it has also been suggested that, on the basis of income elasticities of demand, individual industries could be categorised as being early or late developers, and that the presence of such industries would suggest the level of 'maturity' in an economy. Later still, the idea was taken down to the level of individual products in some of the marketing literature, where products losing ground to competitors were said to be in a 'mature' phase. Each of the industries studied in

Chapters 6 and 7 exhibit some of these varieties of maturity. The discussion begins with automobiles and steel which are two of the largest and more well established industries in the advanced countries. Chapter 7 provides an analysis of two more recently maturing industries, consumer electronics and oil refining, as well as an examination of advanced electronics which, by comparison, is a newly emerging industry.

The automobile industry

In recent years the auto industry had come to resemble a number of others, being characterised by fast-growing capacity while faced with sluggish growth in worldwide sales. But beyond this simple fact there are few parallels. First, there is a wide diversity of experience and prospects among the firms comprising the auto industry, whereas in industries like oil refining, weakening demand has had effects upon the operations of most if not all firms. Second, for all the talk of its global reach and international investments, the expansion of the auto industry has, since its inception, been very heavily conditioned by national tariff and trade policies; it has been severely subject to what, in another context, Harry Johnson referred to as 'economic nationalism in old and new states'. Third, and perhaps most important, the auto industry is distinguished from most others by its vulnerability to the shifts in taste and preference between many different product lines. The purpose of this section is to show how some of the industry's largest firms got into difficulties in the early 1980s and to suggest what options or industry strategies might be available in the next five years or so.

Early history and post-war period
The literature on the history of the auto industry is voluminous, and two points only need to be raised here about the industry's pre-1939 phase. First, it is a curious fact that soon after the first firms entered the field they became multinationals. By 1914 the Ford Motor Company had plants in Canada, France and the UK, as well as the USA, and only 15 years later the firm was assembling its cars in no fewer than 20 countries (Maxcy, 1981, p. 69). General Motors (GM) followed suit, operating 19 plants in 15 countries by 1928. A second important historical characteristic is that, despite this proliferation of plants, the USA was the only significant market in this period. In 1930, for example, US sales were 3 million units or 84 per cent of the world market. During these years 'all roads led to Detroit' and the emergence of production capacity in Europe and Japan (where Ford

began production in 1924) was certainly not motivated by comparative cost considerations. Indeed, in the mid-1920s, average unit costs in the USA were only one-half the estimated European level. Instead the industry's moves were plainly dictated by the trade policies of the host countries. In 1919, for instance, tariffs on the imports of built-up cars were extremely high, amounting to 25 per cent in Japan, while in Europe they ranged from 88 per cent in the UK to 212 per cent in Italy (Maxcy, 1981, pp. 74–6). The major US companies, then, were not willing multinationalists; rather, they accepted the fact that in order to share in the anticipated growth of foreign markets they needed to set up operations inside the protective walls erected by foreign governments.

The post-1945 period began with a similar set of forces at work. Defensive investment continued as the initial levels of the EEC's Common External Tariff ranged from 17 per cent in Germany to 45 per cent in Italy. Other forces also emerged during this period that gave rise to new European assembly operations. The critical dollar shortage which inhibited imports of consumer goods and the evident unsuitability of US models to European conditions were the two most important reasons.

By the early 1950s the European market had become significant and domestic firms as well as the offshoots of the big three American companies, GM, Ford and Chrysler, could all earn satisfactory rates of return. European auto registrations had reached 3.6 million (or 21.4 per cent of world sales) by 1960 compared with a US market of 7.9 million. For Europe, this represented a density – that is, ownership of cars per 1,000 inhabitants – of 68. Although a comparable level had been reached in the USA as early as 1918 (in 1960 the US density was 344), the European market was growing at a healthy pace of 8.4 per cent per year in the 1960s. Meanwhile the Japanese market was also picking up. Following the expulsion of foreign auto firms in 1936 and the devastation of the war, the establishment of an indigenous auto industry became a priority of government policy. American investments in Japanese firms were blocked while MITI tried to arrange mergers between Japanese companies in apparent preparation for the liberalisation of imports at some future date. But in 1969 and 1970 the plan was upset when Mitsubishi established links with Chrysler, while Isuzu and Toyo Kogyo made similar arrangements with GM and Ford respectively. Subsequently, this deviation in the timing, although not the spirit, of the MITI scheme did not seem to harm the Japanese industry notably.

Market growth continued and, by 1973, European auto density was 225 with sales of 9.4 million. Similarly, US sales totalled 11.3 million and the density had reached 476. That year, with its attendant oil price rises, brought the first serious reversal of the industry's fortunes since the war. The number of units sold in the USA declined by 23 per cent in 1974, while European purchases fell by 14 per cent. These circumstances gave rise to considerable confusion, both within the industry and outside, over the effects of the oil price rise and the impact of the subsequent recession on the automobile industry. For years critics of Detroit's design policies had argued that some crisis would eventually put a stop to the industry's allegedly wasteful behaviour. Segal's view, that 'the progress of the motor car offered less the long-pledged liberation than a predatory despotism' (1968, p. 280), was typical and, combined with a general concern about the ultimate exhaustibility of natural resources, led many observers to conclude that the US industry might have to adjust to a very different set of circumstances.

Change after 1973
Assisted by the fact that real rates of interest plunged to levels below zero, Western economies recovered quickly from the 1974–5 recession. Car sales in Europe resumed their long-term upward trend; each year between 1976 and 1979 marked a new sales peak, with 10.7 million units being registered in 1979. By then the average density in Western Europe was 298 but it was considerably higher in some of the richer countries such as West Germany (374) and France (344). Despite the resumption of a normal pattern of growth in demand, the years after 1974 were not exactly comparable to the 1960s. Three important differences, each of which was later to have at least some bearing on the crisis of the early 1980s, were by then developing.

    The first difference was the emergence of Japanese firms as major worldwide competitors. Up to 1963, annual levels of production in Japan were below 1 million units, far less than the levels attained in France, Germany, Italy, the UK and the USA. Consequently, Japan's share of world production of automobiles was only 6.2 per cent in 1963. However, by the mid-1960s, MITI's guidelines for its nascent car industry were clearly taking effect; annual rates of growth in domestic demand were 20 per cent between 1960 and 1973 and they supported a vigorous industry of eleven major companies. Relentless investment and massive productivity gains (discussed below) permitted producers to enjoy increasing economies of scale. By 1979 Toyota had become the world's fourth biggest car manufacturer (with sales of 3 million units, worth $12.9 billion) while Nissan (Datsun) was the sixth largest (sales of almost 2 million units valued at $10.9 billion). In 1980 Japan emerged as the largest single producer of autos, supplanting the lead held by the US since the beginning of the industry (see figure 6.1).

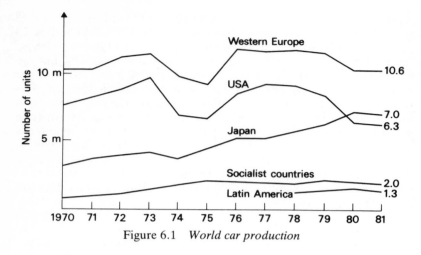

Figure 6.1   *World car production*

A second factor distinguishing the 1970s from earlier years was the progressive elimination of export opportunities in third markets. European firms anticipated that exports of fully assembled cars would continue to grow for years to come, and their previous experience, when exports rose from $4.8 billion in 1963 to $22 billion in 1973, appeared to bear out this optimism (GATT, 1979, p. 74). But, although world trade in autos continued to grow, the shares of most European and US-based firms fell back. After supplying nearly 70 per cent of the value of world exports of autos in 1963, European firms claimed only 43 per cent in 1981. The American firms' share (excluding sales to Canada) also declined, from 26 per cent in 1973 to around 12 per cent by 1979. Although they had sold 744,000 units abroad in 1963, US firms managed to export only 672,000 in 1978. The explanation for this change was, of course, the export success of Japanese producers whose share of world auto exports rose from 2.9 per cent in 1963 to 19.1 per cent in 1980. Japanese gains were particularly evident in the fastest-growing markets, the LDCs, where they supplied 6.5 per cent of these countries' imports of autos in 1963, but by 1978 had attained over 28 per cent of this trade flow. Japan's proximity to the Asia-Pacific region was convenient once Nissan and Toyota began to expand into these countries. By the late 1970s the dealership and parts networks of Japanese firms in Indonesia, Malaysia and Thailand were much more comprehensive than those of competitors and, by 1979, Japanese firms possessed no fewer than 38 assembly plants in Asian LDCs.

The problem of shrinking export prospects for established European and American firms was exacerbated by the traditional desire of LDC governments to impose local content agreements and to develop indigenous auto assembly plants rather than importing fully assembled units. Characteristic of such moves was the network of restrictions which were imposed by the members of the Andean Pact (Bolivia, Colombia, Ecuador, Peru and Venezuela). Beginning in 1969, these countries tried to establish their own auto industry, sharing out the responsibilities for the assembly of components in order to achieve greater economies of scale. In practice, the plan has been undercut by several bilateral agreements, such as one whereby Ecuador and Venezuela co-operate in the production of components rather than allowing the location of capacity to be restricted to one country. The result is almost certain to be high-cost production, and when the industry is ready to supply a significant share of the countries' markets, a high tariff of around 115 per cent will be used to exclude imports. Serious doubts, for instance over the extent to which the Andean arrangements allow or encourage rapid technological progress in auto design and manufacture, have also been expressed (Behrman, 1972, pp. 123–48; Gwynne, 1980, pp. 160–8).

A third distinction between conditions during the industry's post-1973 recovery and its rapid growth of the 1960s is associated with the first oil price rise. The impact of this move was most evident in the USA, which continued to be the world's largest market for autos. Concerned over the possibility of future oil boycotts and in an effort to diminish the country's oil-import dependence, the US government's Energy Policy and Conservation Act of 1975 instituted fleet economy regulations. The Act requires that, by 1982, cars sold in the USA should travel twice as far (24 miles) per gallon of petrol as they did in 1974. The 1985 target of 27.5 mpg refers to new cars; for the US fleet as a whole a target of 19 mpg applies.

To what extent did these regulations merely reinforce trends apparent before the 1970s? The answer to this question is exceptionally complex and concerns the way in which the US market evolved since the late 1940s. While it is true that 'the 1973 oil embargo came just as the American auto industry was making its most inefficient range of cars since World War Two' (Brown et al., 1979, p. 29), the compact car was no stranger to Detroit. The first US-made economy models were sold in 1930 and many were being imported from European affiliates of American firms. Sales of compacts grew from 1.7 per cent of the market in 1956 to 10.2 per cent only three years later, and throughout the 1960s the big three continued to market their own compact models (GM, 1974, pp. 26–8). This apparent paradox may be attributed to two contradictory trends. First, the growing affluence of the US consumer throughout the 1950s and 1960s encouraged car makers to market increasingly lavish models. In 1965, for instance, air conditioning was sold on 21 per cent of new US cars; by 1973 it featured on 72 per cent (AN, 29 Apr. 1981). Despite these trends, car prices fell by approximately 33 per cent in real terms between 1959 and 1974. (The US price index, as compiled by the Bureau of Labor Statistics, adjusts for quality changes.) In consequence, the typical new car cost just over 50 per cent of median annual household income in 1959 but, by 1973, was equivalent to only 35 per cent of this figure (GM, 1974, pp. 79–80). Simultaneously, an opposite trend was forcing the industry's planners to think along different lines. The share of the US market accounted for by compacts grew to 27 per cent in 1961, before falling gently and then rising again to 43 per cent by 1973. This shift in demand coincided with a rise in imports which claimed 15 per cent of the US market by 1971, with Japanese firms taking nearly 5 per cent of all sales (GM, 1974, p. 24).

It is not easy to explain the coexistence of these two trends. The former is probably best interpreted in the light of the persistent growth in real disposable household income coupled with a drop in real prices that resulted from greater economies of scale. The latter trend is a consequence of several factors: the reduction in the US tariff on imports (from 9.5 per cent in 1959 to 2.9 per cent by 1972), the movement of American households to the suburbs which necessitated the purchase of second and third family cars, the increasing proportion of younger, first-time buyers in the market (an inevitable consequence of the rapid growth of the under-25 age group in the total US population), a relatively over-valued US dollar before the 1971 devaluation and VAT rebates on European firms' exports (GM, 1974, pp. 32–5). Other factors which might be noted include the ability of foreign firms to buy a share of existing dealer networks ('dual franchising') and trends in comparative cost. The last of these factors is in itself a complicated question and will be pursued shortly.

So far, then, it can be seen that a variety of somewhat contradictory circumstances resulted in a long-term shift in US demand patterns, and that these, coupled with the emergence of sophisticated car-manufacturing capacity in Europe and Japan, led to a rise in US imports. The rapid growth of Japanese exports to LDCs, the fastest-growing markets in the world, allied to the tendency for the governments of these countries to limit – sometimes severely – imports of fully-assembled autos, put further pressure on the longer-established producers.

Crisis in the 1980s
The 1970s ended with two exceptionally good years in terms of sales and profits. In 1978 worldwide registrations exceeded 12 million units

and in 1979 they totalled 11.65 million. Moreover, the oil price problem seemed (until early 1979) to have disappeared; increases in the real price of petrol were substantially less than the rise in oil prices in all countries. For instance, between January 1970 and August 1979 the real price of petrol rose only 3.3 per cent in Canada while the 37 per cent increase in Italy was the largest in any major country. The USA experienced a comparatively large increase in the price of petrol, 35.1 per cent, although American prices were always much lower than those in Europe, and even in 1979 were only around one-third of European levels. Indeed, tax as a share of the retail petrol price fell in the USA, from 30 per cent in 1970 to only 15 per cent in 1979 (*The Economist*, 1 Mar. 1980, p. 73; Tate and Morgan, 1980, p. 358).

It is now necessary to examine in some detail the emergence of the crisis which overtook most of the world's auto companies in the early 1980s. To do so one must not only decide what the exact nature of the crisis is, but determine why it occurred at all, and why it occurred when it did. As to the crisis, the symptoms were plain by mid-1980. Huge operating losses were reported by the major US firms. Between them, the four largest American firms made $3 billion in 1979 but lost $4.2 billion in 1980 and $1.3 billion in 1981. In Europe, after an exceptionally profitable year in 1979, Ford, GM, Fiat and others all reported losses in 1980. As a consequence of the losses and the sales collapse which precipitated them, lay-offs increased rapidly, particularly in Michigan. Another symptom of the crisis was the imposition, in April 1981, of a three-year voluntary export restraint (VER) on Japanese autos which, by that time, accounted for nearly three-quarters of all American imports. The VER restricted Japanese sales to 1.68 million cars per year. In Europe similar strains were evident, as the Commission in Brussels was under growing pressure to restrain imports of autos – as well as other manufactured goods – from Japan.

If these were the symptoms, what were the causes of the crisis? The most significant factor was unquestionably the severe downturn in the volume of sales. The record year of 1973 saw US sales at 11.4 million. In 1977–9 sales averaged 10.7 million annually, but slumped to only 9 million in 1980, while 1981 brought a further decline to 8.5 million. Furthermore, 1981 sales by domestic firms in the USA were 6.2 million, the lowest level in twenty years. Three factors contributed to this. First, the international recession which affected all OECD countries after 1979 hit real disposable income quite seriously. The sudden rise in oil prices in 1979, feeding through the current account deficits of OECD countries, led to higher rates of inflation and later to recession as deflationary government policies were adopted. One result was that aggregate demand in the major seven OECD members – Canada, France, West Germany, Italy, Japan, the UK, the USA – rose by only

0.2 per cent in 1980 and 0.5 per cent in 1981 (OECD, 1981, p. 15). Fiscal policy was already fully extended, since few governments had restored their budgets to anything near to balance after the reflations in 1974–5, and so could not serve as a means of stimulating demand. These conditions, coupled with tighter US monetary policy after 1979, pushed up US interest rates and began a phase of competitive interest-rate bidding as other countries tried to offset the inflationary impact of a stronger dollar.

The second important contributor to the fall in sales was the very rapid increases in auto prices in the USA after 1978. Earlier it was noted that, despite the growing sophistication of Detroit's products, their real price had been falling for years. Between 1973 and 1981, however, wages grew by 79 per cent while auto prices increased by 145 per cent. Moreover, federal regulations allegedly added $700 to the cost of each car after 1975 and retooling for new models grew increasingly costly.

A third contributor to the slump in demand was associated with the oil supply shortages in some parts of the USA in 1979. These appeared to upset the entire psychology of the market as uncertainty, not only over oil availability and prices, but also about the trade-in values of traditional cars, all served to delay replacement purchases. (This factor is by no means insignificant, for in all consumer durables markets in advanced economies, replacement sales overwhelm sales to first-time buyers. Thus purchasing can be easily postponed and planners in mature markets face an additional element of uncertainty less apparent in immature, and faster-expanding, markets.)

Together these three factors help to explain the slump in demand which was the predominant characteristic of the auto industry after 1980. A second set of circumstances, however, was also at work to exacerbate the industry's problems and involved the shift in tastes, or the product mix, demanded by consumers after 1979. The steady encroachment of small cars into the total market has already been charted and, clearly, was no new phenomenon by 1979. However, that year saw a sudden turnaround which left Ford and Chrysler very badly placed, for neither had ideal models prepared. GM, fortuitously, had introduced the high-economy X-car in May 1978, and was therefore insulated to a degree. Nevertheless, the main beneficiaries were foreign manufacturers, whose sales in the USA reached a record high: 26.7 per cent of all sales in 1980 and 27.3 per cent of sales in 1981. (For a detailed discussion of the effect of high oil prices on demand for cars by size, see Mogridge, 1978.)

Moreover, in attempting to meet this new pattern of demand throughout the next two years, US firms were to find themselves persistently wrong-footed. The apparently capricious behaviour of con-

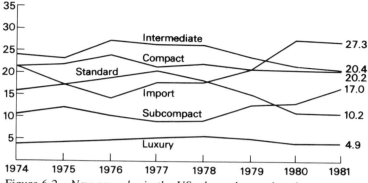

Figure 6.2   *New car sales in the US: shares by market class, 1974–81*

sumers who returned in large numbers to full-sized cars after 1974, as the real price of petrol slipped, had already surprised companies. Assembly plants for full-sized cars were working to capacity during 1978, and Ford's policy of concentrating its reinvestment on full-sized rather than economy models seemed completely vindicated. In 1982 a marketing executive was quoted as saying that 'before, you had a cycle every three or four years; now you have a cycle every few months . . . these market shifts are playing havoc with the cars on the drawing board' (*New York Times*, 17 Feb. 1982). Figure 6.2 confirms this view, and shows just how complicated the demand shifts between segments have become. This complexity is indicated by the fact that standard and luxury cars accounted for 18.5 per cent of sales in the first five months of model year 1982, whereas they took 16.8 per cent of sales in the year before (*New York Times*, 21 Feb. 1982). Not only were fears over oil prices easing once again, but the recession had a greater impact on lower-income workers who would typically drive the more fuel-efficient cars. Thus, the mix of demand in the market once more shifted towards larger cars.

Such capricious behaviour could not, of course, have come at a worse time. For, following the collapse of the overall market and planners' interpretation of this as evidence of a permanent shift in tastes, unprecedently large investment programmes had been started. GM alone embarked on a $40 billion investment scheme for 1980–4; the rest of the industry worldwide committed itself to a further $40 billion of outlays. Investment programmes, which required massive cash flows, were handicapped by lower overall sales, lower US sales within total sales, a smaller proportion of sales in large (high unit profit) models, and (until 1981) a more aggressive pricing policy by the Japanese importers.

Table 6.1 *Indices for output, earnings and wages in the manufacturing sector, selected countries, 1972–81 (1975 = 100)*

| | | | | *Output per person-hour in manufacturing* | | | |
	US	Canada	Japan	France	Germany	Italy	UK
1972	93	92	87	94	89	91	94
1973	96	96	102	100	94	102	101
1974	98	98	104	103	96	106	102
1975	100	100	100	100	100	100	100
1976	106	104	110	111	107	109	105
1977	108	108	115	115	110	108	106
1978	110	112	124	121	113	111	107
1979	112	114	134	129	118	122	109
1980	115	113	142	131	116	127	107
1981	119	114	146	. . .	119	130	113

| | | | | *Hourly earnings in manufacturing* | | | |
	US	Canada	Japan	France	Germany	Italy	UK
1972	79	70	53	62	76	52	56
1973	85	76	66	71	84	64	64
1974	92	86	87	85	92	79	78
1975	100	100	100	100	100	100	100
1976	108	114	109	114	107	121	116
1977	118	126	117	128	114	155	127
1978	128	135	123	145	120	180	146
1979	139	147	131	164	127	214	169
1980	151	162	142	189	135	262	203
1981	165	181	151	212	142	324	232

| | | | | *Wage costs per unit of output* | | | |
	US	Canada	Japan	France	Germany	Italy	UK
1972	85	76	60	67	86	57	59
1973	89	79	64	71	89	63	63
1974	94	87	84	83	96	75	77
1975	100	100	100	100	100	100	100
1976	102	110	99	101	100	111	111
1977	110	117	102	112	103	143	120
1978	117	117	100	120	106	161	136
1979	124	129	98	128	108	176	155
1980	132	143	99	145	116	207	189
1981	139	159	103	. . .	119	249	206

Source: NIESR Review (1982), May, p. 88.

Despite their need for extra financing, the prices of US firms were being increasingly undercut by importers. The power of the big three to set US car prices has long been alleged – and for as long denied. Senator Estes Kefauver cited car makers as one of the most egregious offenders in his Senate investigations of US monopolies, noting that 'the auto industry . . . is a tribute to the intensity of non-price forms of competition in an industry where effective price competition is effectively barred' (1965, p. 102). The manufacturers naturally denied this, arguing that 'no motor vehicle manufacturer has control of any part of the market' (GM, 1974, p. ii). However, the fact that Japanese firms were apparently able to land their cars in the USA at a cost differential of up to $2,000 per unit suggests that they severely constrained the pricing policies of American competitors. How then did such a large cost differential arise?

Explanations for the erosion of the competitive position of US firms are complicated. Table 6.1 shows trends in the manufacturing sector for output per person-hour, hourly earnings and wage costs per unit of output in various countries since 1972. It is apparent that Japanese wage costs per unit have barely risen whereas US wages have increased by around 40 per cent. Table 6.2 shows that after 1955 production of autos per man-year scarcely changed in most countries, whereas in Japan it increased roughly seven-fold. These facts would be sufficient to result in a formidable cost differential, but they were supplemented by a depreciation in the real rate of exchange for the Japanese yen that led to a 21 per cent improvement in the country's competitive position between October 1978 and early 1981 (BIS, 1981, pp. 132–4). Efforts by US producers to identify the source of Japanese cost advantage have stressed that fewer labour hours are required to produce each car and that lower wage-rates (both direct

Table 6.2   *Productivity growth in selected countries' auto industries, 1955–78*

| Year | UK | Producing country: cars per employee-year | | | | Japan |
		Germany	France	Italy	US	
1955	4.1	3.9	3.6	3.0	19.3	2.2
1965	5.8	6.4	6.2	6.3	23.2	5.9
1973	5.8	7.7	6.9	7.1	31.6	13.1
1978	4.7	8.6	6.6	6.2	20.9	16.3

Sources: D. T. Jones (1981), p. 101; *The Economist*, 23 Aug. 1978, p. 89.
Notes:
i   Output adjusted for the weight of each car produced.
ii   Output by Japanese firms varied in 1977 from 54.4 at Toyota, 40.4 at Nissan to 22 at Isuzu.

and indirect) are paid per hour. In comparison, other cost considerations are of little consequence. Even the cost of shipping a car from Japan to the USA (put at $300 per unit in 1981) only slightly offsets a $1,500–$2,000 per unit cost advantage while the US tariff, 2.9 per cent, is hardly significant.

A major reason for the Japanese advantage is their extensive use of outside suppliers and low inventory-output ratios. Whereas US firms typically manufacture 50 per cent of the value of their cars in-house, 70 per cent of the value of Japanese cars is bought in. Toyota, for instance, depends on 44,000 outside firms (virtually all of them in Japan) which together supply parts accounting for 71 per cent of all the hours spent constructing a car (*Fortune*, 11 Aug. 1980, p. 109). That different practices are significant in reducing overheads can be seen from Table 6.3, which shows that nearly one-fifth of the ex-works unit cost in the USA reflects fixed costs.

Industry strategies in the 1980s
Although an assault on higher unit costs is underway in the USA, there are doubts as to whether this strategy will be sufficient. Ironically, the options available to US firms to improve efficiency may be limited by the very strength and scale of the industry. Even after a

Table 6.3   *Estimates of US firms' production costs: compact models*

		cost per unit, $1982
a	*Assembly plant*	
	Body	552
	Engine	311
	Transmission	90
	Chassis	501
	Assembly of vehicle	533
	Total	1,987
b	*Overheads*	
	fixed costs @ 40%	795
	profit target @ 10%	278
	R & D, special tooling	1,236
	Total	2,309
c	*Sub total*	4,296
d	*Dealer markup @ 22%*	1,212
e	*Retail price*	$5,508

Source: Study by Rath & Strong Inc., quoted in *Business Week*, 1 Mar. 1982, p. 95.

one-third attrition since 1979, American automobile firms employ one million workers. They manufacture in virtually every state in the union. Firms have links with other enormously powerful industries in the country, of which steel, rubber and glass are only three examples. Moreover, the industry is of strategic importance, in that defence equipment of various sorts is made by some auto firms. All this power invites obligation. And the signs in the early 1980s are that powerful interests want to retain as much of the US-owned auto industry within that country's borders as possible. These circumstances may prevent US firms from implementing their cost-cutting strategies to the extent required if they are to match the Japanese in competitive ability.

Recent efforts by US firms to reduce their costs have taken two forms. First, a variety of schemes are already in progress to cut labour costs. The United Auto Workers (UAW) and Ford agreed on cost-cutting measures early in 1982, and GM was able to negotiate a considerably tougher pay agreement for 1982–5 than the 1979–82 one. At Chrysler, 'Detroit's new pragmatists', as *The Economist* has referred to the UAW (15 Aug. 1981), agreed to wage concessions of $600 million to help keep the company afloat. These concessions have not always been overwhelmingly popular among the workforce. Among GM's unionised employees, the vote for accepting the company's offer was only 52 per cent, and 48 per cent against. At Ford plants the vote was higher, possibly reflecting the fact that Ford announced losses of $1.5 billion in 1980 and $1 billion in 1981, while GM managed to record a profit of $333 million in 1981. Second, companies have put pressure on their suppliers to roll back earlier price increases. Henceforth, GM also intends to buy in its steel on price tenders rather than on long-term contracts. By cutting variable costs in this way, and by mounting similar assaults upon fixed costs, particularly the overhead of the executive staff, firms have managed to reduce, sometimes considerably, the rates of capacity utilisation at which they can break even. Chrysler, for instance, halved that rate in the three years to 1982; the biggest three firms together are thought to have reduced their break-even volume from 12.2 million units per year to 9.1 in 1982 (BW, 21 June 1982). Another means of cutting costs will occur as car sizes continue to shrink. Quite simply, less material will be used, although the absolute weights of some higher-priced materials will grow. Table 6.4 shows the intended changes to be introduced by 1985.

To supplement these efforts, however, US firms will increasingly have to consider other strategies as well. The major options are summarised in Table 6.5. First, the industry, or more correctly, its owners and their political representatives, could attempt to preserve

Table 6.4   *Inputs of materials for US-built cars, 1975–85 (in pounds)*

	1975	1980	1985	%change 1975–85
Steel	2,420	1,834	1,356	−44
Iron	626	458	216	−65
Plastics	168	184	252	+50
Rubber	160	124	180	+13
Aluminium	86	124	156	+81
Glass	94	80	72	−22
All others	416	276	168	−60
Total car weight	3,970	3,080	2,400	−40

Source: Study by Arthur Anderson & Co., cited in *Business Week*, 15 June 1981.

the status quo by limiting Japanese sales to a certain share of the market, possibly with floor and ceiling values to cope with changes in the size of the market over the business cycle. But with so much existing unused capacity, even at current levels of Japanese penetration, this approach would not yield a stable solution. The obvious problem of trying to impose a quota in perpetuity is that it leads the thwarted exporter to add more value to the items he can export, thus posing a threat to the higher-priced segment of the protected market as well. This tendency has been documented in the case of garment makers in South Korea, for instance, who are attempting to circumvent the constraints placed on them by quotas (*FT*, 10 Aug. 1981). The same practice is apparent in the automobile industry and, as later discussion will show, can be observed in other industries as well. As the strong rise in the yen against the dollar during the first half of 1978 reduced Japanese sales in their major overseas market, their immediate response was to turn to higher value models. Although, in view of subsequent exchange-rate changes, it was perhaps premature to claim that 'the cheap imported Japanese car is dead' (*The Economist*, 23 May 1978), the strategy set in motion about that time will increasingly appear at the retail level. Indeed, as early as 1979 the average price of an imported car in the USA matched that for a domestic car. By 1981 imported cars, on average, sold at $9,318 (a 357 per cent rise over their 1961 price) while domestic cars sold at $9,012 (a 207 per cent rise). The effect of this switch in price characteristics on importers' profits has been substantial (USNWR, 8 Mar. 1982).

Alternatives to Trade Restrictions
Based on this reasoning, some strategy in addition to one of imposing stringent trade restrictions on Japanese imports would seem to be preferable in Detroit. One option reflects the desire of the UAW

(who have seen approximately one million jobs in their industry disappear since 1978) to protect employment. The UAW has long argued that Japanese capacity should be built in the USA to boost jobs, albeit not at the pay levels set by Detroit, where auto workers enjoy a wage differential of up to 66 per cent in excess of the average for manufacturing. VW set up a plant, able to produce 200,000 units annually, in mid-1978, but in 1982 it postponed plans for a second plant indefinitely. This reflected the change in the DM/$ exchange rate, ironically the very factor which prompted the establishment of the first plant.

Although economic forces in the 1970s dictated that VW establish capacity in the USA or resign itself to selling fewer cars in that market, the same forces are not so compelling for the Japanese. There is little reason to expect Japanese competitors to invest $500 million in a plant employing workers that are relatively expensive and less quality-conscious than in Japan. The Japanese reluctance may also result from the fact that such a plant would come on stream just as all three US firms, plus an American Motors now reinforced by Peugeot, are improving their own ability to supply economy models. While there is evidence that Japanese management success is transferable and, consequently, a Japanese-run plant could achieve better financial results than a domestically-run plant in the same industry, the view from Tokyo reflects all the ambivalence with which the auto industry has traditionally viewed foreign investment.

Reports commissioned by US firms have shown that in inventory control, direct labour costs and quality control, the advantages of Japanese plants are such that only a part of their competitiveness can be readily transferred overseas. By relying upon outside sub-contractors for up to 70 per cent of the value of their cars, Japanese firms carry very little inventory. US car firms are estimated to carry $775 in stocks and work-in-progress per unit produced, equivalent to five times the corresponding Japanese figure. Thus Japanese plants can be physically smaller, quicker to build and cheaper to heat (WSJ, 7 Apr. 1982). In direct labour costs, 14 man-hours were used to build a car in Japan compared to 29 in the USA in 1981. This is a differential which could be reduced only with difficulty (USNWR, 8 Mar. 1982) while the quality control systems may be still harder to transplant. Indeed, consultants in 1982 advised that what is involved is far more than setting up 'quality circles' in US plants; it is 'getting the whole workforce-management picture straightened out' (AN, 15 Feb. 1982).

Nonetheless, Japanese firms have reluctantly started to produce cars and light trucks in the USA. Nissan has a plant for assembling pick-up trucks at Smyrna, Tennessee, and Honda of America will use

40 per cent local sourcing for its Marysville, Ohio, plant. In doing so the Japanese firms were reacting to a wider range of considerations than the VER imposed on them in 1981, although the timing of the Nissan investment decision, barely a week before the first report of the International Trade Commission (ITC) into the problems caused to Detroit by car imports, was unlikely to have been a coincidence. They were also responding to the growing support in the USA for local content rules, similar to those imposed in virtually all LDCs. Both labour interests and manufacturers warmly endorsed this move during 1981 and 1982, and one Congressman collected over 200 co-sponsors for a bill requiring up to 90 per cent local content for cars by 1985 (*NJ*, 22 May 1982). Other trade reciprocity bills have been proposed – among them the so-called Two Way Street Bill, which calls for tariffs to be imposed on Japanese car exports to the US (*FT*, 24 Feb. 1982). The UAW proposals, as announced by President Douglas Fraser in mid-1982, include an element of US content in every single imported car. This, he argued, would by 1985 create 868,000 new jobs in car and supplier firms (*The Times*, 4 June 1982).

A mitigating change would be for the Japanese to liberalise their own imports. As yet, foreigners have sold few cars in Japan: in 1981, US firms sold 7,742 units or 20 per cent of the import market. Imports in 1981 took 0.7 per cent of the market. Moreover, so long as only a trivial amount of imports are permitted, there is no incentive to alter the cars offered there to right-hand-drive and this in turn constitutes another barrier (*BW*, 15 Feb. 1982, p. 39). Although Japanese officials maintain that their market was effectively liberalised in 1965, arguing that 'an increase in effective demand depends primarily on the efforts of foreign automakers' (JETRO, 1976, p. 27), they have recently admitted that standards and testing regulations still inhibit sales. The requirement that each imported car be individually tested at the dockside was not relaxed until late 1981, when the first type approval certificate was granted to the VW Golf (*FT*, 3 Mar. 1981). Certainly the UAW were not impressed by the Japanese liberalisation measures announced in 1982: Douglas Fraser referred to them at the House Foreign Affairs Committee as 'a delaying tactic', which had 'nothing for the US car industry and little for anybody else'.

An alternative to a strategy of simply relying upon greater trade restraints is the 'captive import' option, whereby US firms would resume the practice of bringing in, from their overseas affiliates, the models they are unable or reluctant to manufacture themselves. As early as 1981 Ford sold Lynx models in the USA which, having been engineered in West Germany and assembled in Spain, were sold in Europe as the Escort. A variant of this strategy is to import units from the Japanese affiliates which were acquired in the late 1960s.

Chrysler, for instance, imports 110,000 cars per year (13 per cent of its sales) from Mitsubishi, and Ford is planning to use its Toyo Kogyo affiliate similarly. Moreover, in early 1982 GM announced that after 1984 200,000 per year of a new subcompact will be imported from its Isuzu affiliate. This is the first venture into full overseas procurement by GM – the cars will be entirely built in Japan – and has naturally aroused fears among the UAW membership. The 6,600 GM workers employed to make the closest US-built substitute, the Chevrolet Chevette, are particularly concerned. Arrangements were also made to source very small one-litre cars from Suzuki during the mid-1980s.

These developments reflect the increasingly complicated pattern of interests in the US car industry, and it is worth describing their evolution during 1980–2 in some detail, since they illustrate admirably the way that some coalitions can dissolve as options change and as perceptions of risk alter through time. Early in the sales slump, in 1979, there appeared to be substantial common ground between the union and the employers; both saw imported cars as a major threat. The attitude was shared by supplier industries that also had considerable interests at stake and, as the discussion of the steel industry will show, had their own extremely sophisticated lobbying apparatus. The automobile complex, including suppliers of steel, glass, rubber, plastics, machine tools and spare parts, employed 2.5 million Americans in 1978 and, when that figure began dropping towards the 2 million mark, objections were not long delayed (*Fortune*, 14 June 1982, p. 116). A more dispersed but no less articulate group who had 100,000 of their number laid off as early as mid-1980 were the car salesmen (*The Economist*, 14 June 1980). At that time the only source of tension between the various interest groups was the level of prevailing wage rates in US auto factories. GM, which had just signed a 30 per cent three-year wage award that was almost immediately regarded as extremely damaging to competitiveness, was seeking opportunities to cut labour costs. Ford and Chrysler meanwhile turned to Washington and made a case for import controls for the car industry. At one stage, even the infant industry argument for import controls was advanced, on the grounds that building small cars was a new and untried skill for American companies.

Gradually the principles at stake became clear. First, US managers had begun to lose confidence in their ability to make successful economy cars. The reception of the 1978–9 economy models, particularly the GM X-car, was generally favourable but later models like GM's first 'world car', the J-car, were thought to be overpriced, underpowered, unexciting and still of unsatisfactory quality. Second, as the slump in sales continued, the US firms' financial resources were stretched thinner and the risks of launching further subcompact cars were regarded as excessive. Thus the captive import strategy came back onto the agenda. An early hint that some form of captive imports were likely to be sold through GM's Chevrolet marketing channels came with the announcement – confirmed in February 1983 – that Toyota would collaborate with the American firm to develop jointly a small car. Once again, Japanese interests were uneasy about the problems of transplanting their operations to an alien culture (IHT, 9 Mar. 1982). On the other hand Toyota was keen to build up its dealer network (*The Economist*, 13 Mar. 1982). Chevrolet has six times as many US dealerships as Toyota. An outsider interpreted the GM decision as follows:

> In aborting its US S-car project, GM is almost certainly reflecting a view that no matter how much of the subcompact sector it might capture . . . and no matter how cost-effectively it might mechanize production, the foreseeable labour content and labour cost would make the S-car a financial loser . . . Thus, the most technically resourceful and financially healthy American automaker seems to have concluded that US factories cannot profitably compete in the largest volume segment of the US passenger car market, if not permanently then at least for the next decade. (*WSJ*, 26 May 1982)

This line of thinking will, obviously, dull the enthusiasm of auto firms for the trade reciprocity bills under discussion, now that they are convinced of the need for captive imports as part of their recovery plans. Thus the Motor Vehicle Manufacturers' Association, bearing in mind that the international sourcing intended by its members would be hampered, is not backing any of these restrictive proposals. Also ill-disposed towards local content rules are the National Automobile Dealers' Association, whose 58-member board of directors decided in June 1982 to oppose such rules on the grounds that they would be inflationary and would have a deleterious effect upon car sales. Although the UAW wishes to see these issues discussed as matters of fundamental principle – one UAW executive said in 1982 'what you are seeing is the deindustrialization of America' – few of the other interest groups in the industry agree (*WAW*, May 1982, p. 44).

If the appeal of the Japanese tie-up is so strong – and the opinion just quoted regards it as an imperative – why not make greater use of yet cheaper labour sources? As part of the 'world car' strategy embraced by the US firms in the late 1970s, there was to be much more use of international sourcing, and GM's new investments in Austria and Spain as well as further commitments in Brazil, Mexico and other Latin American subsidiaries, confirm that this is underway. What is not so clear, however, is how far the process will be carried. To date,

US firms have made only modest investments in LDCs which mainly serve as suppliers for parts to be sold in the USA. As Maxcy (1981, p. 157) has noted, 'international sourcing in low-wage developing countries for use by parent companies in their home markets is insignificant'. What reasons are there for this hesitance?

A major part of the explanation concerns the large differential in the USA between the wages of auto workers and those of the average manufacturing worker. In September 1980 hourly earnings (excluding overtime) for all manufacturing workers in the USA averaged $7.86, while in transportation equipment they were $10.04 or 28 per cent higher (BIS, 1981). Benefits extend the differential to as much as 66 per cent. Thus American car-makers are well aware that substantial savings in labour cost economies could be realized without moving overseas. The prospect that the gap between hourly wages in the auto industry and the manufacturing sector can be eroded may have been a consideration which prompted the chairman of GM to remark that 'we don't have to go to Japan, we don't want to go to Japan' (GM News Media Briefing, Detroit, 29 Jan. 1982). The preference expressed, that for the time being US firms would prefer to rely primarily on domestic suppliers, brings the analysis full circle and back to the reluctant multinationalism of the 1920s.

The LDCs and the auto industry

It will be apparent that so far the role of the LDCs has been considered only in terms of their capacity as importers of fully assembled and knocked-down cars and – to a very marginal degree – as manufacturers. In advanced countries other than Japan the ratio of car imports to sales have risen quickly (Batchelor *et al.*, 1980, p. 42), although exports from LDCs have not been responsible. Indeed, the total imports of cars and components to LDCs rose from $5.8 billion to $21 billion between 1973 and 1979 while their exports amounted to a mere $1.7 billion in the latter year. What factors then, have limited the involvement of the LDCs in the auto industry?

The fundamental point for the auto industry in the Middle East, Africa, Latin America and Asia is that a number of these countries are only now approaching the stage of development where motorisation will grow explosively. Once *per capita* income reaches $1,000 – a level now attained by countries such as Jordan, Morocco, Syria and Tunisia – the demand for cars may expand at a rate up to four times as great as the growth of income. Thus a country where real income is growing by 7 per cent per year will double its income in ten years while auto density per 1,000 can soar from 15 to around 100–120. Already many Asian markets are significant in size. Auto registrations in Indonesia in 1981 reached 205,000 and, in Malaysia, totalled

125,000. Sales in the Philippines were around 45,000, while sales in Thailand and Singapore were 92,000 and 37,000 respectively. Even this volume of business could be overshadowed in the early 1990s by some Middle Eastern markets. There, sales rose by 15 per cent per year between 1970 and 1980 while in the same decade sales in the Asia-Pacific region grew by 2 per cent per year and the African market expanded at a rate of 3.2 per cent per year (*WSJ*, 15 Feb. 1982).

Naturally, this growth of demand can be awkward to manage, particularly if all cars are imports and if expansion of the market fails to boost domestic output or to nourish a wide range of supplier firms (UNIDO, 1978, p. 1). Mention has already been made of the failures of the Andean Pact members' auto efforts, and the example of the Maruti project, associated with Sanjay Gandhi in India, is another poor precedent (*FT*, 29 Oct. 1980). The lesson of these projects might appear to be that the capacity to design and build a car at an attractive price is not readily transferable outside the ten or so countries where it is part of the industrial tradition. Yet there is no serious question about the success of the eleven Japanese firms that matured under the aegis of MITI. Nor do the Taiwanese or South Korean firms now laying down substantial manufacturing capacity appear likely to suffer from the Andean Pact group's problems. What then are the lessons from these projects?

The first step for most newcomers to the industry has tended to be heavy state involvement. Indeed, it is usually the state's own actions – in setting prohibitively high tariffs and local content rules – which provide the impetus to set up the industry. This can be useful in two ways. First, the natural tendency of the long-established firms to compete with one another in any market so as to maintain their overall market share can result in a proliferation of models. Firms in Thailand and Indonesia have produced models in runs as low as 2,000 per year. Given that the annual target of car-makers in advanced countries is around 250,000 units, such levels of output will clearly not yield economic unit costs. As a result, domestic markets will be restricted and will hinder local suppliers in gearing up for more ambitious production runs. The second attraction of state-managed rationalisation is that offering the market to an individual firm can be traded off against a range of concessions such as higher local content levels than might otherwise be obtainable. In Morocco, for instance, the process of rationalisation has some way to go: eight firms together only produced about 20,000 cars annually between 1980 and 1982. Tunisia is a similar case where five firms share an even smaller volume of output, while Turkey hopes to eliminate some of the fourteen firms operating there. The Chilean government tried to slim down its auto industry from nine firms to one, and the Argentinian government had reduced the twenty-two firms operating within its borders to nine by the early 1970s (Behrman, 1972, pp. 33–40). Predictably, perhaps, this process has gone furthest in South Korea where, by 1980, the government had eliminated all but two firms, aiming for maximum possible output from each. The importance of this factor will, clearly, vary between countries. In planning for exports right from the start (at the rate of 100,000 per year by 1988) the Taiwanese government is pursuing a different path from Tunisia where the matching of local demand is the first priority. There is an obvious link between these objectives, in that experience demonstrates overwhelmingly the importance of exposing import substitution projects to international competition to ensure efficient resource allocation.

This strategy of ensuring a fair degree of concentration in the industry is not the whole answer, however. For despite being a relatively 'mature' industry, in the sense that technologies for manufacturing and assembly can be readily transferred to most countries, newcomers obviously face the problem of intense price competition. The need to match the most competitive prices set by the established producers means that 'best practice' technologies must be adopted from the outset. Here, too, the joint venture approach would appear to be the most promising. A further reason for wishing to involve the multinationals in a new venture is access to the former's marketing network. In an international economy overlaid to a considerable extent by barriers to trade in manufactured goods (see Chapter 8), access to established marketing apparatus (and, by implication, to the lobbying efforts that will have gone into its creation) is of paramount importance. Recognising this, the Taiwanese government insisted that the firm it would eventually select to operate (with Ford, Toyota and Nissan all bidding) must undertake to sell half of its Taiwanese output through the multinational's own dealer network. As the official responsible for the policy stated 'we don't want to be confined to Africa and South America . . . we want to be able to export worldwide' (*AN*, 15 Feb. 1982, p. 28). The rationale for this decision, which involves $2 billion of investment and is Taiwan's biggest industrial project in recent years, is instructive. Experience shows that if an indigenous auto manufacturer begins without foreign assistance he is unlikely to be successful; joint ventures are desirable to acquire the technology without which cost and quality can not match international competition. Acquisition of the technology is part of a negotiating process that focuses on domestic issues such as the rules for local content but, quite apart from this opportunity to trade off involvement and risk, the host country partner will obtain access to the multinational's sales apparatus. This last point is important.

Clearly, the attractions of using established marketing networks are by no means restricted to partners in LDCs. Recent instances have involved firms in advanced economies. In 1980 VW and Nissan announced a scheme to boost the VW's sales in Japan. Already VW supplies 30 per cent of Japan's imports and the volume of additional sales could be substantial, possibly a five-fold growth to 200,000 units annually (*WSJ*, 15 Jan. 1982). Another attraction is access to the established Nissan sales network of 3,400 outlets, as the huge cost of such a network has long been a deterrent for exports to Japan (*The Economist*, 6 Dec. 1980). To Nissan, the greatest benefit will be the prospect of breaking the nascent EEC-wide import barriers on Japanese autos. As the French government's Tokyo trade representative, M. Missoffe, commented, 'the Germans always had second thoughts about the united front of European auto manufacturers in Tokyo'. For the West German firm, taken aback by the speed with which Japanese sales penetrated the West German market, the attraction is the prospect of replacing the lost domestic sales with exports. In turn, the Japanese firm hopes to defuse the European protectionist clamour while at the same time gaining better access to the European market. This type of relationship is sufficiently new for there to be no established nomenclature for it. There is no serious commitment to technological co-operation, nor to joint ventures in third markets such as the US. Spokesmen for Nissan have denied that the scheme was a joint venture, calling it a 'new concept in business' (*FT*, 4 Dec. 1981).

Where to now?

It is apparent from the foregoing discussion that automobile firms in Europe and the USA are having to adjust to a very quickly changing trade environment. The volume of sales, as well as their pattern, have altered considerably. The intensity of competition, as regards both price and non-price factors, has changed even more markedly. The late 1970s saw a series of major adjustments being initiated. Belated realisation of lagging productivity growth spurred renewed attention to re-equipping and to cutting back overhead costs. Realisation that quality deficiencies had become a focus for consumer dissatisfaction prompted a certain amount of re-equipping but also a search for new methods of organising tasks in the assembly process. The burden of financial difficulties, as revenue fell but interest rates rose, simultaneously forced firms to seek out ways of reducing inventories and farming out some of the tasks which, in an earlier era, would have been performed in-house.

This last point is perhaps the single most pervasive theme for the automobile industry. As preceding sections have illustrated, the traditional image of the auto firm producing its own product range to sell

Table 6.5 *Problems and strategies in the US auto industry*

Problems	Possible strategies				
	A *Increase exports to Japan*	*B* *Cut US car production costs*	*C* *Subcontract e.g. to developing countries*	*D* *'Tied imports' e.g. from Japan*	*E* *Continue trade restrictions indefinitely*
1 Sales stalled because prices are too high	Only minor aid via greater economies of scale	Underway but Japanese advantage remains significant	Major possibility; not as yet important in planning	Helps profits; opposed by the UAW	Only helps insofar as restructuring is behind closed doors
2 Japanese share of market is too high	As 1A	As 1B	As 1C	As 1D	Combats but does not solve problem
3 Capricious shifts in consumer demand	No help	Slight help	Slight help	Enhances flexibility	At least stalls import sale while US firms re-gear
4 Japanese plans to move up-market	Significant volumes would help	Imperative if US is to retain full-size car segment	Helps in retaining full-size car segment	Helps; but then where is US domestic comparative advantage?	As 3E
5 Shift to (lower profit) economy models within total sales	Slight help	Helps boost margin on economy sales	Helps boost margin on economy sales	Helps boost market sales	As 3E

through its own tied dealerships is being reshaped. As Table 6.5 suggests, a number of the more significant US and European-based firms have opted for a strategy which includes a more aggressive search for bought-in components as well as fully assembled cars. This is a strategy in which the need for new products can only be satisfied – at least at acceptable risk levels – by forging new links with outside producers.

Thus, the production effort is being dispersed – in some cases internationally and between firms – while the marketing effort becomes more concentrated. The following case study analyses an industry in which few, if any, firms can exercise this option readily. Although a portion of the inputs necessary for producing steel can be bought in, most producers have tended to retain all such processes for themselves in order to capture as many economies of scale as possible. While acting as an importing agency and abandoning domestic steel production is, in principle, an option open to firms, the following discussion will show that there are a host of constraints when adopting such a strategy.

The steel industry

Starting around 1870 the steel industry in advanced countries enjoyed a full century of growth and expansion, spurred by the construction of vast shipping fleets, railway systems and machines. By the time planners and governments in LDCs began to place their development hopes on manufacturing, the existence of a steel industry was widely regarded as a prerequisite for successful industrialisation. By virtue of its long-standing prominence, the industry's history abounds with examples of interest group reactions to deep-seated structural forces and efforts to alleviate adjustment pressures. The organization of Western interest groups has had decades in which to evolve. The International Steel Cartel (ISC), founded in 1926, and its present successor, Eurofer, are well-known examples. Other national and international bodies like the International Iron and Steel Institute (IISI) provide co-ordinating functions or work to achieve political and policy objectives.

A long-term perspective
The widespread importance given to the development of a national steel industry, coupled with expanding domestic demand, meant that the pattern of world production was continually undergoing change. The UK was the world's predominant steel producer up to 1900 when it was replaced by the USA. American leadership reached its zenith

around 1920 when it accounted for 60 per cent of world production. Since then, the US share has steadily fallen, declining to 15 per cent by the late 1970s (UNIDO, 1978b, p. 42). Latecomers like the USSR and Japan are now the premier steel-producing nations. In 1980, these two countries accounted for 21 and 16 per cent of the world's crude steel production respectively (*ISE*, Aug. 1981, p. 60).

The violent fluctuations in steel prices that preceded the Great Depression led to the formation of the ISC and its lesser-known counterpart, the Steel Export Association of America. In general, however, there were few problems as the demand for steel followed a steady upward path until the 1970s. This trend was marred by occasional cyclical fluctuations, four of which occurred in the high-growth period between 1946 and 1970 (ECE, 1976, p. 8). Buoyant domestic demand meant that producers were not plagued by contractive problems arising from excess capacity, the threat of substitutes or declining profits. Thus, the global spread of steelmaking capacity posed no real problem to established producers during this period.

Steel's eventual transition from a growth industry to a mature one changed all this. Basic changes in long-term patterns of demand and production provided the impetus for steel's conversion to a mature industry. Because the demand for steel is derived from the demand for steel products, structural changes within the manufacturing sector altered the industry's demand pattern. In advanced countries today's major growth areas are telecommunications, energy, aerospace and computers, and, unlike the leading industries during the first two-thirds of this century, these new fields are not intensive users of steel. Thus, at least in advanced countries, steelmakers are dependent on a set of steel-using industries which, themselves, are losing ground relative to overall economic activity.

Other structural changes that were economy-wide in their scope had a similar effect on demand. Because the service sector's share in GDP in advanced countries has tended to grow relative to the production of material goods, investment has given way to consumption in the expenditure of national income. Both services and consumption are less steel-intensive than investment in the production of material goods; thus the steel industry's share in output and employment is prone to decline further. These contractive effects of demand have been reinforced by basic changes in production processes and, in particular, by technical advances that have dramatically reduced the requirements of steel users. West German figures for steel inputs per 1000 kg of finished product suggest the extent of the cutback between 1970 and 1977: in electrical machinery the use of steel declined by 10 per cent; in shipbuilding by 23 per cent; in rolling stock by 9 per cent; in nuts, bolts and similar products by 11 per cent (UNIDO, 1980, p. 18).

New production techniques have also led to the substitution of aluminium, plastics and highly resistant glass for steel in many traditional uses. Not the least of these is automobiles, where 44 per cent less steel and 65 per cent less iron will be used by 1985 in a typical US model compared to its 1975 precursor (see Table 6.4). Steelmakers themselves have also cut back on their requirements of crude steel per unit of finished steel through technological advances and improvements in rolling and finishing. By the early 1970s the net effect of these forces had unmistakably altered the industry's prospects. There had been a definite departure from the long-term growth trend that could not be attributed to cyclical factors or to the destabilising impact of energy prices. Between 1973 and 1980, consumption of steel in advanced market economies actually fell 13 per cent although GNP and industrial production rose by about 15 per cent (GATT, 1981, p. 55).

Long-term shifts in demand also affected the basic pattern of world trade. In 1950 exports were less than 11 per cent of world production of steel. However, this share rose steadily and exceeded 24 per cent by 1977 (IISI, 1980, p. 14). The growing variety of products demanded by steel users encouraged firms to specialise in particular products, a practice that boosted trade between steel-producing countries. By 1980, for example, intra-EEC trade accounted for nearly 19 per cent of steel production by these countries (*The Economist*, 7 Feb. 1981). Another significant trade stimulant was the emergence of excess capacity in many advanced countries; the slump after 1974 forced producers to turn to foreign markets in an effort to maintain customary rates of capacity utilisation. Finally, the demand for steel in the LDCs has steadily risen and, coupled with a long-term decline in transport costs, has contributed to the growth in world steel trade. As a result of these factors, net exports of steel increased between 1973 and 1980 although consumption declined.

Casual observers are inclined to assume that an air of perpetual crisis had hung over the world's steel industry since the mid-1970s. A more accurate assessment is that the crisis is largely confined to steel makers in the EEC and USA. This fact is borne out by the figures in Table 6.6 which show the levels of production in 1950, 1965 and 1980. Significant increases in production were recorded by steelmakers in LDCs and in several of the smaller advanced countries such as Belgium, South Africa and Spain. These latecomers have managed to weather the present crisis or even maintain an impressive rate of expansion. In fact, steel production in the LDCs grew at annual rates exceeding 9 per cent throughout the 1970s. The steel needs of an embryonic manufacturing sector, coupled with high rates of investment in construction, equipment and infrastructure, led to an abrupt rise in steel consumption in LDCs. The industry's growth path has been stylised in the form of a 'steel intensity' curve that relates apparent consumption of steel to *per capita* GNP. The expansion path is often approximated by a flattened, S-shaped, curve beginning when

Table 6.6   *The global distribution of crude steel production for selected countries and country groupings, 1950, 1965 and 1980 (in millions of metric tons)*

	1950	1965	1980
Advanced market economies	150.4	270.5	399.1
of which:			
Austria	0.9	3.2	4.6
Belgium-Luxembourg	6.2	13.7	16.9
Canada	3.1	9.1	15.9
Finland	0.1	0.4	2.5
France	10.6	19.6	23.2
Italy	2.4	12.9	26.5
Japan	4.8	41.2	111.4
Netherlands	2.4	3.1	5.3
Norway	0.1	0.7	0.9
Portugal	—	0.3	0.6
South Africa	0.8	3.2	9.1
Spain	0.8	3.5	12.7
Sweden	1.5	4.7	4.2
West Germany	12.1	36.8	43.8
United Kingdom	16.6	26.7	11.3
USA	87.8	119.0	101.7
Advanced socialist countries	35.9	119.6	196.0
of which:			
USSR	27.3	91.0	149.1
Less developed countries	3.5	26.9	123.6
of which:			
Argentina	0.1	1.3	2.7
Brazil	0.8	3.0	15.3
Chile	0.1	0.5	0.7
India	1.5	6.4[a]	9.5
Mexico	0.4	2.5	7.1
South Korea	—	0.2	8.6
Turkey	0.1	0.6	2.5
Venezuela	—	0.6	1.8

Source: for 1950 and 1965: ECE, 1976, Table III.1; for 1980: *Iron and Steel Engineer*, August 1981, p. 60.
Note: [a]   ingots only.

steel consumption and GNP are very low, rising rapidly, stabilising and then declining (IISI, 1980, pp. 39–43). Because many LDCs are in the second phase, demand has increased disproportionately and steel consumption has usually outstripped supply capabilities. For example, in 1955 the LDCs accounted for only 1.6 per cent of world production of crude steel although they consumed 6.1 per cent (UNIDO, 1976, p. 76–7). Corresponding figures for 1980 were 9.8 and 12.3 per cent respectively (Taniura, 1981, pp. 4–7). In fact, virtually all LDCs were net importers of steel throughout the post-war period.

The industry's development course in LDCs is reminiscent of earlier experience in advanced countries. The construction of industrial plants, harbours, railroads and highways has generated demand for non-flat iron and steel products, while industries like automobiles, shipbuilding, and electrical machinery require flat iron and steel products. The construction sector accounts for 50–60 per cent of steel consumption in the typical LDC, followed by manufacturing, with other sectors absorbing only a minor portion. Other characteristics in addition to differences in patterns of domestic demand serve to distinguish producers in LDCs from their counterparts in advanced countries. First, few LDCs (South Korea is an exception) are significant exporters of steel products, whereas many Western firms have begun to sell in foreign markets as a means of alleviating contractive pressures. Steel producers in LDCs are often encouraged to increase capacity in response to growing domestic demand and their governments' desire to replace imports. Second, in relative terms, the intersectoral linkages involving steelmakers in LDCs are probably more extensive than those found in Western countries. This characteristic, which reflects the more diverse range of users in construction, transport and infrastructure at lower income levels, influences the composition of the relevant interest groups. Finally, steelmakers in LDCs have a history of close, often formal, involvement with the state. The high priority that governments originally accorded to industrialisation, and to steel in particular, led to this longstanding relationship. By contrast, continuous public involvement has not been the case in most advanced countries. Western governments refrained from such entanglements when the industry was expanding although their involvement was evident during the Great Depression and re-emerged only in the 1970s as contractive pressures mounted.

Characteristics such as these affect the interrelationships between various interests and the degree of influence which they may exert. Because the political and economic circumstances differ – between LDCs and advanced countries as well as among countries in each group – the resultant policies and industry strategies reveal a similar diversity. Likewise, other factors that are more purely economic in nature can be country-specific and will affect the choice of an industry strategy. Before discussing some of these industry strategies, however, it is useful to examine some of these techno-economic characteristics in more detail.

A techno-economic profile

Post-war advances in steel technology were only part of a longer continuum. The fact that the industry enjoyed a full century of steadily expanding demand influenced its pattern of technological development, in particular the search for greater economies of scale. The first moves toward larger-sized units began around 1860 in response to the development of a railway network in Europe. By 1900 annual plant capacity in many integrated iron and steel units was 100,000–200,000 tonnes. Plant size was continually expanded and, in 1920, a typical rolling mill had an annual capacity of 600,000 tonnes. The advent of huge open pit mines and the later shift from open hearth furnaces to oxygen conversion hastened the move to larger unit size throughout the entire production process. By 1970 the Japanese were building integrated units with capacities of 3–10 million tonnes. Investment costs rose dramatically as plant size increased. The relative increase in these outlays meant that investors were heavily committed to the chosen technologies through the new plant's lifetime. A further complication was that firms had only a limited ability to make alterations in production processes once new capacity was in place.

These characteristics – the continued enlargement of optimal plant size and the steady rise in investment costs – have had a lasting impact on the steel industry and the pattern of interest group behaviour. The heavy financial outlays for new greenfield capacity sometimes made it difficult for producers to incorporate technological advances as they became available. Although the international transfer of technology was relatively easy, the diffusion of 'best practice' techniques has been very uneven. Simultaneously, long-term increases in plant size made it essential that all capacity – new and old – be operated at rates of utilisation as high as 90 per cent.

The reluctance of some steel producers to introduce new technological advances has posed a problem of growing complexity throughout the post-war era. Even during periods of buoyant demand such as 1950–70, some risk was associated with such large-scale investments. Major additions to capacity could later prove to be ill-timed if technological breakthroughs took place shortly after construction. This situation occurred in the American steel industry which undertook its major expansionary push in the 1950s, just before several significant technological advances (Kawahito, 1981, p. 237). Because of the long time-period for investment amortisation, much of the existing capacity in advanced countries is obsolete by modern standards. A typical example of the uneven pace of technological diffusion is the prolonged use of ovens to produce coke, an important raw material for steel production. Today, about one-third of US coke oven capacity is at least twenty-five years old, while in the EEC a similar proportion is at least twenty years old, despite the fact that such operations are now outmoded (*ST*, Dec. 1981, p. 663).

A second complicating factor was that many firms in advanced countries incorrectly interpreted signs of decelerating demand as another cyclical aberration with no prolonged structural impact. Massive investment programmes, typified by the British Steel Corporation's expansion programme and the French Fos development on the Mediterranean coast, rolled on. Surprisingly, the rate of growth in world steel capacity actually accelerated in 1975–7, even though major markets had already begun to contract.

Finally, steelmakers found that it was far cheaper to increase existing capacity than to build new plants. Technological improvements were introduced at the same time, although there were several reasons why this practice did not always provide for lasting gains. Modifications sometimes led to bottlenecks at subsequent production stages. Moreover, the improvements were often marginal and any competitive gains were soon eroded by subsequent advances elsewhere. Overall profitability was still contingent on higher rates of capacity utilisation than were practical in a contracting market.

The problems described here are largely attributable to a misplaced faith in the continued growth of demand. Steelmakers' long-term expectations for the stability of prices for raw materials and energy proved to be equally erroneous and gave rise to additional problems. The data in Table 6.7 provide rough indications of the cost structure in different countries during the period 1964–80. There are several explanations for the systematic differences in the cost structures of the LDCs and the advanced countries. First, because of the wage gap, labour's share in total costs is 2–5 times greater in advanced countries than in LDCs. Second, although raw materials are everywhere a major cost component, their share is particularly high in many LDCs. This is because many LDCs import most of their iron ore, coke and related materials at prices higher than those paid by their counterparts in advanced countries who have easy access to domestic supplies. Steel scrap, another basic raw material for certain processes, is widely available in advanced countries, whereas producers in LDCs usually purchase scrap on the open market where prices are volatile and supplies are unreliable. Third, energy generally accounts for a small share of costs in LDCs because of differences in sources. For example, many steelmakers in LDCs practice charcoal ironmaking, using local wood rather than importing coal for later use as coke. Brazil, Latin America's leading iron producer, obtains about 36 per cent of its iron by this manner and this share may be increased. Because the method is relatively labour-intensive and yields a high quality iron, it is common in many LDCs.

Owing to these systematic differences in input prices and production practices, the structure of costs bears some relationship to the level of development. Raw materials, labour and energy are significant cost components for producers in advanced countries whereas, in LDCs, the first of these inputs tends to be the predominant cost determinant. Not surprisingly, the industry's priorities for R & D have reflected the cost structure in the advanced countries. Thus, over

Table 6.7   *Cost structures in the iron and steel industry, selected countries and years (percentages)*

Country (year)	Installation/product	Labour	Raw material	Energy	Other
Argentina (1964)	flat rolling mill	1	56	5[a]	38
Brazil (1965)	steel products	10	31	22[b]	38
Chile (1965)	non-flat rolling mill	3	73	8	16
Indonesia (recent year)	industry average	4	81	1	14
Malaysia (1980)	primary products	15	43	17	25
Malaysia (1980)	secondary products	3	91	2	4
Philippines (1979)	industry average	4	82	4	10
South Korea (1980)	industry average	6	71	4	19
Thailand (1980)	electric arc furnaces	7	56	7	30
Japan (1980)	industry average	13	57	31	9
United States (1965)	steel products	35	37	14[b]	14
Western Europe (1965)	steel products	18	44	17[b]	21
'Hypothetical' advanced country (1975)	carbon/specialty steels from continuous casting	27	28	11	34

Sources: for Argentina, Brazil, Chile, US and Western Europe, Baer, 1969, pp. 124, 145 and appendix III; for Indonesia, Sugiarto, 1981, p. 93; for Malaysia, C. D. Fong *et al.*, 1980, p. 104; for Philippines, E. Velasso *et al.*, 1981, p. 42; for South Korea, H. Y. Pyo *et al.*, 1980, p. 16; for Thailand, N. Akrasanee *et al.*, 1980, p. 19; for Japan, T. Taniura, 1980, p. 86; for hypothetical country, UNIDO, 1978b, p. 176.

Notes:
a   includes repairs.
b   includes maintenance and internal transport.

time, a variety of technological innovations have been intended to reduce the input requirements for one or more of these three components.

Competitive pressures on the more obsolete producers mounted during the 1970s. Although the increase in energy prices received the most attention, rises in wage rates also had an impact. This is suggested by the experience of the US steel industry where increases in unit labour costs were, on average, 50 per cent higher than those for all manufacturing in the period 1957–77 (Anderson and Kreinin, 1981, p. 204). The plight of some producers deteriorated further with the rise in energy prices. By 1981, firms relying on dated methods of production often found that energy accounted for 30–40 per cent of all costs. Changing economic conditions rendered many existing production processes even more cost-ineffective. The rising costs of various inputs meant that steel production could no longer be described simply as a capital-intensive industry.

Gradually, the priorities governing technological development and expenditures on R & D began to change, moving away from the design of larger-sized plants to focus on increased production flexibility and capacity rationalisation. One example is the method of continuous casting of molten steel directly into slates and billets. The process, which bypasses the ingot stage, saves energy and labour by avoiding expensive reheating and handling of ingots. A second significant advance is the direct reduction of ore into iron, thus eliminating the need for a blast furnace. Afterwards, the iron can be processed into steel by new electric-arc furnaces. These and other innovations offer lower capital and operating costs, smaller optimal sizes and greater flexibility than the more traditional plants of the 1960s and early 1970s.

Despite contracting demand and dramatic changes in the cost structure, many producers were still reluctant to scrap existing capacity. The adoption of methods of continuous casting is a typical case. Almost 31 per cent of the world's crude steel was produced by this method in 1981 – more than double the corresponding share in 1975. Although such figures suggest that the conversion is occurring rapidly, few major producers (exceptions are Italy and Japan) have made real headway. Among the countries producing most of the world's steel, only a modest proportion of crude steel is obtained by continuous casting; in 1980, the figures for the USSR, USA and UK were 12, 20 and 27 per cent respectively. In contrast, this method currently accounts for more than one-half of all crude steel production among countries such as Argentina, Austria, Denmark, Finland and South Africa, while others – Brazil, Portugal, South Korea and Taiwan, for instance – are approaching that level (*ISE*, Aug. 1981, p. 61).

Because of the great diversity among national steel industries, the choice of strategies and policies varies widely. The following discussion examines some of the strategies chosen by steel industries in several different countries.

Defensive strategies: the US trigger price
Defensive protection as practised in the steel industry is a somewhat more elaborate strategy than versions found in other industries. Earlier discussion has shown that many of the major steel firms in the EEC and the USA were the slowest to adapt to changing circumstances. Thus it is not surprising that protectionist fervour was largely concentrated in these two markets. In many ways, however, the American and European applications of the strategy are distinct, reflecting differences in political, cultural and economic conditions.

Interest groups in the USA have closely associated their appeal for defensive protection with the increased penetration by foreign suppliers. The country first became a net steel importer in 1959 during the course of a prolonged strike by steel workers. At that time steel imports were only 6 per cent of apparent consumption, but they increased steadily, reaching 16.3 per cent in 1980 (AISI, *Annual Statistical Report*, various years). Protectionist sentiments grew stronger as imports rose and, in 1969, VERs were negotiated with both the EEC and Japan. However, free trade was restored with the Trade Act of 1974 which abolished the earlier VERs. Following this setback, steel interests resumed their anti-import campaign which differed in several respects from earlier efforts. Significantly, the campaign took place in the midst of the worst recession since 1930 and thus benefited greatly from public sympathy. Advocates of protection stressed the consequences of unfair trade practices and predatory dumping rather than the more naive arguments of cheap foreign labour, adverse balance of payments effects or foregone tax revenues. Serious attempts were also made to document the charges of unfair practices and anti-dumping complaints. The protectionist drive succeeded during the Carter administration in the establishment of a trigger price mechanism (TPM) in 1978. This set a minimum price for imports based on 'constructed costs' using Japanese data. Foreign steel could be imported into the USA at or above these minimum prices but imports at prices below these levels would prompt an immediate government investigation into dumping practices.

The minimum prices were raised periodically at the government's discretion. However, American steel interests remained dissatisfied with the TPM's levels of protection. They called for a two-tier system of constructed costs – one based on Japanese data and another derived from European figures. The proposal, which was not accepted, would have led to much higher trigger prices for European exporters whose costs were higher than the Japanese (although their landed American prices were sometimes lower). The industry's position continued to deteriorate; demand continued to fall and the minimum prices for imports were being raised too slowly.

In 1980 the US Steel Corporation filed an extensive anti-dumping petition against several European producers. This action violated a closed door agreement between the administration and the industry which had led to the creation of the TPM, in return for an industry pledge not to file anti-dumping petitions. Consequently, the TPM was suspended. After further negotiation US Steel withdrew its anti-dumping petition and the administration reinstated the TPM with a 12 per cent increase in the minimum price of imports and new quantitative restrictions. However, conditions continued to deteriorate and, by mid-1982, the industry's operating rate was 42 per cent of its production capability, the lowest level since 1938 (*The Times*, 9 June 1982).

Seven American firms again violated the informal agreement by filing anti-dumping charges against foreign producers and the TPM was suspended for a second time. The legal battle became more heated when US Steel filed nine petitions against imports that were alleged to be heavily subsidised. The petitions implicated a host of suppliers in Brazil, France, Italy, South Korea and West Germany, and included some categories of steel products that were new to the dispute. The legal cases involved 85–90 per cent of the steel exported to the USA by the EEC (*The Economist*, 15 May 1982). American steelmakers are obviously dissatisfied with the TPM – which, at present, is suspended – and hope to force the administration to introduce more effective trade restraints against European exporters. The US Commerce Department has recently issued a preliminary finding in favour of many of the instances contained in the anti-dumping petitions; estimated margins of dumping range up to 40 per cent. US importers of these products are liable for the retroactive collection of anti-dumping duties on all imports entering the country after the preliminary finding, provided that the final determination of the Commerce Department agrees with its preliminary decision and that the US International Trade Commission concludes that these (dumped) imports cause, or threaten, injury to the US industry.

The ebb and flow of the US protectionist battle provides some insights into the role of various interest groups. At least some parts of the US bureaucracy were reluctant to endorse the protectionist drive. Their concern for wider-ranging trade relations with the EEC was apparent and retaliation in the form of trade restrictions on American exports of chemicals, textiles or agricultural products was feared. Certain industrial interests have also opposed the protectionist campaign. The American Institute for Imported Steel pointed to the fact that demand for specific products, notably pipes and tubes, often exceeded domestic supply capabilities. Equally important, much of the increase in imports was in the form of semi-finished steel slabs, the sole importers of which were large integrated American mills – the same firms that were complaining about steel imports. The emergence of organised, albeit limited, opposition to the protectionist campaign suggests some interesting possibilities for new steel producers with export ambitions. For example, potential exporters in LDCs may find that they can eventually exert some leverage on protectionist debates through the strength of their own importing markets. Alternatively, they may find 'friends in court' by aligning themselves with other industries whose self-interest would be served by cheaper imports.

Little precise information is available on the role played by politicians and policy-makers in the American protectionist campaign. At the height of the protectionist drive, a steel caucus of about 150 Representatives and Senators demanded that the administration produce an effective means of import restriction by the end of 1977 (Kawahito, 1981, p. 234). Significantly, the TPM was introduced early in 1978. Government agencies have attempted to assist American steelmakers in other ways. The US Economic Development Administration (EDA) has provided assistance to some companies for modernisation and new investment. The practice has caused controversy among rivals who complain that taxpayers' money is used to finance new capacity while excess capacity already exists.

Among producers, the American Iron and Steel Institute (AISI) has been in the forefront of the protectionist campaign. The Institute filed a petition in 1976, charging that Japanese producers had unfairly diverted shipments of steel to the USA after agreeing to restrict exports to the EEC. The AISI also attempted to document various charges of unfair practices (AISI, 1978, 1980) and forcefully advocated the need for stronger import restraints if producers were (belatedly) to modernise. Individual firms have increasingly turned to the courts in an attempt to force the administration to replace the TPM with a stronger form of import restraint, often co-ordinating the submission of their changes. The zeal with which individual firms have participated in the protectionist campaign varies, depending in part upon the nature of their overall operations. Several, for example, have long-term commitments to foreign producers to import specific types of steel that are in short supply. A few have undertaken to diversify – into oil refining, chemicals, or activities outside the manufacturing sector – and their enthusiasm for protective measures by such firms is less vigorous as a consequence. These firms, however, remain a small minority among steelmakers.

With regard to labour, the United Steel Workers Union represents workers throughout the industry and has actively supported the anti-import campaign. The position of steelworkers differs from that of some producers, however. The union, along with some of the smaller producers, hoped to have a system of quotas introduced while some of the larger integrated firms preferred to seek relief through duties first. Unions have also made attempts at wage restraint to help alleviate the industry's worsening position. The labour movement has good reasons for working to preserve American steelmaking capacity. Their position is influenced by the favourable wage conditions attained by steelworkers over the past twenty years. For instance, in the mid-1960s, steel wages were only 30 per cent higher than the average for manufacturing but, by 1980, the gap had widened to 70 per cent (Kawahito, 1981, p. 248). Non-wage compensations – unemployment insurance, worker compensation and fringe benefits – provided to steelworkers increased even more rapidly, as noted before, so that hourly labour costs in the USA significantly exceed those of major competitors. In 1981 hourly direct costs plus benefits among US firms averaged $19.42; in Japan, $10.05; in France $9.74; and in West Germany $11.46 (*BW*, June 1982). As with the automobile and refining industries' employees, these gains would be jeopardised if the industry were to contract significantly resulting in massive layoffs.

European cartelisation and the Davignon Plan
Although numerous commodity agreements for particular steel products were attempted previously, the International Steel Cartel (ISC) was the first supranational scheme for the entire industry. Founded in 1926, it functioned with varying success until 1939. The steel slump in the mid-1970s recreated an economic milieu similar to that in the 1920s. European producers were shackled with excess capacity and faced vigorous competition from more efficient producers in Japan and elsewhere. State involvement was already extensive; many steel firms in Belgium, France, Italy and the UK had been nationalised or were only nominally in private hands, while state subsidies to privately owned firms were an established practice elsewhere. Thus the resumption of a cartel approach was not a significant departure from existing policy.

In 1976, the industry commissioner of the EEC, Viscount Davignon, proposed a voluntary steel cartel. The purpose of the cartel was to promote market stability by agreeing on levels of crude steel production, setting a minimum price for imports and fixing duties to prevent dumping. In return, producers were expected to rationalise their plants and to reduce excess capacity with the help of cash payments from the EEC. Observers have noted remarkable similarities between that proposal and the original ISC, 'indicating perhaps that cartel thinking itself has not changed much over the years' (K. Jones, 1979, p. 149).

The cartel, known as Eurofer, has been plagued by the internal disputes and bickering that are common to many cartels. These disputes, which were aggravated by a continued fall in demand, have concerned intra-EEC price wars and dumping charges, the extent of public subsidies provided to various steelmakers, and the need for compulsory rather than voluntary controls to enforce the cartel. As a result no consensus could be reached on several of the provisions such as the voluntary guidance prices and minimum price controls. To a large extent these problems reflect the heterogeneity of the European steel industry. National differences in the level of public involvement, the degree to which firms specialise in the production of bulk steel, specialty steel or steel products, and the extent to which steelmakers have been integrated into the country's industrial structure, have also handicapped efforts to forge a common policy.

Issues such as these are national in character but the central problems of cartelisation involve the existence of considerable excess capacity and, to a lesser extent, the failure of certain European firms to stay abreast of the latest technological advances. Regarding the first problem, demand forecasts of many European firms, like those of their American counterparts, proved to be serious miscalculations. Encouraged by government support, they made significant additions to capacity during the early 1970s. A typical example is the experience of British Steel Corporation: in 1971, the government endorsed plans to expand productive capacity to almost 40 million tonnes by 1980. Ironically, 1980 began with a tripartite dispute between government, industry and labour regarding a production level of 15–16 million tonnes (*The Economist*, 12 Apr. 1980). The extent of the misjudgement was compounded as, by mid-1982, actual capacity was only 14 million tonnes (*The Times*, 8 June 1982). Such misadventures have aggravated the general problem of overcapacity and have hampered firms' ability to modernise.

The overall effectiveness of the cartel strategy has been greatly influenced by the EEC's changing fortunes in the 'steel war' waged against American interests. Most European producers would probably have preferred to see the continuation of the original American TPM provided that the trigger prices were not set too high. This would have allowed them access to the US market without any formal investigation of the extent to which their operations are subsidised. However, as the more militant protectionist groups in the USA continued to make headway, European objectives were scaled down and the prospect of negotiating VERs became more attractive. The closure of the American market to European exporters would mean that the six million tonnes of steel being exported to the US would be diverted back to Europe. Under these circumstances the EEC's ability to agree on price levels, production cuts and modernisation programmes would be seriously jeopardised. In response to the American threat, Eurofer's export officials, known collectively as the London Committee, have attempted to persuade steelmakers to accept self-imposed export restraints. Because the firms that are most severely handicapped by excess capacity have continued to export at prices below the TPM, the committee's efforts have, however, met with only modest success.

The inability to find workable solutions to the problem of excess capacity was probably exacerbated by the extent of state-owned or state-supported steel firms. The Community itself has tried to act as an information broker to promote greater product specialisation, the joint use of plants, co-ordination of investment plans to eliminate duplication and common purchasing of raw materials. Efforts to scrap obsolete capacity have relied on cash inducements and gentlemen's agreements to limit national subsidies to inefficient firms. In conclusion, the injection of a supra-national element into European steelmaking has had only marginal success in encouraging firms to adjust to the new realities. Basic problems have persisted as EEC steelmakers added 43 million tonnes of effective capacity in 1970–9 while US capacity was almost unchanged during the same period (OECD, 1980, p. 4). The Community's results appear even more dubious once the comparison is extended to Japan and the extent of adjustment demanded by its industry strategies.

A consensus strategy – the Japanese approach

An examination of the Japanese steel industry reveals a set of industry strategies, most of which complement or reinforce one another. The features described here largely apply to the Japanese steel industry; other strategies are shared with steel producers elsewhere and are considered later. Perhaps the most unusual characteristic of the overall approach followed in Japan is the complex system of consultation between industry, labour and government that can be traced back to the 1950s. This practice grew out of the concerted drive for national recovery and was largely identified with the government-controlled Yawata steel works, now part of Nippon Steel, which is the world's largest steelmaker. Consultations between the three groups concerned wage levels, production targets and modernisation plans, and included all of Yawata's main competitors. Wage rates negotiated by Yawata set the norm for the industry, prices were agreed upon, and 'reasonable' rather than maximum profits were the aim of this team approach.

These consensus tactics proved to be an effective means of achieving long-term improvements in Japan's competitive position. The industry's solution to its supply problems is an example. In 1956, Japanese steelmakers imported two major inputs, coking coal and iron ore, at prices more than double those charged to American competitors. By 1976, the situation had changed completely; price levels had equalised or even favoured the Japanese (Kawahito, 1981, p. 237). A decline in ocean freight rates relative to inland rates was one explanatory factor. A more significant factor, however, was that the Japanese themselves contributed to this shift by extending financial and technical assistance to foreign sources for exploring and opening new mines, by designing more efficient bulk carriers and by constructing steelworks at coastal locations. Government-initiated consultations were also effective in preserving other cost advantages over major competitors. A comparison of hourly labour costs of Japanese and American steelworkers revealed a steadily widening gap in favour of the Japanese throughout the period 1956–76 (Federal Trade Commission, 1977, Table 3.3).

In stark contrast to the internal differences that have plagued the European cartel, the homogeneity of the Japanese steel industry paved the way for such a consensus strategy. The five major producers – which, together, account for 70 per cent of Japan's steel output – are all efficient and have similar cost structures. Many raw materials are bought through joint negotiations between these companies and their suppliers. Although the product mix of each firm differs, the total market share of each of the five major producers has remained constant over time. With the exception of a short-lived cartel in 1971, successful control of production has been achieved through close consultation. Today the framework for consultation is elaborate, including the provision of monthly voluntary guidelines by MITI and weekly meetings attended by executives of the five companies and MITI officials.

Participants in the consultations demonstrated flexibility in their reactions to the first oil crisis and the later maturity of the steel industry. Investment priorities were revised quickly to suit the new conditions. Emphasis was on the modernisation of capacity rather than cutbacks. Japan soon became the world's leader in the use of continuous casting and the proportion of output accounted for by this method rose from 20 to 60 per cent between 1973 and 1980 (*ISE*, Aug. 1981,

p. 61). This advance yielded significant reductions in energy use and other improvements in efficiency. More recent developments, many of which are still at the pilot stage, may lead to the eventual conversion of Japanese steelmaking into a continuous-process industry with a straight, logical flow from input to output. Significantly, this subject is reported to recur in the frequent consultations held between government, industry and labour interests (*The Economist*, 9 Jan. 1982).

The Japanese approach seems well-suited to an industry like steel where international negotiations and disputes have become a major policy determinant. Although the Japanese lead in technology provides one important negotiating edge, the ability to enter international policy debates with a single, unified position amounts to an additional advantage. This contrasts with the American and European situations where stringent anti-trust laws and the heterogeneity of the various interests prevent the emergence of a common position before international negotiations begin. The remaining industry strategies described in this section apply to subsets of firms operating in Japan, Europe, the USA and LDCs. Japanese participation, however, is in every case an outgrowth or complement to the consensus strategy sketched here.

Product diversification

A strategy of product diversification reflects a desire to lessen the firm's dependence on crude steel production. Among the alternatives available to steelmakers who choose to diversify is the shift into the production of higher quality steels. Another possibility is to move downstream from crude steel, through integration, into steel-using operations that are more closely related to engineering. A third version, diversification into non-steel producing activities, has already been noted among American firms and is tantamount to a partial exit from the steel industry.

The popularity of a diversification strategy reflects the consequences of the slump in demand and the rise in production costs which occurred during the 1970s. Producers of bulk steel suffer disproportionately in any slump; moreover, the structural changes that occurred in the 1970s gradually brought the realisation that steelmaking was not likely to reach pre-1975 levels again. Diversification into higher quality or specialty steels offers better demand prospects and a lesser threat from competitive substitutes like aluminium or plastics. Alternatively, producers who choose to move downstream into engineering activities are usually part of large, integrated firms. Their steel-using operations are of a sufficient size to absorb demand fluctuations and to subsidise losses. This arrangement works to the benefit of the firm because the engineering and metalworking phases of the operation are assured that they will obtain the types of steel they require.

Japanese steelmakers quickly moved into the production of 'high-strength' steels that would compete with aluminium in the manufacture of automobiles, containers and other mass-produced items. Japan's consumption of specialty steels rose steadily in the 1970s as the use of ordinary steels declined (UNIDO, 1980, p. 18). A French plan to boost production of sophisticated steel products (currently 15 per cent of the industry's output) is also under way and is expected to create a homogeneous group from France's dispersed makers of special steel. Government interests are also involved through the provision of low-interest loans to streamline the production of special steels. The move downstream into steel-using activities is best illustrated by the larger German firms (Mannesman, Thyssen and Krupp) where basic steel production now accounts for only about 30 per cent of company sales.

A potential drawback is that if too many firms should choose to diversify, competition will be increased in the new product fields. For instance, producers of special steels in Sweden now account for one-third of national output (compared with only 1 per cent of British steel output) and increased competition in these higher value-added items has driven a number of firms out of business (*FT*, 2 June 1982). Moreover, regardless of the particular tactic adopted, the huge investment costs required for diversification are a major constraint. The general reluctance to modernise on the part of some producers in the USA and the EEC suggests that they have even less incentive to diversify or move downstream.

Expanding indirect exports of steel

Because of the defensive strategies prevailing in the world's major markets for steel, some groups have attempted to avoid trade restraints through indirect means such as exporting steel-intensive products. As it became clear that increased exports of finished steel products such as plates, coils, bars, rods and sections would be increasingly difficult, steelmakers in Japan, South Korea and elsewhere turned their attention to indirect exports in the form of ships, vehicles and other manufactured goods. Significantly, the volume of world trade in these products rose over 50 per cent in 1970–9 as restrictions on steel exports have spread.

The success of this strategy depends on the degree of collaboration between steel-using exporters and steelmakers. Self-discipline is required of steel producers since an increase in their own exports could jeopardise the strategy. The transition from direct to indirect exports also depends upon the ability and willingness of steel-using

industries to co-operate and to undertake an expanded export programme of their own. The strategy holds some attraction for steelmakers and planners in the exporting country since there is more
value to be added to steel by exporting vehicles and other manufactures than by exporting of steel itself.

Japan and other Asian countries began the shift from steel to
indirect exports midway through the 1970s. There is in all likelihood a
link between the rise in steel protectionism and the import competition encountered by car-makers in the same Western markets. If the
expansion of indirect steel exports should continue, it could provide
the basis for stronger political opposition to the protectionist pressures brought by steelmakers. A perverted application of the strategy
can be observed in the diversification of several European (mainly
West German and British) steelmakers into shipbuilding. Their purpose is mainly to obtain access to the government subsidies provided
to hard-pressed European shipbuilders (*FT*, 27 Oct. 1980).

The internationalisation of steelmaking

For many industries the TNC serves as the primary channel for international investment and the transfer of technology. But unlike consumer electronics or automobile manufacture, steel is not an industry
where this organisational form predominates. The extent of public
ownership or state control of the steel industry limits the opportunities for a TNC presence. Moreover, steelmaking has traditionally
been geared to meet domestic needs and many firms have never
developed the international orientation necessary for TNC operations. In the absence of TNCs, an international network of information flows, trade agreements or joint ventures might be expected to
provide many of the same functions, but the proliferation of protectionist measures has probably discouraged such firm-to-firm contacts.

More recently, these types of international initiatives have been on
the increase. Despite criticism within the industry, some American
firms have begun to search for foreign technical assistance leading to
'a multitude of agreements . . . between Japan's big five and the
USA's top ten' (*ISI*, Apr. 1981, p. 55). Another variation of this
approach may involve firms from two or more advanced countries –
frequently Japan and West Germany – that collaborate in the expansion of steel plants in an LDC.

A distinctly Japanese version concerns overseas ventures that are
designated to be 'national projects'. Through official aid provided by
the Overseas Economic Co-operation Fund, the government
becomes the major stockholder in investment companies set up by a
consortium of firms involved in each project. Low-interest loans are
then provided to both the Japanese partners and the host countries.

In the case of steel the Japanese hope that, in return for help in building the steelworks and infrastructure, they will receive preferential access to the host country's resources. Japanese-Mexican negotiations concerning the exchange of oil for steel technology and finances are one example. Under the auspices of MITI, for instance, a petroleum import company was formed with the participation of thirty-six Japanese firms including refiners, distributors, trading firms and financial institutions. In exchange for Mexican oil, several Japanese steelmakers simultaneously proposed that they should participate in three large Mexican steel projects (*FT*, 12 July 1980). Similar negotiations with the Argentine government involve technical and financial assistance to expand a state-owned steelworks. The total cost of the project is put at $2 billion. Acting on an industry-wide basis, Japanese steel firms proposed that the negotiations be designated a national project on the grounds that Argentina is a major food supplier (Ozawa, 1980, p. 13).

The net effect of all these contacts may not be as random as the reader might expect. At least in the Japanese case, the intent would appear to be to provide LDCs with technological and financial aid to meet most of their domestic requirements. Emphasis is on the use of mini-mills and electric-arc furnaces. Japanese companies actively support research by the LDCs in these fields. Simultaneously, assistance in the development of large-scale operations (including continuous casting) is avoided. Thus new LDC capacity would be efficient but would probably not lead to a significant export potential. In this way the Japanese have attempted to avoid the creation of additional competition on international markets while at the same time pursuing a tactic sometimes described as their 'new resource diplomacy' (Ozawa, 1980).

Involvement of the LDCs
The prevailing trend within the LDCs resembles a 'national champions' strategy which is more frequently associated with science-intensive industries in advanced countries. However, in the case of the LDCs, government involvement is almost exclusively through state ownership rather than a less direct form of state control or public assistance. Steel industries in Algeria, Libya, Morocco, Peru, Saudi Arabia, South Korea and Tunisia are expected to be entirely state-owned by 1988; comparable estimates for Argentina, Brazil, India, Turkey and Venezuela exceed 75 per cent (Walter, 1979, p. 157). A widespread pattern of state ownership is supplemented by a variety of state regulations and forms of assistance. Typical examples are the South Korean and Thai governments' participation in pricing decisions (Pyo *et al.*, 1981, pp. 71–3; Akrasanee *et al.*, 1981, p. 53),

import licenses and fiscal incentives in the Philippines (Velasco and Almario, 1981, pp. 72–3) and a variety of government incentives like accelerated depreciation allowances and the reimbursement of import duties such as are practised in Malaysia (Fong *et al.*, 1981, pp. 52–7) and elsewhere. Such policies are representative of the approach adopted in most LDCs towards the steel industry.

Although few LDCs have yet become significant producers, the prospect of new capacity in these countries has been an important consideration in the industry strategies of the steel interests in advanced countries. In turn, each of these strategies will affect the industry's development in LDCs. The protectionist approaches adopted by American and European steel interests have obvious consequences for new producers in LDCs. Even though European or Japanese exporters were the initial targets of the American campaign, trade restrictions were soon applied to secondary suppliers as well. Thus the original VERs negotiated by the USA with Japanese or European producers were extended to exporters in Argentina, Brazil, Indonesia, Mexico, South Korea and elsewhere. Similarly, the EEC has attempted to bolster its effort to establish a cartel by a network of quotas which covers 85 per cent of the Community's steel imports, including some suppliers in LDCs (UNIDO, 1981a, p. 141).

American steelmakers clearly hope that the TPM will be replaced with a more stringent set of measures such as global quotas or an international trading arrangement modelled on the Multifibre Arrangement for textiles. Such an approach would effectively 'lock out' producers in LDCs who have yet to develop their export potential. In view of their pre-eminent position in world trade, the most vigorous international opposition to this move might be expected from Japanese steelmakers. Ironically, however, the Japanese appear to be more amenable to some form of sectoral trade negotiations than their less successful European counterparts (Walter, 1979, p. 184; Kawahito, 1981, pp. 242–4). This attitude may reflect the Japanese confidence in their ability to implement strategies such as the expansion of indirect steel exports and diversification into higher quality and specialty steels.

The subsidies offered by governments of advanced countries have sometimes pitted the interests of steelmakers against those of other industrial groups and the resultant policy debates have altered the prospects of producers in LDCs. The controversies over the credits provided to LDCs by the US Export-Import Bank for the purchase of American steelmaking equipment are one example. American exporters of capital goods have long pressed the Bank to be a more aggressive lender and to match the terms offered by its European and Japanese counterparts. Many American steelmakers, however, have opposed this move, arguing that the long-term effect would be to create unwelcome competition and that the policy would permit new competitors to buy US-made equipment with subsidised interest rates while American firms would not have access to similar benefits. The predominant part played by the state means that most international contacts involving steel producers in LDCs are between governments or, at least, government agencies operating on behalf of the LDC and a major firm in the advanced country. Among advanced countries, the Japanese motive for collaboration is often a desire to secure long-term supplies of key natural resources like oil. In exchange, they offer technical assistance and access to modern technologies. As has been noted, the Japanese approach is intended to upgrade technology and to improve efficiency while avoiding the creation of large-scale plants with subsequent export potential. There are indications, however, that the Japanese tactic has gone awry at times. Producers in several LDCs – Argentina, Brazil, Mexico and South Korea – have acquired know-how and equipment while simultaneously developing sufficient capacity to sustain exports. The governments of many LDCs have become familiar with the way Japan uses its formula for resource diplomacy and have begun to take advantage of it (Ozawa, 1980, p. 12). The prospect of additional export-oriented capacity in LDCs can only heighten the potential for conflict with producers in advanced countries so long as a defensive strategy prevails in the latter markets.

Conclusions

As was noted at the outset of this section, the steel crisis is largely confined to producers in the EEC and the USA. Moreover, there are immediate problems of excess capacity as well as plant obsolescence that cannot be separated from longer-term adjustment requirements. Both these characteristics suggest that unique or simple solutions are unlikely. The analysis of the steel industry's post-war experience revealed two related characteristics with a significant impact on the choice of strategies and policies described here. First, the fact that many of the world's major steel producers failed to anticipate the consequences of emerging maturity and decisions made in the early 1970s continues to have ramifications today. Second, the prevailing pattern of operating technologies is very uneven; sizeable chunks of productive capacity are woefully obsolete but continue to operate in competition with the latest and most efficient production methods. The misplaced faith in a continuous growth in demand led steelmakers in advanced countries to embark on a long-term programme of plant expansion in order to reap greater economies of scale. As the investment costs of new plants rose, firms found themselves heavily committed to technological processes that were not suited to the new market conditions and were soon to become obsolete. The effects of misjudging future demand were complicated by the creation of new capacity throughout the world and unexpected shifts in the relative prices of steel inputs.

The firms for which this description is most applicable – mainly European and North American – were faced with a relatively stark choice between voice and exit and, for several reasons, chose some version of the former response. First, because many firms' investments in over-sized plants were so great, any form of exit was a painful decision. Second, the workforces in the steel industry, being relatively large, well organised and politically influential, have strongly opposed any form of exit. Third, there was already a history of state involvement in many advanced countries and this improved the prospects for political support. Finally, the slump in steel markets coincided with a worldwide slowdown, which meant that the attitudes of both the state and the public were sympathetic to the plight of contracting industries like steel. For such reasons, steel interests in several advanced countries have increasingly chosen to give voice to their plight by resorting to political pressure and lobbying tactics as an alternative to adjustment and contraction or eventual exit. The tendency to resort to voice in order to postpone the contractive effects of adjustment has coincided with an emphasis on the industry's short-term or immediate problems. Furthermore, the thrust of interest group activities has been diverted away from basic solutions such as the research and technological dimensions of the adjustment process.

Table 6.8 looks at several strategies in terms of their effectiveness in dealing with some of the industry's major problems. Clearly, the problems listed there are long-term; as the synopsis implies, stop-gap measures like protectionism or cartelisation hold little promise if they are not coupled with more far-sighted attempts to remedy some of the problems arising from the diverse range of technologies and ownership patterns in the EEC and the USA. Moreover, effective solutions to the prevailing problems cannot be addressed purely in a domestic context. For instance, a strategy of modernisation and attempts to upgrade production technologies will be more effective if they are coupled with a systematic effort to expand the network of firm-to-firm contacts with producers in the LDCs. Such an 'outward orientation' would be an important link between potentially competitive steel interests in distinctly different markets and should be conducive to a more acceptable division of labour within the industry (for both sides). The adoption of this approach seems unlikely, however, without enlightened guidance from government in

Table 6.3 An overview of problems and strategies in the steel industry

Problems \ Strategies	A Stronger protective measures; cartelisation	B Move away from production of bulk steel	C Closer affiliation with LDCs	D Modernisation; up-grade production technologies
1 Excess capacity	Combats but does not solve the problem	Move downstream into engineering products would reduce problems of cyclical demand; requires high investment	Would help in long term by co-ordinating development of new large-scale capacity	Improve flexibility; pave the way for further co-ordination by reducing the range of the problem facing different producers
2 Obsolete capacity	Stop-gap solution; diversity of producers hinders agreement on forms of protection sought	No help	No help for immediate problem	Same as 1D
3 Long-term contraction in home markets	No help	Reduces competitive threat from substitute materials but competition between suppliers is sometimes fierce	Slight help if contacts serve to reduce import penetration	Will help but result will still depend on producer contacts in advanced countries to avoid serious supply-demand imbalance
4 Emergence of new competitors in LDCs	Little help; markets in LDCs will be lost anyway	Move upstream to special steels could help, particularly since major markets are in advanced countries	Same as 3C	Improves competitive ability but excess capacity on a global scale could still emerge

Solutions

the advanced countries and, in fact, would run counter to current trends where the politicisation of the steel industry has taken a distinctly national focus, as evidenced by the proliferation of defensive strategies.

The Japanese experience during the 1960s and 1970s showed that successful adjustment could take place with a judicious choice of long-term strategies that take account of both technological considerations and the emergence of potential competitors in other countries. Significantly, that adjustment process occurred during a period of fairly rapid growth in output – something European and American producers cannot expect in the 1980s. Moreover, Japanese successes were probably assured by the simple fact that American and European competitors failed to follow suit. In this connection it should be noted that the period of relatively free trade enjoyed by steel producers during the 1950s and 1960s was an exception rather than the norm (Turner *et al.*, 1982, p. 95) and that the trade restraints and anti-crisis measures prevailing today are likely to continue in the 1980s.

The preference for smaller plant size is likely to grow and should provide for greater flexibility on the part of steel producers. In the long term, this move would lessen the dependence of American and European steel interests on lobbying tactics and the use of political voice. Until that time, large portions of the world's steel industry will continue to be subject to intense pressures to contract and the need for long-term strategies such as diversification, modernisation or closer affiliation with producers in LDCs will be paramount.

7

Engines for Growth or Survival – A Tale of Three Industries

This chapter looks at three industries – consumer electronics, advanced electronics and oil refining. In various countries each of these industries occupies the enviable position of being a centrepiece for the government's industrial aspirations. Consumer electronics, for instance, was one of the priority industries which Japanese policy-makers chose to foster in the early post-war period. Today, that industry is accorded a similar position in the industrial plans of many Asian LDCs. During the era of cheap energy, oil refining emerged as a key field for industrial progress in the advanced countries and it continues to enjoy a favoured position in those countries that are endowed with abundant supplies of crude oil. Finally, according to many observers, advanced electronics promises to be an essential field for continued industrial progress and has already claimed a favoured position in the opinions of many policy-makers and planners.

Because the prevailing economic and political circumstances in each industry are unique, the discussion introduces new material and amplifies the types of industry strategies described in Chapter 6. The analysis of each industry reveals several salient characteristics that have influenced its development and have helped to shape the strategies associated with it. Consumer electronics, for instance, is generally thought of as being a light industry – a phrase implying that it is not particularly capital-intensive. While such a description is not completely accurate, that characteristic does serve to distinguish the industry from others studied in Chapters 6 and 7. As in the case of autos, the TNC plays a prominent role in the consumer electronics and oil refining industries, while the state figures significantly in the development of advanced electronics as it has – in some countries – for the steel industry.

Finally, it is hardly necessary to add that the three industries taken up in Chapter 7 can be distinguished in terms of the demand patterns and adjustment pressures which they are experiencing, in terms of the legacy of past investments and the evolution of production technologies used, and in terms of their political involvement. These and other characteristics add to the uniqueness of each subject and help to determine the range of strategies that can be observed in each industry. The chapter begins with an examination of consumer electronics. It continues by looking at developments in advanced electronics and concludes with an analysis of the world's refining industry.

Consumer electronics

An overview of the industry
Consumer electronics defined here to include familiar items like television and radio receivers, phonographs, stereo and sound equipment, tape recorders, electronic calculators, several major components such as picture tubes, and new products like video-tape recorders and video-discs. Beginning immediately after the Second World War, the industry established itself as one of the most dynamic growth centres within the manufacturing sector. Producers benefited from the rapid expansion of post-war demand (notably for radio and television sets) which was due to the rise in real incomes. The spread of national broadcasting networks, the development of colour television, FM broadcasting and international events such as the Olympic Games, also contributed to the rapid emergence of worldwide markets. The industry benefited in yet another way as wartime advances in communication and electrical equipment were readily adapted to consumer applications.

Rapid expansion continued until the mid-1970s when consumer electronics reached a mature stage of development. Its pre-eminence has only recently been overshadowed by the expansion of industrial electronics – mainly electronic applications equipment such as computers and automated machine tools. In 1978, Japanese producers of consumer items still accounted for 35 per cent of the value of all their country's electronics production; corresponding figures for Western Europe and the US were 27 and 14 per cent respectively (IDE, 1980, p. 11). Thus, the pattern of interest group behaviour and the evolution of industry strategies occurred during a prolonged period of expansion.

The early pace of innovation was maintained in later years. Successive waves of technological advances enabled producers to avoid the limitation of market saturation by reducing prices and by introducing new products or improved models. Moreover, the new production processes were transferred rapidly from one country to others. This characteristic contrasts with practices in advanced electronics where strict export controls on commercial technologies are imposed by the state or the developer in order to limit their acquisition by foreign competitors. Today production facilities are widespread, giving the impression of an industry advancing on a genuinely global scale. This impression, however, is somewhat misplaced, since a vast proportion of world demand for consumer electronics is confined to advanced Western countries and that pattern is likely to persist in the next 10–15 years.

The significance of technological advancement for consumer electronics can not be overemphasised. One consequence has been a tendency to 'compress' product cycles, particularly with regard to more recently developed products like video-tape recorders, and to shorten the life of models and product lines. The high priority given to innovations has had other lasting consequences for the industry. For example, the conceptual stage of consumer electronics has always required large amounts of skilled labour and substantial outlays on R & D. As the relative costs of these inputs rose, the comparatively brief life of most products began to pose a problem for manufacturers. Major firms tended to compensate by developing highly diversified product lines. The technologies used to produce different products were similar and the practice helped to spread the financial burden of R & D across a wider product range. An unintended result was that major firms found it easy to adjust to a drop in competitiveness in one or two product lines by shifting their operations to other items (Walter and Jones, 1980, p. 28). The relatively high development costs incurred by most firms also had an impact on the structure of firms within the industry. Today consumer electronics is dominated by a few large firms, most of which are vertically integrated from the conception of the product to its final sale. The export orientation typical of many producers also follows from their need to reduce the unit costs of R & D through high turnover.

Probably the most profound impact of technology has been on industry sitings. Production of most items fits easily into three stages. The first includes the conception and development of new products and processes and requires substantial engineering skills as well as significant outlays for R & D. A second stage is the capital-intensive production of components, usually with large production runs. The third stage, which is primarily labour-intensive, entails the testing of parts and components and their assembly into finished goods. Clearly, the factor requirements associated with each stage differ significantly and improvements in production processes have accentuated these distinctions. Advances in the production and assembly of television sets provide one example. Today these products require only one-third the number of components used in 1970 while over 70 per cent of chassis assembly is automated. As a result, production time has been reduced to one-tenth of its former level (*FT*, 18 Nov. 1980). A similar trend can be seen in the production of electronic calculators where the number of components has been reduced from 5,000 to fewer than 40, thereby simplifying the assembly process and reducing the amount of skilled labour required (Majumdar, 1979, pp. 562–3).

The purpose of these developments was to achieve improvements in quality and to realise greater economies of scale. However, their implications for the dispersal of the various production stages should also be noted. One effect was to exaggerate the differences in factor requirements between the second and third production stages. The unit costs of circuitry and components fell substantially, making the labour costs of assembly even more significant. The simplification of production processes also enhanced the ability of the TNC to manage and to control different stages that were widely dispersed. In so far as requisite skills were available, low-wage countries became desirable locations for labour-intensive stages while operations in advanced countries concentrated on those activities requiring considerable human or physical capital. The steady diffusion of technological advances, coupled with a widening differential in wage rates between countries, led to far-flung production sitings.

Logically, observers might expect that, in an industry so prone to abrupt competitive shifts, a coalition of vested interests would be at work to reduce the related adjustment pressures. In fact, the opposite is true, since firms have responded with a market-oriented reallocation of resources. This has been attributed to the distinctly lower private costs of adjustment in consumer electronics relative to other industries (Walter and Jones, 1980, p. 28). In other words, opportunities for adjustment have been created by the nature of the production processes and the market itself, the organisation of the industry and the latitude for intra-industry specialisation and diversification.

The foregoing description leaves little doubt of the TNCs' importance in determining industrywide patterns of investment, the location of productive capacity, expenditures on R & D and product development – in other words, the features that characterise the industry's strategies. Reasons for this are not difficult to find. First, the conceptual and mass-production stages of the industry require large outlays of human and physical capital. These requirements largely preclude small- or medium-size firms as an effective force in shaping the industry's development. Similarly, the practice of locating labour-intensive stages in LDCs means that large firms which are not multinational have difficulty matching the prices of TNCs in an industry that is known traditionally for its fierce price competition. In general, the TNC's influence derives from its ability to develop, disperse and control the technologies upon which the industry depends. The successive waves of technological advance that characterise the industry have served to strengthen the TNC's role at the expense of national competitors (large or small).

Related circumstances explain the minor role played by labour interests in fashioning the industry's strategies and influencing its growth pattern. Unskilled and semi-skilled labour is used sparingly in those production stages that are located in Western countries. This does not mean that labour interests have had no impact on industry policies and strategies. Their influence, however, is limited in comparison with TNCs and is not industrywide. The extent to which investment practices of TNCs have undercut the unions' ability to influence the industry is suggested by Asian data. In 1979 the number of consumer electronics firms in Asian LDCs that were affiliates of TNCs was twice the combined total of Western European and American firms producing in their home markets (IDE, 1980, p. 58).

In contrast to advanced electronics, the direct involvement of the state in consumer electronics is limited. With the possible exception of France (discussed below), public ownership, control or financial assistance in Western countries has been minimal. One reason for this is that, until recently, the industry enjoyed a steady rate of expansion. Another reason is that the labour force is relatively small in comparison with other industries like textiles where labour groups are politically vocal. Thus when financial collapse has seemed imminent, the state has rarely intervened.

Neither their technological orientation nor their adjustment facility enabled producers of consumer electronics to escape the negative effects of the recent economic malaise. The sluggish growth of markets, excess production capacity and fierce price competition had affected all producers by the late 1970s. In the West, these conditions led to the closure of many firms and the merger of others so that, by the late 1970s, important segments of the market were showing clear signs of having reached a saturation point. Eventually the industry's responses to prevailing conditions may add new approaches, or variations, to their existing inventory of strategies. These, along with more familiar methods, are surveyed below.

Offshore processing

Beginning around 1965, internal developments in the industry led firms to undertake a feverish search for low-wage locations for the later stages of production (Keesing, 1978, p. 54). The growth in world demand outstripped supply capabilities and, in response, numerous firms (mainly Japanese) undertook aggressive export programmes. Foreign penetration of the US market contributed to an emerging pattern of fierce price competition that eventually became a world-wide hallmark of the consumer electronics industry. The Japanese advance began with monochrome television sets in the early 1960s. A few years later that success was repeated with colour television sets. Simultaneously, Japanese firms began moving assembly operations to South Korea (and, later, to Singapore and Taiwan) in order to reduce the wage component in their production costs. US firms countered in several ways but, most often, resorted to the same tactic. American producers moved many of their assembly operations to Mexico and South-East Asia, and offshore processing became a common strategy throughout the industry as price competition spread to other products and markets.

The existence of aggressive price competition is not sufficient, however, to explain the strategy's popularity among producers of consumer electronics; other industries facing similar conditions have not necessarily turned to offshore processing. In fact, it is the industry's ability to separate physically the production stages, coupled with the nature of the technological developments described above, that make the strategy viable. Presently, only 30 per cent of all production sitings in the electronics field (including industrial goods and components) are not determined by strategic, technical or marketing considerations (Interfutures, 1979, p. 344). Thus TNCs enjoy considerable leeway in selecting their locations. Almost all these firms operate offshore facilities for mass production as well as sites for assembly and testing. However, variations of the strategy, among both Japanese and American adherents, are numerous. Some apparently used it as part of a positive approach by sloughing off ageing, uncompetitive products, and providing themselves with cheaper components or a new, low-cost export base. Other firms took a more defensive slant and undertook to relocate purely for reasons of cost.

The European version of offshore processing in the all-important television market is an example of a case where the existence of a NTB meant that firms pursued the strategy less aggressively. The unique European transmission/reception technologies – SECAM in France and PAL elsewhere – have provided an effective, if deteriorating, buffer to foreign competition. Licences for the PAL system will expire in the 1980s but they were first used in the 1960s to restrict manufacture to European firms. Although Japanese competitors have gradually acquired licences, they still can not supply, in quantity, television sets of twenty inches or more. As a result, European firms have been slow to develop offshore processing sites. For the same reason, perhaps, Europeans have been slow to undertake

many cost-cutting measures or to develop any serious export programmes. This trait, which may also reflect the built-in protection
afforded by transmission/reception technologies, has led to a fragmented production pattern with many small and sometimes uneconomic units. Viable production of television sets is put at an annual
minimum of 400,000 units, yet several dozen European plants make
only 10,000 units per year. For the production of picture tubes a
break-even point is about 1 million units, while more than a dozen
European factories produce a combined total of less than 7 million.
Under such conditions it is not surprising that the production costs of
Philips, Europe's largest manufacturer of consumer electronics, are
twice the level of those incurred in the Japanese plants of its competitors (*The Economist*, 20 Feb. 1982).

   The smaller size of European firms may have restricted their ability
to transfer the labour-intensive phases of their operations to LDCs.
There is also indirect evidence that once European firms begin
offshore processing, they focus on the assembly of consumer items,
although many of their competitors are equally concerned with the
standardised production of components and parts such as semiconductors or high technology components. The contrast between
different groups of Western producers will become clearer after
examining several other industry strategies.

Moving upstream

A second strategy often identified with consumer electronics is that of
moving upstream. The choice seems logical since one consequence of
the industry's omnipresent technological development has been to
extend both the range of products and their functions. Given the wide
technological gap that originally existed between Western countries,
the strategy was well-suited to Japanese producers. Immediately after
the Second World War, firms in Japan began at the bottom of the
technological range by exporting small transistor radios. The
Japanese version of the strategy was imitative; at that time they had
no possibility of moving upstream through technological advances of
their own making. This approach served them well throughout the
1950s and 1960s. Initially, they made use of a labour cost advantage
since the relevant wage rates were roughly one-fifth the prevailing
scale in the USA (Majumdar, 1979, p. 563). Later, they successfully
combined their imitative practices with extensive offshore processing.
The composition of Japanese exports steadily changed, eventually
including television sets, tape recorders, stereo equipment, and all
their principal components. Japanese successes were made easier by
the fact that Western competitors placed a much greater emphasis on
advanced electronics than on consumer products (IDE, 1980, p. 14).

Today, Japan's manufacturers are poised to take a commanding lead in video recorders where they already account for 95 per cent of world sales. The opportunities for moving further upstream, however, are no longer simply a matter of imitation; Japanese technological capabilities can match, if not surpass, those of any competitors.

The attempts by Western firms to adopt a similar strategy of moving upstream have been partial and, sometimes, half-hearted. US firms did introduce the first pocket-sized calculator but later lost much of this market to the Japanese. Producers of television sets and picture tubes tried to move upmarket by specialising in large-screen units. European transmission/reception technologies helped to make this an attractive, albeit short-term, solution. In doing so, European producers probably suffered a considerable cost because they ceded much of the market for small sets to the Japanese. Today no colour picture tubes for sets smaller than twenty inches are produced in Europe although all smaller tubes account for at least one-third of the cost of a finished set (*FT*, 18 Nov. 1980). All these components are imported – chiefly from Japan.

There were several reasons for the failure of many Western firms in implementing this strategy. First, the extensive degree of competition that has characterised consumer electronics – in pricing policy, product development and innovational advances – forced the more aggressive TNCs to stay abreast of the industry's general advances. Thus significant opportunities for an imitative effort to move upstream were available only to late-starters like Japan. Second, the highly diversified range of products supplied by firms further reduced the chances of finding a safe market niche, whether upstream or otherwise overlooked by competitors. Third, many firms interpreted the strategy solely in terms of its marketing implications and attempted to push consumers toward the upper and more profitable ends of their product lines. They abandoned the lower range of their product lines to imports and gave little attention to improvements in productivity or to the development of new products (Turner *et al.*, 1982, p. 56). Finally, trade in consumer electronics had been relatively unencumbered by tariff or NTBs, leaving producers little opportunity to adopt an artificial strategy of moving upstream into product lines that were more sheltered from foreign competition. The reasons for this last characteristic are explored below.

Defensive protection
Given the extensive degree of import penetration by Asian manufacturers, the failure of home-market interests to erect a fully-fledged programme of defensive measures may seem surprising. In the USA,

for instance, imports of radio sets had claimed 94 per cent of the American market by 1976, while imports of television sets accounted for 56 per cent of total consumption (Walter and Jones, 1980, p. 35). Although Japan remained the main supplier, over one-third of these goods were imported from manufacturers in Hong Kong, Mexico, Singapore, South Korea and Taiwan, and the latter countries' share was rising. Trends in the EEC were similar.

By the late 1960s, Japanese successes in American markets had led to sporadic charges of dumping and a number of lawsuits. One of the most noteworthy of these suits concerned colour television sets. Filed in 1968, it was not settled until 1980 when Japanese manufacturers agreed to an out-of-court settlement of $76 million (IDE, 1980, p. 7). Most suits arising during this period, however, were dropped eventually or the defendants were cleared of any dumping practices. American interest groups did, however, become more active and an organised lobby of labour unions and manufacturers launched a protectionist campaign in the 1970s. They brought more anti-dumping suits and pushed for legislation that led to an orderly market agreement (OMA) with Japan for 1977–80. This achievement was followed by the negotiation of VERs with Japanese firms located in Taiwan and OMAs with the South Korean producers of television sets.

In Europe, protectionism has focused on the market for television sets. Although the best protective device has been the different transmission/reception technologies used there, a variety of trade restraints can be also found. Some are bilateral – for example, a privately negotiated VER between the UK and Japan dating back to 1973 – while others are unilateral restrictions such as those imposed by France and Italy. The EEC has also introduced restrictions on behalf of certain countries, often with the intention of reducing Japanese imports entering via other member countries (Shepherd, 1981, p. 383).

There are several factors which explain the limited success of protectionist initiatives. First, the markets for consumer electronics were expanding rapidly and growth proved to be an important ally of free trade. Widespread appeals for defensive measures did not occur until emerging market weaknesses forced a drop in levels of operating capacity. Moreover, protectionist campaigns were generally restricted to those product lines such as expensive durables that were the hardest hit. Second, the TNCs themselves have a long history of responding to competitive pressures by resorting to a strategy of offshore processing. It is natural that these firms strongly favour free trade in the finished and semi-processed items exported by their own subsidiaries, associates and affiliates in LDCs. Zenith, for example, was the only major US firm to take an active role in the American protectionist campaign. It supported the union-sponsored move to repeal the offshore assembly provision of the US Tariff Act of 1930 and endorsed the efforts of a lobbying group called the Committee to Preserve Colour Television. Other American TNCs may have had tacit reasons for supporting import restrictions on Japan because such restrictions promised to shift the major source of foreign supply to Asian LDCs where these TNCs had established their own affiliates. It is significant, however, that Zenith was the only major American producer which had not opted for the strategy of offshore processing (Walter and Jones, 1980, pp. 37–8). Third, industrywide protection in consumer electronics has not yet emerged since interest groups have been unable to construct a politically influential coalition. Because the industry's political impact is relatively diffuse, the necessary degree of protectionist sentiment to marshall an industrywide campaign has not yet been achieved and defensive measures continue to be product-specific. Although the pressure for new defensive measures has made only modest headway, the emergence of these tactics has had a more subtle effect on the investment patterns of major exporters. These are discussed below.

Export-replacing investment
Conditions in the consumer electronics industry have increasingly favoured a strategy of replacing exports by direct investment in the major consumer markets, and this practice is becoming widespread among manufacturers in the major exporting countries. Clearly, Asian investment and acquisitions in the EEC or the US are not undertaken in order to reduce overall labour costs; the strategy is distinct from one of offshore processing. Instead, exporters have attempted to defuse any defensive sentiment by moving behind the importing countries' trade barriers. An early example of this strategy was the Japanese investment in Western Europe, undertaken with the intent of acquiring PAL licences. The UK has been a recent investment target and, after some initial reservation, has become a virtually open market for Asian investors (Shepherd, 1981, p. 383).

The slump which hit consumer electronics in the late 1970s uncovered many opportunities for foreign acquisitions in American and European markets, and Asian-based firms, in LDCs as well as Japan, responded quickly. The industry's great diversity, its pace of innovation and its rapidly changing market opportunities, meant that troubled firms often suffered from ill-advised decisions of a managerial or marketing nature rather than from the effects of import penetration (Walter and Jones, 1980, p. 40). The recent literature provides ample evidence of successful cases such as the acquisition of a West German television firm by a Yugoslav conglomerate, the purchase of a Motorola television division by a Japanese firm, and the erection of US plants by Hitachi, Mitsubishi, Sharp and Sony. With proper management, the strategy is viable. In this sense, consumer electronics differs significantly from other industries like steel where troubled firms or contracting markets offer the investor little prospect of a return to profitability.

The degree to which host markets are willing to permit foreign acquisition varies. The American market, given the longer acquaintance with Japan, seems most prepared to accept the practice. The UK may be a particularly attractive base for Asian manufacturers to reach EEC markets, because of its regional subsidy programmes, relatively low wages and skilled labour force. Belatedly, that country has come to accept foreign takeovers, partly because several of its small independent producers are anxious to benefit from Japanese technology. Ready acceptance of an Asian strategy to invest in the major consuming markets is not unanimous, however, as is suggested by the alternative strategy described below.

Promoting a national champion

Consumer electronics has not been a probable candidate for selection as a national champion. In contrast to advanced electronics, the production of consumer items has only remote links with national defence and is not a likely field for the sort of technological breakthroughs that have strategic national importance. The French government, partly as a reaction to the UK's more ready acquiescence to foreign takeovers, is unique in this regard. The government has actively supported a programme of aggressive expansion on the part of Thomson-Brandt, its main television manufacturer.

The French strategy, which calls for heavy investments to automate and streamline existing operations, is more a consequence of planners' decisions than of pressure from producer or labour interests. In fact, Thomson officials are reported to prefer a more lenient version of the strategy (*The Economist*, 20 Feb. 1982). The government's approach is part of a wide-ranging programme to launch an era of advanced communications systems. For instance, its plan to supply telephone subscribers with a simple computer terminal linked to an electronic telephone directory will require millions of picture tubes and associated circuitry. The government's plan for Thomson to lead its *dirigiste* economic policy in electronics also calls for the company to recapture the French market for consumer electronics. For example, the newly-nationalised firm has agreed to begin home production of hi-fi equipment that was hitherto produced under licence in Japan. Some elements of this same strategy can be found in the approach of the LDCs which are described below.

Consumer electronics in the LDCs

The involvement of LDCs is limited to specific types of consumer electronics that are produced in significant numbers by only a small number of countries. The field is dominated by Asian suppliers who specialise in the production of sound recorders, television and radio sets; in 1978 Asian LDCs respectively accounted for 18, 55 and 13 per cent of world production in each of these three product categories (UN, 1981). A closer look at the producing countries shows that two groups may be distinguished according to degree of export orientation. Foremost among the exporters are Hong Kong, Singapore, South Korea and Taiwan. Exports claim over 90 per cent of all production in each of these countries except for South Korea where the share exceeds 70 per cent (IDE, 1980, p. 56). Malaysia seems likely to join this group as producers elsewhere are shifting many of their labour-intensive operations to that country. In other Asian countries such as the Philippines and Thailand the attention of producers continues to be focused on the domestic market.

Among the strategies reviewed here, the possibility of moving upstream is most frequently cited as an appealing choice to low-wage LDCs. While based on the successful Japanese experience with the strategy, such advice may be overly optimistic, for two reasons. First, unlike their Japanese predecessors, in most LDCs the choice of a strategy is not the province of a government-producer coalition but is a decision to be made by the TNC. Thus many of the current LDC operations are no more than appendages to TNCs. In the production of colour televisions Singapore has been described as a 'front' for Japanese firms, while Taiwan depends heavily on Philips and RCA (Turner *et al.*, 1982, p. 55). Second, Japanese efforts to move upstream occurred during a prolonged period of rapid growth in demand. Given the present slowdown and the likely prospects of increased saturation in major markets, any widespread repetition of the strategy might exceed the threshold for protective reprisals – by TNCs if not by Western interest groups affiliated with the production side.

There is evidence that the development of consumer electronics suits sectorwide objectives such as employment generation of export promotion. Such objectives, however, are neither industry-specific nor an outgrowth of any interest group initiatives. Given the TNCs' predominance and the embryonic state of the industry, active interest group participation in LDCs has not really taken shape. Instead, governmental support – in the form of extensive tariff protection, fiscal and non-fiscal incentives and, occasionally, direct government participation – caters to a nebulous and more broadly based audience in the industrial workforce and the emerging middle classes. In general, the discussion of this industry suggests little likelihood of effective interest group pressure emerging in LDCs in the near future. This situation contrasts with that in other industries like petrochemicals, steel or automobiles, where interest groups in LDCs may exert a significant influence on policy choices. Perhaps the only current alternative for LDCs to exert some influence on the industry's development path is to follow the example of Taiwan's largest manufacturer, Tatung. This firm, which currently operates subsidiaries in various LDCs, in the UK and in the USA, produces a wide range of home appliances as well as televisions, picture tubes and stereo equipment. Such a step would require that firms are nationally (LDC) controlled and have access to the necessary capital, technology and distribution facilities.

Summary and conclusions

Consumer electronics exhibits several distinguishing characteristics, each of which exerts a powerful influence on the industry's development path as well as the choices available to national policy-makers and industry strategists. Technological innovations have made the global dispersion of production a reality by accentuating differences between the respective factor requirements of each production stage. These advances in production technology, in conjunction with parallel efforts in product development, have shaped the choice and content of available industry strategies. The long-term emphasis on improvements in technology has extended the TNCs' ability to chart the industry's development and has reduced the influence of other interest groups. National labour interests have had little incentive or scope to act as a countervailing force during the long period of steady growth and expansion. Although the industry may have reached a more mature stage where a relative contraction and a cutback in the labour force may occur, labour has yet to fashion any coherent response, particularly to those strategies like offshore processing that may be detrimental to the domestic worker's interests. This hesitancy contrasts somewhat with labour's response in other industries like textiles where its negotiating power more closely approaches that of major firms and where trade unions have become increasingly vocal critics of offshore processing agreements.

Table 7.1 relates several of the industry's major problems to possible solutions. Neither set of considerations – problems or strategies – are mutually exclusive. For instance, constraints like market saturation and excess capacity are experienced by a large number of firms in different countries, while strategies such as offshore processing or moving upstream may be pursued simultaneously by the same firm. In general, the strategies that appear to offer the best prospects for

Table 7.1   *An overview of problems and strategies in the consumer electronics industry*

	Solutions			
Problems	*A* *Offshore processing*	*B* *Product development, moving upstream*	*C* *Defensive protection*	*D* *Foreign investment to replace exports*
1 Excess capacity	No help	Of limited benefit	Possible short-term benefit; jeopardises long-term solutions	Can help when problem is due to poor managerial or marketing decisions
2 Fierce price competition	Improves ability to compete on basis of price	Of limited benefit	No help	No help
3 Market saturation	Of very little benefit	Helps to alleviate problem	No help	No help
4 Continued penetration by low-cost, foreign suppliers	May help if partial control of exporters is obtained by firms in major importing markets	Helps to alleviate problem	Combats but does not solve the problem; may conflict with strategy A	Effective way for Asian producers to penetrate Western markets

alleviating problems are those that include some technological dimension or those that are international in scope. This is, of course, natural in an industry where technological dexterity and the ability to relocate to low-wage countries have been long-standing traits. In contrast, strategies that are purely national hold less promise of making a positive contribution to the problems at hand. The involvement of governments is, perhaps, likely in any industry where adjustment pressures are triggered by the emergence of 'super-competitors' like Japan or Taiwan and this tends to give a domestic slant to the strategies adopted. However, consumer electronics is not a highly political field and, in comparison with some industries, government intervention has seldom gone so far as to seal off the domestic industry from technological advances or foreign competitors. In those instances where industry pressures have successfully contributed to policy decisions the results have still retained an element of market forces. For example, the ready acquiescence of some countries to a Japanese strategy of supplanting exports by foreign investment represents an effort to acquire know-how and to improve performance in both domestic and foreign markets while minimising the adjustment costs of contraction. Although the actions of various national interest groups, including the government, are key determinants of industry policy, they are not so pervasive as to supplant the role of the market. This position contrasts with that in the following discussion of advanced electronics where the role of government is shown to be extensive.

Advanced electronics

The advanced electronics industry as treated here consists of electronic applications equipment such as computers, automated machine tools and electronic testing and measuring equipment, as well as semiconductor devices and integrated circuits which are the main components used in such equipment. Beginning from a negligible base in 1950, advanced electronics has expanded rapidly and, in several countries, has overtaken consumer electronics as the predominant subsector in electronics. Thus, by 1978, the value of industrial products and components accounted for 68 per cent of all electronics production in the USA. The corresponding figure for the EEC was 53 per cent, while the share in Japan was lower but rising rapidly (IDE, 1980, p. 11). When examined in terms of its end-uses, the industry appears to be a conglomeration of products and production techniques. In another sense, however, these activities are closely linked. For instance, technological advances in electronic components or computer hardware can dramatically improve the versatility and effectiveness of the electronic tools and equipment used by manufacturers. Conversely, the recognition of new industrial applications for electronic equipment quickly feeds back to the producers and designers of circuitry, components and computers.

There are several reasons why many governments regard the industry's development as a high priority. First, the industrial applications of advanced electronics are expected to improve greatly the reliability and quality of products. Manufacturing activities consist mainly of making materials, forming them into various shapes, joining the bits together, and then assembling these parts into finished products. A product's quality and reliability are mainly dependent on the performance of these tasks – whether welding, brazing, soldering, glueing or riveting – and electronic capital goods and computer control of manufacturing processes are expected to do a far more consistent job than people. Second, the cost of a manufactured product largely depends on the level of efficiency attained in the joining and assembly phases and, in comparison with humans, electronic capital goods can be expected to excel. Third, the high priority accorded to the industry is part of a more general response to recent trends in productivity in the advanced countries. A decline in productivity has been experienced in many fields of manufacturing since the mid-1970s (Interfutures, 1979, pp. 113, 131; UNIDO, 1981a, p. 15; Sachs, 1982, p. 57). As the productivity gains to be achieved through the applications of additional capital have diminished, the search for profitable investments has gradually turned to the development of new systems of capital goods, and advanced electronics may eventually serve as the basis around which many industries may reorganise (Interfutures, 1979, p. 349). Finally, various governments attach a high priority to the development of advanced electronics because of the close links these activities have with their country's defence and military interests.

Electronic components – the emergence of a new industry
The production of active electronic components – semiconductor devices and integrated circuits – has a comparatively brief history, beginning only after the Second World War. Transistors, which were invented in 1947, quickly replaced the vacuum tubes that had been used in electronic equipment. The electric current connecting the electrodes in transistors flows through solid materials known as semiconductors. Full-scale production of semiconductors began in the late 1950s in California's Santa Clara County, now nicknamed Silicon Valley. This phase was quickly followed by the development of the first integrated circuit in 1959. Each circuit, or 'chip', contained many

discrete but interconnected functions such as transistors on a piece of silicon and made it possible to produce products that were fully transistorised.

The ability of producers to increase the available circuitry implanted on a semiconductor, or chip, was an essential first step in developing the electronic capital goods which would become the nucleus for new production systems. Researchers succeeded in doubling the number of transistors or logic functions on a chip in each year during the period 1959–80. Today firms may produce over 200,000 components on a pea-sized chip of silicon compared with only 10 transistors per chip in the early 1960s. The ability of chip-makers to miniaturise their product promises to widen enormously the range of industrial applications, both to electronic capital goods and to computer-based systems of production. Developments in these two fields (discussed below) have contributed to the tremendous growth in demand for semiconductors and integrated circuits.

The producers of semiconductors and integrated circuits passed through a comparatively brief period of adolescence. World sales were $1 billion in 1970 but totalled $10 billion by the end of the decade. Simultaneously, the volume of output doubled in every year during the 1970s as a miraculous growth in demand was matched by drastic price cuts. The price of a transistor dropped from $10 in 1960 to less than one cent in 1980, while the price per integrated circuit function declined, on average, by 27 per cent per year during the 1970s. Thus, price reductions as well as product improvements were instrumental in establishing a worldwide market for semiconductors, electronic circuitry and machines that used them.

The structure of firms within the industry changed drastically during these years. Silicon Valley had been dominated by many small firms or even individual entrepreneurs, and sufficient venture capital was readily available for producers with new ideas. Significantly, two of today's largest producers, National Semiconductor and Intel, entered business in the late 1960s with only $1 million to $3 million in capital (UNIDO, 1981b, p. 102). However, the cost of entry soared as demand grew and larger economies of scale became necessary if new entrants were to match the prices of competitors; by 1980, the capital outlay required of a new entrant for a basic chip making facility was $50 million (*The Economist*, 1 Mar. 1980). While Silicon Valley continued to be the centre of innovation and development, Japanese production was started up, mainly in newly-created divisions of large conglomerates that were supplying a wide range of electrical products. This organisational arrangement partly explains why Japanese firms were the first to use semiconductors in consumer electronics and calculators. American producers concentrated on selling a broad range of devices to cover a large segment of the market while Japanese suppliers specialised to meet in-house requirements.

The industry's first crisis occurred around 1975 when the demand for chips and integrated circuits plummeted. Annual variations in demand, often amounting to 10 to 20 per cent, had been common. However, the industry had by then arrived at a point where the burgeoning costs of R & D, product development and capital investment started to make it difficult for firms to adjust. Many chip-makers cut back on investments in new plant capacity and development programmes and, when demand resumed its upward trend, consumers were faced with a serious shortage of components and circuitry. Japanese firms were, perhaps, more fortunate than their American competitors since they were able to fund investments from the profits of other (much larger) production divisions while the major US producers were solely dependent on revenues earned from the sale of chips and integrated circuits.

An atmosphere of crisis recurred in later years and delayed the production of computers and numerically controlled machines which used the components. Reasons for the bottleneck are more complex than a simple supply-demand imbalance. First, during the period 1970–80 the capital investment required by chip-makers rose from 12 per cent of sales to 21 per cent (*FT*, 17 June 1981). This trend was complicated by the fact that each new generation of installed equipment has a shorter lifespan than the previous vintage. As a result, investment costs have become a major deterrent to new entrants. Second, with the growth in worldwide capacity, each subsequent downswing in demand brought a more vigorous round of price-cutting. Since 1975, rates of return have dropped by almost one-third and venture financiers have shifted out of chip production. Third, major users of chips such as IBM have set up their own facilities. Production problems have been widespread – largely because of the users' inexperience – and these firms have been forced to buy chips on the open market.

A new trend of market segmentation also emerged during the 1970s. Greater market segmentation was due to the convergence of designs for circuits and systems along with the growing number of suppliers and end-users, each of which had developed a complex set of interrelationships. A UNIDO study (1981b, pp. 73–5) notes the existence of five different types of semiconductors: standard devices that are technically indifferent to their final use; exclusive devices which are indifferent to final use but are supplied by a firm having a technological monopoly; specific devices that are mass-produced for a pre-determined market; customised devices for a particular client; and microprocessors which are circuits that can be mass-produced and used for many purposes. The trend to greater market segmentation has complicated the pattern of demand for semiconductors and made predictions considerably more difficult. Producers have also found it necessary to improve their distribution networks in order to reach new users and to broaden the range of devices which they supply.

As the relationship between chip-makers and their users continues to evolve, the maturing industry can expect additional complications to arise because producers will be required to perform new and unfamiliar tasks. For instance, development of the more intricate chips means that the job of designing and producing them becomes more complex and time-consuming while the skilled personnel required for these tasks is expensive and in short supply. Moreover, suppliers will experience growing pressure from their buyers to provide additional services. They must supplement the engineering skills on which their growth has been based by new service-orientated functions to help buyers adapt products to their needs. Examples include the design of the microprocessors which use the basic chips and the development of subsidiary chips to suit the needs of different customers. Another complication results from the growing range of applications for chips and microprocessors. In the past, increases in production runs led to a spectacular decline in unit costs. However, there has been a steady increase in the costs of developing the software for each new application, perhaps ten-fold during the 1970s, and this cost component may soon outweigh the fall in per unit costs of production.

The outline of a new industry – flexible manufacturing systems
Many new systems of capital goods are still in the planning stage, while others exist in only skeletal form. Although the systems will eventually be tailored to each user's needs, they will all rely on a computer-controlled network of automated machine tools and other forms of computer aids. The objective is to develop flexible manufacturing systems using a combination of robots and numerically controlled machine tools. The systems of the future will be expected to meet at least three basic requirements. First, if a system is to be economic it must be capable of producing a variety of parts; capital investments cannot be justified when a system is designed to produce only a single part. Second, in order to produce a sufficient range of products, machines must have the ability to switch, under computer control, from one production step to another. Finally, a robot or, alternatively, a conveyor mechanism will be necessary to speed the passage of materials from one machine to the next. The importance of this last function is indicated by the fact that materials are worked on for

only 5 per cent of the time they are in a factory; during the remainder of the time they are pushed from place to place or lie idle (UNIDO, 1981a, p. 154).

The computer, which is to be the key element in these systems, was remarkably altered during the 1970s owing to the advances made in semiconductors. The fall in prices of computers during the 1970s and the new range of models now available reflects the chip-makers' ability to cram more components onto the small pieces of silicon. Accordingly, the cost of computer memory dropped and smaller versions of hardware – the minicomputer and the microcomputer – became available. These changes promise to make it technically and economically feasible to develop computerised control of factory plants and processes. In such a system a network of small computers would be located close to line operations and would communicate with a central computer or mainframe.

A second element in these systems will be numerically controlled machine tools and industrial robots. Numerically controlled tools are standard machines which usually perform specific tasks and have been adapted to respond to instructions from a microcomputer. The first of these was developed by a US firm in the early 1960s to perform welding tasks. Robots normally replace a human skill; their tasks involve some movement and they are typically designed for a specific industry. Although programmable, the present generation of robots is not very intelligent and is dedicated to simple, straightforward tasks like spray-painting or lifting heavy castings. However, as electronic components have become more compact and powerful, the ability of these machine tools and robots to perform their tasks has gradually improved. The same advances have made possible the introduction of the microprocessor – essentially a complex type of integrated circuit that is programmable – to the factory floor. This innovation permits the sequence of instructions to be followed by a component or a robot to be changed. Today such machines are common in the automobile industry, where they perform the simple but boring tasks listed above, and in the electronics industry, where they are used to assemble parts, to insert components and to move materials. Robots have also found limited use in other fields like shipbuilding and textiles.

In 1981, Japanese manufacturers were reported to be using over 14,000 industrial robots. Less than one-third of this number was found in American factories, while West Germany was the only other country with a robot population that exceeded 1,000 (*The Economist*, 19 Dec. 1981). The Japanese lead in computer-controlled robots appears more impressive when account is taken of the fact that more than 95 per cent of its robots are domestically produced. In contrast, roughly one-half of those used in Europe and America are imported.

The high cost of robots, as well as their limited flexibility, has prevented more widespread adoption. Based on costs and wage rates in 1971, a Japanese company would have required over twenty-two years to recover its investment in a robot that was operated on a single shift basis (*FEER*, 4 Dec. 1981). In 1980, a basic robot was still thought to cost $50,000–$60,000, while depreciation, interest charges and maintenance charges added an additional $20,000–$30,000 (*The Economist*, 1 Mar. 1980). The eventual replacement of minicomputers by cheaper microcomputers will reduce these costs. Microcomputers are expected to serve as the supervisory computer or brain for a whole system of machine tools.

A look at the structure of firms engaged in making robots provides an interesting comparison with the pattern among producers of electronic components. In Japan, robots are often custom-made to suit particular requirements and the initial requirements are minimal. Hence, the Japanese industry is widely dispersed and supplies a broad range of automated machines. The American situation provides a stark contrast; there are only two major producers which, together, account for more than one-half of the market. These differences reflect a combination of factors, mainly the infancy of the industry and the different strategies pursued by producers.

Experience to date suggests that there may be several ways to develop systems which meet these requirements. The Japanese have moved quickly by relying on existing technology and by making extensive use of conveyors, rather than robots, to transfer parts and materials from one machine to another. Cutting and grinding of parts is done in machining centres by machine tools that can perform a variety of steps. Although the same approach can be found in some Western factories, most firms have opted for a more gradual approach. Instead of creating machining centres, companies use their existing machine tools in combination with robots. As the system is extended, the Western plan allows for the robots to be reprogrammed rather than having to rebuild the conveyor. An advantage of the gradual approach is that it avoids large capital investments and production bottlenecks owing to poorly planned automation systems. However, in comparison with the Japanese version, a more advanced technology is required because the system uses a greater variety of machine tools and a larger number of machines.

Two other applications have yet to be perfected but may eventually have a significant impact on manufacturing systems and production costs. One of these, computer aided design (CAD), would provide technicians with the ability to design, draft and analyse parts or assemblages on a computer screen. This advance would eliminate the labour-intensive task of drafting and would avoid the need to produce expensive test versions of products and components. Moreover, if the necessary computer programming has been done, the designer could test the results of his work by subjecting products to electronically simulated temperature changes, mechanical stresses or other conditions that would impinge on actual performance. To date, CAD has found only limited applications in a few heavy industries. Examples include the design of hydraulic tubing for large aircraft and tests for structural flaws in the design of huge turbine blades and automobile bodies.

Even greater potential is foreseen if CAD is combined with computer aided manufacture (CAM). When the linkage works smoothly, on-screen designing and testing will generate a bank of computer instructions for manufacturing a product or making the tools, dies and moulds used to manufacture it. Integration of the two systems would shorten the time between design and production and reduce the cost of introducing new models or customised products. The importance attached to the perfection of integrated and flexible systems is reflected by the fact that 60–70 per cent of the current costs of manufacturing are thought to have nothing to do with the physical tasks involved but depend on the planning, scheduling and control of the equipment and the people who operate that equipment (*Fortune*, 5 Oct. 1981).

Although manufacturers have been slow to consider CAD/CAM, there are several forces at work that may eventually ensure a greater degree of acceptance. Most important, perhaps, is the growing preference for materials that require moulding (plastics, ceramics or composites) in order to realise reductions in cost and weight and to simplify assembly tasks. This trend has given rise to a disproportionate need for toolmakers since the throughput of moulding machines is slower than metal forming or stamping. The growing shortage of toolmakers can not be easily rectified and some of the demand is being transferred to suppliers of CAM systems. Another attraction is that such systems are valuable in preparing speedy estimates and in executing contracts to a tight schedule. Finally, planners hope that CAM systems may ultimately become available to small firms in a field of manufacturing that has hitherto proven unsuitable for such techniques. Roughly four-fifths of all manufactures are currently made in small batch lots of 10–15 units, and the operating costs of these firms are much greater than those incurred when mass-production techniques are used.

With the exception of electronic components, virtually none of the activities identified as being part of advanced electronics have existed for a sufficient period of time to allow for the development of a distinctive set of industry strategies. Nevertheless, the extensive involvement of one important interest group – the state – is readily apparent in the following discussion of these strategies. Unlike the experience of other industries, the state has played an active role from the industry's very inception. In the USA, and to a lesser extent in Western Europe, state involvement can be partially explained by the obvious importance of advanced electronics for military and defence activities. This is suggested by the fact that, in the USA, the 'electronic content' of R & D for defence is projected to rise from 39 to 46 per cent during the 1980s (*The Economist*, 12 Jan. 1980). However, close government–industry relationships extend beyond military considerations. Another important explanation is that most governments regard advanced electronics as essential for maintaining some measure of technological independence and international competitiveness (Interfutures, 1979, pp. 341–4) and no industry strategy really precludes the role of the public sector.

Promoting a national champion
In most advanced countries the state's involvement began with the development of the computer industry which was an early choice for a national champion. The provision of state funds for R & D, preferences in public procurement for domestic firms, government-assisted mergers, and favourable loan terms, were only some of the policies employed by the governments of France, Japan, the UK and West Germany to spur the take-off of computer firms in the late 1960s and 1970s (Warnecke, 1978, pp. 39–40, 135, 212–13). Governments also played an indirect role in fostering the industry's development. In addition to the large proportion of defence expenditure on microelectronics, the US government's stringent regulations on fuel economy and emission controls promise to make the automobile industry one of the largest markets for chips and, eventually, microprocessors. More subtle forms of government intervention are typified by the Japanese government's decision in 1965 to subsidise research on integrated circuits while simultaneously preventing US manufacturers from establishing a domestic presence before local producers were ready to compete.

For several years, the EEC has attempted to formulate an overall plan for the development of computers and the associated microelectronics and telecommunications equipment, as well as a common policy on public procurement. The outline of the programme calls for direct financial assistance to hasten the development of European firms engaged in the production of computers and microchips and for indirect support through the creation of a European network for advanced communications. In addition, public procurement policies would provide for all 'qualified' EEC firms to have the opportunity to tender bids and it calls for governments to allocate a small percentage of their annual equipment purchases to suppliers in other EEC countries. A major flaw is the inability of European governments to agree on the treatment of American subsidiaries. Governments with no domestic computer industry of their own argue that the American subsidiaries qualify as home producers and others, where the American presence is predominant, are under pressure to do the same.

In contrast, the French government opposes the involvement of foreign subsidiaries in any EEC-wide programme. Substantial public funds are devoted to the computer and microelectronics industry, chiefly for the development of large-scale capacity to produce integrated circuits using the most advanced technologies. Such circuits will be specialised in the sense that they are primarily intended for telecommunications. The approach is part of the French strategy to emphasise high technologies that combine the use of the telephone and the computer.

In order to boost its home market for industrial robots, the Japanese government has recently turned to a leasing scheme similar to that employed in the early 1960s to help fledgling computer companies. Because robots have made few inroads in most fields of manufacturing, Japanese producers have been forced to export their new inventions. Under the auspices of MITI and with the support of the Japanese Industrial Robot Association, a robot-leasing company was established in 1980. The government hopes that this step will encourage more – and smaller – firms to accept automation by providing the robots to users at subsidised rates. With this financial assistance, the purchasers of sophisticated robots can depreciate 53 per cent of the total cost in the first year (*FEER*, 4 Dec. 1981). In addition to cheap leasing, the government has directly funded much research by the larger electrical companies and has accepted money from potential users of robots to set up research projects at government laboratories.

Joint ventures and the acquisition of foreign know-how
Their heavy dependence on American and Japanese suppliers has spurred many European governments to take even more aggressive steps to promote home production in key areas of advanced electronics. This dependency is apparent in the market for computers where the EEC accounts for 26 per cent of world usage but only 15 per cent of production in Western countries (*The Economist*, 5 Apr. 1980). The industry's fragmented condition has, as already noted, consistently frustrated efforts to devise an EEC-wide strategy. Their weak position has forced various European governments and producers to look to the Japanese for technology-swapping agreements in order to

withstand the American competition. Recent examples of this trend are arrangements between Siemens and Fujitsu and between ICL and Hitachi.

A similar pattern of dependency prevails in the field of semiconductors where firms in the EEC supply only about 40 per cent of the Europeans' requirements. There are sound commercial reasons for European firms and governments to be concerned about the extent of dependence on foreign suppliers of components. First, there is a history of sudden shortages of key microelectronic components and the vulnerability of users in third markets is great. Second, American and Japanese customers are thought to enjoy commercial and technological advantages because they participate extensively in the design of new semiconductor products. Finally, some Europeans are fearful that a US embargo on high technology exports will be imposed for political reasons.

Most governments control the activities of foreign firms within their borders carefully. The French strategy, designed to encourage joint ventures with the specific intent of acquiring foreign technologies, is one of the most distinctive. Because the leading French firm, Thomson-CSF, lacked the latest technologies to produce integrated circuits, the government stipulated that partnerships with local firms were a precondition for American producers to manufacture circuits in France. The American participants are expected to contribute the technology and process expertise and to train French engineers. In exchange, they are not required to put up any cash and are offered 49 per cent of the equity in the new ventures which receive substantial government funding. In this way, the government hopes to increase production of semiconductors to a level equivalent to the domestic market. These new companies, plus the major French producers, will be the preferred suppliers of chips and circuits for the telecommunications and defence industries.

In the UK most firms specialise in making 'custom' microchips and leave the production of 'standard' chips and integrated circuits to US firms operating in the UK. The state-backed firm, Inmos, is the only potential competitor of the American subsidiaries. The company, which has received $200 million from the state over five years, is expected to produce an advanced version of standard chips but has yet to begin selling. The semiconductor industry in Holland and West Germany is dominated by a few major producers such as Philips, Siemens and AEG-Telefunken, and the role of government is somewhat different. Although these firms have received state aid for development, they have funded much of their own R & D programme and have attempted to gain access to foreign technologies by purchasing American firms.

Co-operative programmes for R & D

At a time when many of the industrial applications of advanced electronics are still at the conceptual stage, access to the results of R & D is crucial. Simultaneously, the heavy and continually rising costs associated with research spending can be prohibitive to all but the largest firms and most generous governments. Under these circumstances, there have been various attempts to spread the cost burden and to share the results of R & D. Two Japanese programmes were successful in pooling the resources and research interests of the public and private sector. Begun in the mid-1970s, the programmes were funded by Nippon Telegraph and Telephone (NTT) and MITI respectively and were intended to develop new generations of advanced integrated circuits, microwave systems and computers. Engineers from NTT worked jointly with experts from three large private companies that received no public funds to cover their participation costs. Instead, the firms expect to receive large orders from NTT for equipment once the programme yields results. The MITI project broke new ground by the creation of a co-operative research laboratory where some 120 researchers from five companies worked together for four years to develop 'very large-scale integrated circuits'. The project resulted in more than a thousand new patents. Private participants are obligated to repay MITI's outlay if and when they start earning money from the patents. However, the firms must first convert the basic know-how into marketable products. In this highly competitive phase each firm is working by itself.

European and American efforts lag behind the Japanese and have a somewhat different orientation. The EEC's attempts to pool research funds have been limited to efforts to persuade the major companies jointly to finance university research in CAD and the development of complex microchips. In contrast to the Japanese, the European strategies have been handicapped by disagreements between governments which have increasingly turned to subsidies in order to defray development costs. American attempts to spread the costs of R & D are at a more initial stage. One co-operative effort, initiated in 1982, is a plan by sixteen large American firms to create a large R & D consortium. In addition to spreading the costs of R & D, the consortium would be a means of sharing scarce talents and avoiding duplication of research. However, the initiative already faces two problems. Differences of opinion between participants have raised doubts about the financial arrangements and it is unclear how the stringent anti-trust laws will be applied by the Federal Trade Commission. A second co-operative programme is a joint venture between American firms and universities that is sponsored by the Semiconductor Industry Association. The non-profit organisation, created to fund long-term research at universities, opens its membership to foreign manufacturers. However, the foreign company must allow all members the right to participate in similar co-operative programmes in their home country and, for this reason, Japanese firms are not expected to join.

Integration strategies

A two-fold integration movement is underway and is expected to continue. Firms concerned with the design and production of electronic components have intensified their efforts to move downstream while the producers of mechanical and electrical capital goods move upstream into automated tools and electronic components. One attraction of vertical integration is that chip-makers are able to specialise and, consequently, enjoy greater economies of scale. A second advantage of a vertically integrated structure is that the large revenues accruing to these conglomerates permit them to concentrate R & D expenditures on technology development for advanced electronics. Thus in 1977, Japan's large and diversified electronics firms devoted nearly 30 per cent of their sales revenues to R & D or to new plants (*The Economist*, 3 Mar. 1982). Third, and perhaps most important, the skills acquired in the production of chips and integrated circuits are valuable in other, more profitable, parts of the market. Despite declining profits, both American and Japanese companies have maintained their semiconductor operations in the hopes of using this knowledge more profitably in downstream activities. This trend will eventually lead to an industry structure that is markedly different from the large number of small firms that dominated the field in the 1950s. Although the diversity of firms served the industry during its infancy and adolescence, the large capital investments and the heavy outlays for R & D that are required today have made expansion, and particularly downstream integration, a necessity.

Integration in the opposite direction – upstream – has occurred among the users of electronic components. Computer manufacturers take up to 40 per cent of all the chip-makers' output. Because their operations are so dependent on adequate supplies, these firms have become major producers of 'captive' semiconductors for internal use. Thus IBM has spent huge sums on research and claims to be one of the world's largest producers of semiconductors. Similar moves are being made by other users of chips and integrated circuits in the automobile industry, in consumer electronics and in office equipment. Although captive operations run the risk of failing to keep abreast of the rapidly changing state of technology, there are two reasons for the growing emphasis on in-house chip design and production. First, very large-scale integration has meant that virtually entire systems are implanted on a chip, leading many equipment-makers to prefer in-house development in order to protect proprietary designs. Second, these newer systemwide chips must be customised for specific applications but the volumes produced for each design will be low.

Evidence of other industry strategies

For the most part, advanced electronics is a new industry that shares few strategic characteristics with other fields of manufacturing. However, American producers of semiconductors have recently begun to mount a modest campaign for protection from Japanese competitors. Representing nearly fifty producers and users of chips, the Semiconductor Industry Association in the USA has charged that Japanese firms are selling below the cost of production. Significantly, the industry association does not include the two leading American producers of chips, IBM and Texas Instruments, both of which have operations in Japan.

A second strategy which is more commonly identified with consumer electronics is offshore processing. The strategy requires that production processes are fragmented or physically separated. Where economic, the most labour-intensive portions of the work are performed in cheap labour-cost locations, typically LDCs. Here again, there is some evidence of this tactic among the suppliers of semiconductors. A move to offshore processing sites occurred during the late 1960s and early 1970s, but since then there has been a decline in this type of investment and a levelling-off of imports from these countries (UNIDO, 1981b, pp. 239–51). While the trend may reflect the growing service orientation of the semiconductor industry, there is also limited evidence that a few firms have returned their offshore operations from South-east Asia to Europe, partly in response to trade union pressure (Dosi, 1981, p. 97).

Implications for the LDCs

For obvious reasons advanced electronics is an industry where the entry of firms based in the LDCs is not imminent or even likely in the medium term. The production of semiconductors is the field offering the most opportunity for the LDCs because the relevant technologies have reached relatively advanced stages of standardisation or maturity. Involvement of the LDCs is largely through offshore chip assembly which began as far back as 1961. The relocation of production facilities to LDCs was concentrated in Asian countries, Mexico and the Caribbean Basin and peaked in the period 1968–73. Since that time, the periodic crises experienced by firms in advanced countries have forced them to cut back on their development of additional offshore processing facilities. Although the value of exports from existing offshore plants continued to rise in later years, their share in value added declined after 1975. A detailed analysis led to the conclusion that these trends do not reflect any significant move to relocate back in the advanced countries (UNIDO, 1981b, pp. 238–42). Instead, the slowdown in investment in offshore facilities is due to emerging financial constraints encountered by most firms and the fact that the technologies in use tend to increase the value of production prior to assembly (largely activities performed in the firm's home market). Such trends may well limit the extent to which producers in LDCs will be involved in the future. Moreover, the growing 'service orientation' of chip makers will increasingly force them to focus on major consuming markets and further slow the movement of production facilities to the LDCs.

Conclusions

A salient fact emerging from the foregoing discussion is that the strategic choices of governments and major producers are guided, to a large extent, by conditions in the electronic components subsector. The knowledge and skills necessary for the design and production of chips and circuits are essential for participants who hope to compete in the future markets for electronic machine tools and flexible manufacturing systems. Despite the steady rise in capital costs and an erosion of profits, many firms – with active government support – continue to develop their capabilities in the field of semiconductors. To industrialists, mastery of this stage holds out the promise of eventual profits in the downstream markets for industrial applications of electronic capital goods. For governments, the growing competition between advanced countries has led them to make the development of the components subsector a top priority. Most governments have apparently concluded that a significant national presence in this subsector, along with a ready acceptance of the new electronic innovations by users of capital goods, are essential preconditions for the preservation of technological independence. The two conditions are, in fact, closely connected: the quality and competitiveness of electronic equipment will largely depend on the aptitudes acquired in the process of designing and producing the components, while the efficient use of automated capital goods will similarly depend on the aptitudes acquired in the production stage.

Table 7.2 looks at the industry's major problems in conjunction with several of the major strategies described above. Because of the predominant role of the state, most industry strategies are distinguishable along national lines. In comparison with other countries, Japan's medium- and long-term programmes for advanced electro-

Table 7.2 *An overview of problems and strategies in advanced electronics*

	Strategies			
Problems	*A* *Joint ventures, technology-swapping agreements*	*B* *Co-operative programmes for R & D*	*C* *Vertical integration*	*D* *Forms of government assistance and funding*
1 Extensive price competition; declining rates of profit	No help	No help for immediate problem	Profitable downstream activities may subsidise costly presence in semiconductor markets	Subsidies do not address real problem
2 Rising costs of capital equipment and rapid obsolescence	Little help	No help	Same as 1C	Generous subsidies, depreciation allowance combat the problem but must be coupled with effective long-term strategies
3 Access to advanced technologies	Effective way to introduce an imitative strategy; firms may still lack an indigenous research dimension	Helps cut R & D costs, avoids duplication; much depends on choice of project and government's role	Leads to development of in-house capabilities at each stage; failure to stay abreast of new technologies is a danger	Government role in conjunction with 3B is important; need to divorce collaborative R & D from market adaptations of results
4 Limited acceptance for industrial applications	No help	Can accelerate R & D for industrial applications	Mastery of component production can hasten industrial applications	Government programmes can reduce cost of users; indirect initiatives to expand market can also help

nics are the most consistent, running the gamut from components through electronic machine tools to flexible manufacturing systems. The strength of the Japanese programme lies in the fact that upstream development in the field of components produces very rapid results in the field of industrial applications. This emphasis is matched by attempts to overcome the reluctance of private industry to accept these innovations and to reduce the economic barriers to acceptance.

Despite the programme's continuity, and contrary to the claims of some competitors, the financial support provided by the Japanese government is relatively modest. For instance, the total funds devoted to the country's research in microchips were estimated to be $1 billion, although only one-half of this was provided by the government and was spread over a period of four years. The industry itself contributed another 12.5 per cent of the total while the remainder came from individual companies that devoted funds to the development of new products. Another example is the Japanese programme for development of highly sophisticated integrated circuits where the R & D investment plan of one American firm is said to match the entire Japanese programme (Interfutures, 1979, p. 341). Thus the success of the Japanese programme is not due so much to public largesse but to the judicious combination of a variety of strategies as shown in Table 7.2. These include co-operative R & D programmes, a continuous search for joint venture opportunities with export possibilities, government guidance for R & D and efforts to develop the home market for industrial applications.

Current trends in the USA provide a stark contrast with those in Japan, primarily due to the differing approaches of the two governments. In the US an important source of public funds for R & D or seed money is the Department of Defense which finances 30 per cent of R & D. Like MITI, the Defence Department is heavily involved in research on very sophisticated integrated circuits, industrial robots and advanced computers. The research funds and development subsidies provided by the Pentagon match or exceed those supplied by MITI. Beyond this fact, however, the influence of the two bureaucracies differs in several important respects. First, MITI's approach encourages firms to co-operate on specific basic research projects but is designed to ensure that they are competitive in marketing. In contrast, the Pentagon tends to award contracts without competitive bidding and contractor overruns are frequent. Second, the Pentagon is most comfortable with large, stable contractors that are to some extent immune from the uncertainties of competition, although no similar pattern is observable in MITI's case. Third, many Japanese projects span a decade or more while Pentagon-funded contracts are subject to the vagaries of politics and national security needs. As

American firms have become aware of this particular drawback they have become reluctant to cater for military users, fearing eventual cutbacks in defence spending and the costs of developing specialised components for this field. Finally, marketing the sophisticated circuitry and the related equipment that uses these components requires a truly global strategy and MITI's assistance includes export financing, subsidies for firms to establish new foreign offices and other incentives. In contrast, US firms are frequently subjected to strict export controls on commercial products and are required to ensure against the transfer of their products to communist countries. Thus the major distinction between the roles of the two governments is not in terms of the extent of public subsidies but in the fact that one government encourages its firms to become internationally competitive while the other may actively discourage this.

European attempts to put together an effective set of industry strategies have suffered because home markets are dominated by American and Japanese competitors while the European industry itself is highly fragmented. In the first instance, the joint ventures undertaken by firms to make up their technological lag have sometimes resulted in no more than the establishment of secondary sources of supply for chips that are made abroad. Similarly, because the European industry is so fragmented, the limited number of firms have attempted to supply a wide range of components. One result is that R & D programmes are widely dispersed and, with few exceptions, results have been modest. A crucial limitation is that, unlike their American and Japanese competitors, the Europeans have yet to gain control of their home market. Perhaps the most effective step would be for these governments to give a higher priority to the development of the European market and to improvements in their production expertise as they now do to promote innovation.

Oil refining

The world oil refining industry provides a most instructive illustration of some of the adjustment problems that can beset even the most modern, technologically well-equipped and – until recently – apparently secure industries. The industry is also of interest because its adjustment activities are worldwide involving both the advanced economies and the LDCs, because the decisions of firms necessarily entail fairly long time lags before fruition, and because, for once, the industry's problems are only very slightly affected by the unemployment issue. Moreover, there is also an interest deriving from the close involvement of a particular group of LDCs – the members of OPEC.

Causes of adjustment difficulty

The story of the crisis in the oil refining industry is at root simple. As long as rates of economic growth maintained their post-war momentum in advanced countries, the demand for the products based upon crude oil expanded at disproportionately rapid rates. Thus between 1963 and 1976 value added by the industry grew at an average annual rate of 5.8 per cent in Western economies, and at 12.6 per cent in socialist countries (UNIDO, 1981a, p. 32). The rapid growth of refining capacity during the 1950s, 1960s and 1970s, is evident from the figures in Table 7.3.

This enviable pattern was reversed after 1974, however, as the growth of demand for oil and for most of its by-products faltered. It has never since been regained. Although the real prices of oil products weakened (particularly for countries other than the USA, which gained from the effect of a weak dollar on import prices) during the 1975–8 period, and brought about a slight revival in demand for some oil-based items, the increases in oil prices in 1979 and 1980 again dampened the long-term outlook. A collapse of demand was the natural consequence of a sharp rise in real prices, but was reinforced by the efforts of many OECD governments to discourage consumption by raising taxes on oil-based items.

Table 7.3   *World refining capacity, 1938–81 (percentages and thousand tonnes per annum)*

Area	1938	1950	1965	1981
Western Europe	4.4	7.6	23.6	24.8
Middle East	3.8	8.1	5.8	3.9
Africa	0.3	0.2	1.5	2.6
USA	61.8	58.0	29.5	22.3
Latin America	11.0	12.3	11.5	11.0
Far East & Australasia	3.8	2.4	9.6	12.2
USSR, Eastern Europe & China	8.7	6.3	13.0	19.5
Other	6.2	5.1	5.5	3.7
World Total	100	100	100	100
	363,700	603,100	1,735,000	4,085,000

Sources: Institute of Petroleum (London) *Petroleum Statistics*, 1981 edition; BP (1982).

Notes:

i   The reported capacity of the Middle East fell by 18 million tonnes between 1980 and 1981, reflecting the fall in Iran's serviceable capacity. In 1980 the Middle Eastern share in the world total was 4.5 per cent.

ii   Figures refer to year-end.

So great was the departure of demand from its long-established post-war pattern that, by 1982, substantial excess capacity had emerged in the refining industries of some advanced countries. Rates of capacity utilisation in refineries in the advanced countries averaged 80 per cent (85 per cent is normally considered the effective ceiling) for most of the post-war period. But, by 1982, utilisation rates in Western European refineries barely exceeded 60 per cent. In the USA, as late as 1978 a rate of 85 per cent was still maintained; two years later it had fallen to 73 per cent. By the first half of 1981 Japanese rates of utilisation were only 56 per cent.

These figures, naturally, reflect the severe downturn in consumption of refined products after 1979. In 1980 world demand for gasoline fell 4 per cent; in 1981 it fell a further 3.3 per cent. The impact of this slump was dramatic. For instance in the UK the consumption of oil products in 1981 was only 65 million tonnes, equivalent to the level in 1966, while capacity stood at 123 million tonnes. The steep fall in industrial output (a 6.6 per cent drop in 1980 over the previous year, followed by a 5.5 per cent fall in 1981) accounted for much of the slump, but price effects were clearly at work too. For Europe as a whole it has been estimated that, even with optimistic forecasts for growth of GDP, no new refining capacity may be needed before 1995 if post-1973 patterns of demand for oil persist (*PE*, Sept. 1980, p. 384). Similarly, studies carried out for the European Community Energy Council suggested that one in four of the refineries existing in 1981 could be mothballed (Europe Energy, 4 Nov. 1981, p. 4). And the International Energy Agency's report in late 1981 suggested that, based on recent trends, excess capacity in member countries could reach an extraordinary level of 62 per cent by 1985 (*The Economist*, 19 Dec. 1981). Shortly before the report was published, Esso Europe announced plans to pull down one of its four refineries (*FT*, 10 July 1981), while soon thereafter Shell announced an imminent halving of capacity at its 8 million tonne Shell Haven installation. These moves followed similar announcements from Burmah Oil, BP (*FT*, 1 Dec. 1981), and Rohm and Haas (*FT*, 2 July 1981).

So far the problem as outlined is similar to that faced by a number of other industries. Here the basic source of the problem is a downward shift in the volume of demand throughout the advanced countries which was precipitated by the energy-saving adjustments induced by the higher oil prices of the post-1973 period. But the slump in refining involves other issues too. Indeed, under scrutiny the industry faces adjustment problems of some complexity, including a pronounced shift in the emerging pattern (not just the volume) of demand; important changes in the conditions of access to the raw material – crude oil – that pose problems for older, established, pro-

ducers; and forces at work that promise to change radically the traditional structure of vertical integration throughout the entire industry.

Aspects of the adjustment problem in advanced countries
A prominent characteristic of refining is the relatively long lead-times
involved between planning and obtaining output from an installation.
One consequence of these lags – which tend to average 5–6 years, but
are typically longer for producers in LDCs – is that even as late as
1981 new capacity was coming on stream, a full seven years after the
first signs of a radical drop in the growth of demand. Plants that were
half-completed during this period have been finished on the grounds
that new refineries are more efficient than old ones. A survey of
capacity in late 1981 established that a further 81 million tonnes (9
per cent of capacity in 1980) is to appear in North America alone
before 1986, whereas in Western Europe only two projects – in Norway and England – are going ahead.

Ironically, there was a growing need to invest in new capacity during this period to match the evolving pattern of demand, despite
plummeting rates of capacity utilisation and falling profit margins as
companies attempted to maintain market shares, and thus to cover
fixed costs. For the longstanding tendency has been for demand for
lighter products (the so-called 'light end' of the distilled barrel) to
grow faster than for heavy products. At the same time, there has
been a trend towards greater supply of sour, or high-sulphur, crude
oils rather than the sweet, low-sulphur, varieties of crude for which
US refineries in particular were designed (*OPEC Bulletin*, Mar. 1981,
p. 14). This factor helps explain the tendency for those US refineries
faced with a need to rationalise to close their smaller refineries first:
these tend to require more of the sweet, high-cost crudes (*BW*, 27
Apr. 1981, p. 25). The same pressures have been observed in the case
of the Venezuelan industry – the OPEC member with the oldest-
established refining installations. A strong effort at tilting Venezuelan
refineries towards the growing heavy oil output of its oil fields has
been under way since 1979 (*OPEC Bulletin*, 15 Oct. 1979, p. 10).

Widely divergent rates of growth in the demand for various refined
products – gasoline, naphtha, middle distillates and residual oils –
have been oberved in the American, Japanese and Western European markets throughout the period since 1973 (*OPEC Review*, July
1980, p. 27). Although the trend towards greater fuel-efficiency in
autos – a process that started in earnest in the USA only in 1977–8 –
will eventually reduce the demand for gasoline, there is no doubt that
its consumption will rise relative to heavier products. Analysts at
Esso have estimated that only 26 per cent of a typical barrel was con-
verted to 'light' products in 1973 but, by 1985, the proportion could

be 36 per cent and is expected to rise to 40 per cent by the year 2000 (*The Times*, 3 Apr. 1981). The process, whereby refiners cater for these different demand requirements by altering the 'slate' created by the refinery, known as 'debottlenecking', will be costly. One recent estimate put the cost of adopting new slates at $2 billion for EEC locations alone (*PR*, Aug. 1981, p. 6), while French estimates suggest that investments of $40 per tonne, over twice the level of earlier costs, will be needed (*L'Expansion*, 5/18 Feb. 1982, p. 69). Although a small refinery can accommodate this change fairly readily, a large one may be closed for as long as two years and the task can cost up to $1 billion. Relatively little new apparatus is needed; the greater part of the change involves the use of different catalysts that are introduced to the refining process. Generally, physical installations are required only in so far as new capital equipment must cope with very different operating conditions, such as temperatures, from those originally intended. Naturally, the need for such reinvestment has caused serious cash-flow problems when demand is slack.

For a time, operators were able and willing to cross-subsidise their refining activities from other parts of their businesses, notably chemicals. For some firms, a reluctance to close capacity also reflected the fact that firms other than their own were involved in the one site: indeed, the majority of the refineries in Europe are owned by more than one company. The size of the subsidies eventually became intolerable, however. One study, which noted that profits in 1979 were 6 DM per tonne for refineries in West Germany, estimated no net income per tonne by mid-1980 and losses of 60–80 DM per tonne by the first quarter of 1981 (*PE*, Aug. 1981, p. 327). With 150 million tonnes of capacity in that one country, clearly the scale of the losses was immense. Indeed, the IEA's 1981 review of the industry referred to losses of $10 billion for that year alone (*The Economist*, 19 Dec. 1981, p. 73). The fact that refineries tend to have been built to capture the greatest possible economies of scale, and are accordingly very large, has been a further deterrent to closure. Nearly 40 per cent of EEC refinery capacity, for instance, is in facilities of more than 7.5 million tonnes annual capacity (Europe Energy, 4 Dec. 1981, p. 5).

New sources of capacity

Falling demand, coupled with a change in its composition, would have been sufficient to pose considerable problems of adjustment for the refining industry. But another phenomenon has also been present. Immediately after the 1973 oil price rise, several of the less industrialised members of OPEC declared a strong interest in adding further value to their crude oil exports. Venezuela, which as recently as 1980 accounted for 23 per cent of all OPEC refining capacity, had long-established facilities; and in Iran capacity had quickly been built up in the 1960s and 1970s. But Iraq, Qatar, Saudia Arabia and the UAE, among others, were able to refine only small proportions of their crude output; in 1979 the percentage of crude production that was refined domestically in these countries was 6.8 per cent, 2.0 per cent, 3.6 per cent and 0.8 per cent, respectively (*OPEC Annual Report*, 1980, p. 155). (Figures for 1979 are quoted here because the output of many OPEC members in 1980, 1981 and 1982 was running well below capacity, and correspondingly their refinery–oilfield output ratios would be misleading indicators of long-run refining capability.)

Acting on the premise that 'it is a natural and logical development for OPEC national oil companies to move into the field of product refining to produce hydrocarbon-based industries' (*OPEC Bulletin*, June 1980, p. 8), plans for substantial expansion in capacity were laid down. By 1984 OPEC members are expected to possess a refining capacity of 9.34 million barrels per day compared with 6.25 million barrels in 1980 and 5.32 million in 1979 (*OPEC Bulletin*, March 1981, p. 17). These steps will follow a decade of already exceptional growth. For OPEC capacity has grown every year since 1970, in line with the additions to world capacity. During the 1960s OPEC members possessed, on average, 8 per cent of world capacity (figures include socialist countries); that share reached its lowest, 6.1 per cent, in 1976, but grew to 7.5 per cent in 1980. Practical problems, as well as the instability of Iran after mid-1978 led to some of the biggest projects there being cancelled. But a so-called second generation of huge refineries is now under construction in the Middle East (*PE*, Sept. 1981, p. 396). Together, these refineries will add a further 3 million barrels per day to processing capacity in OPEC countries. Recent calculations by the OPEC secretariat suggest that between 1981 and 1984 the organisation's share of the increment to world refining capacity will be 32 per cent. This expansion, it is hoped within OPEC, will help to eliminate 'the gap which exists at present between our natural energy resource potential and our involvement in its downstream activities – a truly baffling situation' (*OPEC Bulletin*, 17 Sept. 1979, p. 13).

A number of questions arise from these projections. The most obvious is: why the desire to add so substantially to worldwide refining capacity when the risks, as far as excess capacity is concerned, have been apparent since the mid-1970s? A related question concerns the exact means by which the OPEC members will pursue this intention. To what extent will they, for instance, buy existing refineries in the advanced countries? This prospect leads to speculation as to the future division of labour between OPEC and the oil transnationals.

The first question concerns both the rate at which the larger OPEC states believe their own internal needs for refined oil products will grow in the future, and their choice of a strategy for diversifying their economies away from a high degree of reliance upon oil alone. The interests of individual OPEC member states in proceeding with their downstream investments differ considerably. Venezuela has seen its refining capacity expand since the early 1920s, when US-based firms along with Shell were active in exploration and processing on and offshore. More recently, however, the argument for member countries to process more of their crude oil prior to export simply expresses the desire to retain more of that value domestically. The appeal is particularly strong for those countries which must re-import a portion of their crude exports for domestic use. There is no doubt that demand for refined products within the OPEC members has, in the recent past, been rising very quickly. The annual average rate of growth of refined imports in 1967–79 was 11.6 per cent, far higher than the world rate (5.5 per cent) or, for that matter, Africa's, which is the fastest growing market for refined products in the Third World, where total demand was rising by 63 per cent annually. By 1981 OPEC demand reached 2.3 million barrels per day, and by 1990 the OPEC secretariat has estimated that the same 13 countries may be using 5.8 million barrels per day (*OPEC Review*, Summer 1980, p. 15; *OPEC Bulletin*, 21 May 1979, p. 1; *OPEC Review*, Winter 1981, pp. 68–87). Other figures confirm that, owing to very low domestic prices for energy as well as for other reasons, many OPEC members are emerging as substantial energy users. Data for the period 1974–9 shows that measured energy use in Iraq, Kuwait, Libya and Saudi Arabia grew at an annual average rate of 10.4 per cent, compared with a rate of 6.4 per cent in the more industrialised LDCs (World Bank, 1981, p. 146; *Arabia*, Feb. 1982, p. 90).

The choice of industry strategies in refining
Developments such as these are symptoms of a fundamental change which has affected all operators in the world oil industry since 1960. For it is in the very nature of OPEC as an agency that it should strive for greater control, on the part of its members, over the uses of its crude oil. In 1970, the oil majors still enjoyed direct access to some 90 per cent of the non-communist world's crude exports. Despite having lost some autonomy through the unilateral price fixing imposed by the host country governments at the Teheran–Tripoli discussions, the oil majors could still control the bulk of physical supply. However, the OPEC governments soon realised that the concession system in which they participated yielded little in the way of indigenous spin-offs, ancillary industrial activity, or, more crucially, anything in the

way of production monitoring and control. Recognition of this prompted a series of measures to pre-empt some of the oil majors' activities.

The process of growing control in the 1960s and early 1970s is well-known by now. By 1976 the oil majors had access to only 50 per cent of traded crude oil; by early 1980 this proportion had shrunk to around 40 per cent. Host country governments had correspondingly chipped away at the multinationals' authority over production policy so that by the beginning of the 1980s the position was as shown in Table 7.4. Host countries expected to continue this trend in the future, noting that 'the time is drawing near when OPEC's national oil companies will handle nearly all of their export sales of crude oil and refined products' (*OPEC Bulletin*, Nov. 1980, p. 70). The events of 1979, which saw 'the greatest reorientation of trading relationships between oil companies and . . . OPEC . . . in some years' brought this closer (*OPEC Bulletin*, 25 Feb. 1980, p. 1).

It is important to be clear about the reasons why the OPEC governments – and, indeed, non-OPEC governments, to an increasing degree – wish to take control in this manner. One impulse is simply the growing desire, expressed in LDCs of all political persuasions, to sever those ties with advanced countries and their agencies that savour of colonial or imperial relationships. This desire is particularly evident in the case of foreign-owned oil companies in the Middle East, which have 'managed to preserve their relationship with their host nations in an atmosphere of legal morality which had no legal basis either in creation or in continued existence' (Tanzer, 1969, p. 63). The persistence of such relationships is felt to be a slight upon the strength of purpose and commitment to nationalism of the

Table 7.4   *OPEC national oil companies' control over oil exports*

	million barrels/day	percentage of country's oil exports, 1979
Gabon	0.2	25
Iraq	2.1	60
Iran	1.1	40
Nigeria	0.4	20
Libya	0.5	30
Kuwait	0.2	10
Saudia Arabia	0.8	9
others	0.7	(3)
TOTAL	5.8	average 20 per cent

Sources: J. M. Mohnfeld, (1980); OPEC (1981); own estimates.
Note: The figures above are necessarily only indicators of broad magnitudes.

government. In this respect the desire to grasp control of oil supplies is no different from the desire to take more control over a nation's bauxite mines or any other resource. A second impulse, again common to many LDCs, is the wish to ensure that the contribution of the oil industry, in terms of the revenue it generates and the stimulus it gives to suppliers, is consistent with the intentions set out in the government's development plans. By the same token, there is a desire to ensure as great a degree of congruence as possible within the national plan by determining in advance the industry's requirements for finance, skilled manpower and the like. The prevalence of such national plans, typically ambitious in their goals and comprehensive in scope, therefore reinforces the objective of gaining control over the oil industry.

A related factor is the recognition that the oil industry, like others, is capable of generating substantial revenues which can be used as a source of patronage. The ability to allocate responsible and lucrative posts has an attraction within the LDCs that should not be underrated. Similarly, the governments of oil-exporting countries hope to arrogate more control to themselves because the manipulation of oil can be used as a means to achieve certain political goals. Such objectives as the fostering of regional political solidarity, an image of conscience, or compliance with international agreements regarding boycotts, can be made all the more telling, and dramatic, by the judicious management of oil exports. The political flavour of much decision-making tends to follow from all the foregoing factors. If, in the future, certain member states find that their share of world trade is being eroded and that their influence on OPEC policies as well as the oil market itself is correspondingly diminished, this enhanced opportunity for politicising that proportion of trade which they still control is likely to become particularly attractive.

The tone of much of the writing on this issue implies that, at least in some countries, a bitterly-fought struggle is in progress where the oil majors remain adamant in refusing to relinquish control over their vertically integrated networks of oil production. But there is another interpretation. Indeed, on closer examination it appears that the recent interest of OPEC members in increasing their involvement in the oil industry may be just the change many majors are looking for. There may, in consequence, be a rather easier and less combative type of adjustment process underway in refining than in any other industry.

There are two sets of reasons for believing this. First, as already indicated, a great deal of the oil companies' refining facilities are more of an embarrassment to them than an asset. In consequence, purchase bids from Middle East OPEC states are more than welcome. Recently, the planned enlargement of refining capacity in some OPEC countries has been accompanied by foreign purchases. This desire to buy overseas capacity partly reflected the low purchase price for refineries that prevailed in the late 1970s, as well as the much reduced time-lag involved in acquiring a fully operational facility. In mid-1981 Arab investors were reported to have bought four independent oil refineries in Texas; Venezuelan interests were also believed to have purchased a small facility in Texas (*FT*, 9 July 1981). Kuwait's national oil company, the Kuwait Petroleum Corporation, took a half share in an American-owned Hawaiian refinery, a move which aroused interest among oil stock analysts on the grounds that this was the first public OPEC purchase of a large refining operation. In 1982 this move was followed by Kuwaiti offers (later retracted) for Gulf Oil's European refineries, in an effort to provide more outlets for Kuwaiti crude (*IHT*, 29 Jan. 1982). Hitherto, foreign oil producers were thought to have only small stockholdings in US oil firms (*IHT*, 24 Apr. 1981). A year before, both Saudi Arabian and Iranian interests were well advanced with deals whereby their national oil companies would rent capacity in European and American refineries. While secured access to refining capacity meant that refined products could be reimported to the Gulf whenever domestic demand exceeded supply, the refinery owners received guaranteed access to crude oil for the duration of the agreement. A share of the profits was also negotiated by the Gulf countries. An added attraction for the latter partners is that the arrangement provides a relatively easy way to gain marketing experience in western countries (WSJ, 10 Jan. 1980).

A related development in the early 1980s has been an insistence by crude oil supplying agencies that certain technologies and experience be offered in partial or whole payment for oil supplies. A seminar organised by Italy's state hydrocarbons agency, ENI, along with OPEC in April 1981 set up working groups to assess how far southern European countries could become involved in a network of exchanges of this sort (*The Times*, 10 April 1981). Already Italy and Venezuela have entered a barter arrangement, which, among other things, provides for Italian agricultural assistance in part-payment for 100,000 barrels per day of Venezuelan crude. Similarly, Venezuela has also guaranteed to sell Brazil 50,000 barrels per day of crude in return for a three-year agreement by Brazil to sell 220,000 tons of sugar at less than world prices (*WSJ*, 6 May 1981). Libya and Algeria have also offered crude oil as part-payment for imports, although in 1981 and 1982 this tended to be a way of disguising effective discounts from the official crude prices (*WSJ*, 22 Jan. 1982). The Gabonese government, while controlling only some 25 per cent of oil production through its new Petrogab state firm, runs a scheme whereby oil companies and the government jointly invest up to 10 per cent of the companies' turnover in profit-making projects. So far these investments have included cement, sugar and cellulose works and have totalled approximately $145 million (*Courier*, no. 70, Nov.–Dec. 1981, p. 16). Finally, a number of OPEC governments also require that their national shipping lines be used to carry a certain proportion of crude oil export volume; in Gabon this share is 50 per cent.

A second reason, apart from their willingness to sell off surplus assets, why the oil majors may be willing to accept the sort of new oil industry desired by the OPEC states stems from the latter's assumption of greater control over oil exports during the 1970s. As a result of this change, the flexibility of the market will almost certainly be diminished. A consequence is that running a traditional, vertically-integrated firm will now be considerably more difficult. There will be more centres of decision-making and, for the first time, not all of them will be subject to the oil company's own authority. Moreover, instead of one overriding business objective, there is likely to be a shifting and complex set of objectives, some of them political in character. Previously, the majors' control over oil output and the output-mix, coupled with their sophisticated distribution network, allayed fears of a prolonged supply interruption or a failure to balance refinery runs. By contrast, as decisions regarding the levels of output and output-mix are gradually transferred from the distributors to national oil companies in OPEC, the new decision-makers may be less concerned with the need to eliminate mismatches of supply and demand at the local level, and selling refined products will become more awkward. This applies especially to those OPEC countries preoccupied with lifting heavy crudes in greater than desired quantities.

An orthodox response to conditions of greater risk in crude supplies would be to resort to greater stockpiling and, on occasion, more use of the spot market. Stockpiling carries two costs, however. First, as with all strategic stocks of materials, there is an opportunity cost equivalent to the return which would have been obtained by applying the money needed to retain the stock of inventory in some other use. The second cost is that building up inventories is itself a form of demand. In periods of tight market conditions, the need to stockpile makes a demand-led precipitation of higher spot, if not contract or 'term', prices all the more likely. The effect of stockpiling upon both spot and official OPEC oil prices was an important part of OPEC criticism of the purchasing behaviour of advanced countries in the last quarter of 1980, when the Iran–Iraq war had initially removed around 3.9 million barrels per day from world supply. The IEA members were urged not to maintain stocks at their prevailing high levels but to run them down to fulfil a greater proportion of demand from previous rather than current purchases. Among OPEC circles there was talk of 'irresponsible stockpiling policies' as stocks rose from a 'normal' level of thirty days supply to as much as ninety days (*OPEC Bulletin*, June 1980, p. 14). This irresponsibility on the part of importing countries was attributed to a failure to appreciate that OPEC members would behave in a responsible manner if any sign of oil shortage were to develop. As the article went on to suggest, 'the consuming world has received ample proof that in all delicate market situations OPEC countries have taken the right decisions'. In the view of the OPEC analysts the only clear consequence of stockpiling has been huge windfall profits for the oil companies. Both the majors and the governments of advanced countries, OPEC argues, are, in their stockpiling behaviour, 'quickly gathering a new and unhealthy sophistication' (*OPEC Bulletin*, March 1981, p. 50).

Another consequence of greater host state control of oil exports concerns the frequency of price changes. Notice of thirty days is conventional in the industry but observers expect shorter periods of notice – possibly five days – to become commonplace. Related to this is other evidence that less leeway in government–company relationships may emerge. Although current practices allow for actual liftings to oscillate around an agreed volume so that shipments match regional, seasonal or other client needs, it is thought that these 'contractual tolerances' are likely to be eliminated or tightened up to a degree. Such a move would clearly limit the degree and flexibility of supply responses. It would also certainly affect the cost of doing business. Like the other changes discussed in this section, the preferences of the oil-exporting states' oil agencies will sometimes clash with the majors' objective of cost minimisation.

The same fear is raised by the increasing use of *quid pro quo*s in the business. In these cases the exporting government extracts certain conditions, which may or may not be related to the oil sector, from the intending client. Recent instances involved both OPEC members and non-members. For instance, in 1981 Saudi Arabian officials proposed that each individual investment of one million dollars will be 'rewarded' by guaranteed access for the firm to 500 barrels of oil per day. Such 'incentive' oil schemes, undertaken with the help of Western contractors, will yield 0.75 million barrels per day in Saudi oil entitlements by the mid-1980s. Early instances of 'incentive deals' involve Shell affiliates, who were guaranteed 1 billion barrels of Saudi crude in 1981 in partial return for involvement in the Jubail petrochemicals plant, and a further 300,000 barrels per day for working with a new refinery project (*FT*, 24 Apr. 1981).

Together, these factors point to a very significant series of changes in the oil majors' involvement in the industry. The OPEC members' strategy, referred to in a recent article by the OPEC Secretary-General as 'the gradual displacement of the international oil companies in the upstream area by the OPEC national oil companies' (*OPEC Bulletin*, June 1980, p. 11), is gradually forcing the oil majors into a fundamental reappraisal of their *raison d'être*. For many of them, vertical integration has lost its appeal as a logical and necessary way of organising; instead, as a senior Shell executive recently indicated, 'it may no longer be a tenable approach' (*FT*, 23 Oct. 1981). For one thing, as has just been shown, supply security is no longer assured by vertical integration, since access to the raw material is increasingly determined outside the oil companies. Similarly, observers believe that the parts of the industry where the highest rates of return will be attainable are those which least require an integrated worldwide storage and distribution system. Instead, pure exploration is becoming the most lucrative activity and, to an increasing extent, this is where capital spending of the fastest-moving oil majors is being sunk. Of Shell's £3 billion capital investment in 1980, for instance, 56 per cent was devoted to exploration and producing oil. In 1970 only some 25 per cent was allocated to these purposes (*The Economist*, 28 Nov. 1981). Furthermore, annual reports of the five biggest US-based oil TNCs showed a 28 per cent average rise in exploration expenditures in 1980 compared with 1979 (*PE*, Jan. 1982, p. 3). This shift broadly coincides with expectations in the oil exporting countries. The former Iraqi oil minister, Abdul Aziz Wattari, made the point in 1979 that Western oil companies 'will be left in future with the job of extracting crude which is hard to get, refining highly specialised products and research and development' (*Lloyd's List*, quoted in *OPEC Bulletin*, 24 Mar. 1980, p. 8). An interesting aspect of this development which has recently come to light is the fact that the Kuwait Petroleum Corporation – the OPEC-based national oil company which has so far shown the most aggressive international acquisitions policy – has also acknowledged the need to concentrate on exploration. In a recent interview the firm's chairman noted that 'today the most profitable area is in international exploration', and anticipated spending $600 million per year on that activity alone (*BW*, 11 Jan. 1982, p. 24).

Looking at the industry's prospects in the twenty-first century, Turner has suggested that the breakdown in vertical integration will continue until some companies have very little fixed capital commitments in traditional oil activities: 'in most cases the traditional company will move from being integrated to a form which is best described as a "skills bank" . . . international companies will find themselves in a supporting role, supplying markets, management, technology and finance as circumstances dictate' (Turner, 1978, p. 216).

This is, of course, not to argue that shortly no tanker fleets, storage tank farms or, indeed, oil refineries, will lie within the domain of the oil majors. Such an extensive shift is hardly likely, given that in 1980 the OPEC members owned only 3.7 per cent of the world's tonnage of tanker ships (*OPEC Annual Report*, 1980, p. 135) and, as reported above, a mere 7.5 per cent of world refinery capacity. Instead, a more *ad hoc* takeover by the national oil companies within OPEC is probable. Aspects already noted include the temporary 'renting' of some under-utilised refineries in the West by OPEC oil companies and increasingly frequent discussions between these companies and Western specialists on technology. The Iranian government has, for instance, proposed that Italian contractors working on oil refining and petrochemicals projects in Iran should be compensated with oil (*WSJ*, 22 Jan. 1982).

So far the discussion has been couched solely in terms of the interests of the oil majors and the ambitions of oil-exporting states. This is because one of the most common sources of difficulty for firms during periods of capacity adjustment – opposition from employees and their representatives – has tended to be muted in refining. In fact, relatively few workers are involved directly in refining. In the USA the industry has about 100,000 employees; in Europe there are even fewer. A corollary is that wages tend to account for only about 2 per cent of operating costs (*BW*, 21 Dec. 1981, p. 48) and this fact has meant that workers have captured fairly high wage levels for themselves and have consequently tried to defend their jobs very strongly. Thus, in September 1981, average hourly earnings for US oil industry workers were $10.99 per hour, as against a manufacturing average of $8.14 per hour (*BLS*, 1981). However, when beginning their 1982 bargaining round, negotiators for the oil, chemicals and atomic workers in the USA stressed the issues of job stability and lay-offs, rather than wages once they realised that with so much excess capacity in the industry their priorities lay in securing better layoff terms than higher pay. As real oil prices slid in 1981 and 1982, US oil majors' employees and their union, the Oil, Chemical and Atomic Workers (in which about 60 per cent of refinery workers are enrolled), found a much tougher stance being taken by employers. The union was unable to prevent Texaco from shutting two refineries in February 1982 (*WSJ*, 11 Feb. 1982) and its two-year pay claim for a 27 per cent increase was settled at 16 per cent without receiving any guarantees about future redundancies (*WSJ*, 10 Feb. 1982). Recently, major changes in pension rights were imposed by Texaco on its employees, starting a six-month strike at its largest refinery, at Port Arthur, Texas (*BW*, 5 July 1982). These decisions have been greeted with resignation for the most part, whereas in Europe (notably in Belgium) refinery closures have provoked riots (*L'Expansion*, 5/18 Feb. 1982, p. 68).

The other set of interests involved in the oil refining business are the small operators who lack the large, integrated facilities owned by the major firms. The preferences of small firms differ considerably from those of the oil majors and constitute yet another force for change in the industry. The early part of this discussion demonstrated how some of the larger US-based refiners plan to shift the centre of gravity of their operations. However, that description ignored the fate of the scores of small refinery companies (which were still appearing as late as 1979). Briefly, the problem facing many of these small firms, who have little or no access to crude oil of their own but must buy in from larger companies or foreign governments, is that they are 'creatures of federal policies . . . some of the most elaborate and confusing governmental controls ever imposed on an American industry' (*Fortune*, 12 Jan. 1981, p. 38). Even in 1948 it was evident that US laws on oil amounted to 'a fantastic and inordinately complicated patchwork' (Rostow, 1948, p. 15), with national security imperatives uppermost, although often the result of the laws was the opposite of what was intended (Spero, 1974, p. 126).

The entitlements programme of November 1974 subsidised imported oil and gave various benefits to smaller refiners, as companies with good access to price-controlled US oil had to compensate those which did not. About 170 independent refineries were producing one-fifth of US refined output. Along with a plethora of tiny independents, these firms were nourished on large subsidies and, together, faced oil price decontrols when the programme ended in January 1981. (After 1979, domestic prices had in any case been rising to match world oil prices, so decontrol merely accelerated a trend already at work.) Initially these firms found effective and coherent lobbying difficult, with the American Petroleum Refiners' Association (representing tiny firms) fragmented, and the larger independents' Committee for Equitable Access to Crude Oil, and smaller firms' Alliance of Independent Crude Producers and Refiners, and the Emergency Small Independent Refiners' Task Force all at work (*Fortune*, 12 Jan. 1981, p. 40). It has proved equally hard to disentangle clearly the distribution of gains from this system and thus identify the impulses at work in Washington. One analyst claimed that independent crude oil producers have been outright losers, while independent refiners were the major beneficiaries, and the vertically integrated firms as a group have enjoyed slight benefits (First Chicago Bank, 1981).

It appears that the larger firms, partly by virtue of their established links in Washington and partly because their demonstrated risk-taking in oil searching and innovation is consistent with President

Reagan's ethos, will not be obliged to cross-subsidise smaller 'tea-kettle' refineries, also known as 'bias babies', 'whose sole justification was cashing in on subsidies worth as much as $2 a barrel' (*Fortune*, 12 Jan. 1981, p. 38). This decision is made easier for the government because, first, it can be shown that the larger firms, with enough capital for debottlenecking, can save the USA up to 1 million barrels per day of crude oil imports through their greater efficiency, and second, because the labour lobby is weak.

The problems facing oil refining firms in the advanced countries are set out in Table 7.5 along with a summary of strategies which might be adopted to circumvent these problems. It is clear that there is considerable scope for choosing a viable strategy from the three listed in the table.

Table 7.5 *An overview of problems and strategies in the oil refining industry*

Problems	Strategies		
	A *Shut capacity, starting with least efficient plants*	*B* *Enter technology sales with new refining countries*	*C* *Change output mix of refineries*
1 Steep fall in rate of increase in demand for refined products	Necessary; mitigated by foreign firms' purchasing. Union unable to oppose	At least retains some profit within firm	Combats difficulties if resources are available to finance the reinvestment
2 Change in demand-mix to lighter products	Cuts big firms' market share; eliminates small refiners who cannot afford cost of refurbishment	As 1B	Deals with problem
3 Possibility of subsidised feedstock from OPEC	As 2A	As 1B	Partially confronts problem
4 Existence of hundreds of small refiners dependent upon oil import legislation	Widespread plant closures, although few workers in each	Small refiners unlikely to have technology or contacts to follow this strategy	Small firms unlikely to have resources to pay for such re-investment

Looking first to the problem of producers with established capacity, the steep fall in the growth of demand (indeed, after 1979, a fall in the volume of demand itself) requires that strategy A, that of closing some of the least efficient capacity, be started. If experience can be sold to some oil agencies of OPEC countries, as in strategy B, at least, some of the short-term losses incurred by the industry can be offset. For firms with sufficient confidence in the long-term outlook for refined oil products, strategy C, that of changing their refineries' slate in order to produce a higher proportion of light products from each barrel of oil, is an imperative. To pursue none of these strategies, however, will leave a firm in a very weak position indeed. Strategy C addresses the second problem – that of a steady change in the pattern (as opposed to the volume) of demand. But for those firms which cannot afford the cost of changing their capacity, exit from the industry is the likely outcome. These firms, many of which tend to be small in size, are unlikely to find solace from any of the strategies outlined here. Options B and C are not plausible for small refiners because they require contacts and resources that are probably beyond these firms' reach. The third problem, that some of the larger firms will obtain favoured access to crude oil from OPEC in return for participating in construction and/or distribution projects, is also virtually impossible for small competitors to handle. What they must in consequence hope for is continued legislation of one type or another to assure them access to world oil supplies on terms sufficiently attractive to overcome their intrinsic weaknesses – in particular, the high cost levels which follow from their smaller scale of operations.

In discussing the contrast in the options open to the major oil firms in the 1980s with those open to smaller firms, there is a parallel with the auto industry. In the latter case, the larger firms in Europe and the USA can hope to deal with the major changes in their industry stemming from foreign influence by allying themselves with the source of those changes. Just as GM has attempted to pe-empt competition from other US firms by joining with a Japanese producer to produce a new small car, so some of the larger oil companies will ally themselves with OPEC oil agencies in order to capture a portion of the latter agencies' operating advantages. The implication of this type of move for domestic lobbying behaviour is that, to an increasing extent, a simple antagonism towards competitive imports will be replaced by a more complicated series of interests. Those firms which have decided to import part of their own sales will wish to have relatively liberal conditions of access for imports. Firms in the same industry which do not pursue international sourcing as a strategy will retain the more traditional stance. As the manoeuvrings of the US auto industry in 1980–2 illustrate, shifts of allegiance between partici-pating groups can also take place swiftly. The position held by the management of the major US auto firms regarding imports switched very quickly after the late 1970s, as they lost confidence in their abil-ity to design and master successful subcompact models. This led to a quite different approach to foreign competition. The old cliché, to the effect that if a firm cannot beat its competition it should join it, is uncannily apposite. Similarly, in less than ten years the more verti-cally integrated of the oil companies completely revised their ideas of how they wished to restructure themselves. With surprising speed, integration from well-head to petrol station came to be seen as a danger as much as an index of corporate strength and sophistication.

8

Industry Strategies and National Policies in a Changing World

The preceding two chapters have shown how firms in five industries have coped with adjustment problems of various types. These problems have arisen out of the ebb and flow of different countries' dominance of particular industries and from competition between industries. Clearly the array of forces acting upon one set of firms is quite bewildering, and an exhaustive account of them is well beyond the scope of this book. Rather, the intention has been to cut through the mass of evidence available on certain industries and to identify the fundamental forces that have altered the map of world industry, as sketched in Chapter 5. Another objective has been to draw attention to the manner in which decisions have been made by major firms within each industry. In doing so, the intention has been to illuminate the various ways in which policy-making by a multitude of official and unofficial bodies reacts with industrial structure.

In the course of this discussion, a number of patterns – some predictable, others less so – have become apparent, and the purpose of this last chapter is to draw together some observations under three headings. First, the involvement of TNCs is appraised with particular attention to the increasingly useful role played by these firms in circumventing import barriers. Second, the relationships between industrial structure and policy making are discussed. Enough has been said in preceding chapters about the relationship between public policy and the behaviour of firms to dispel the idea that the two can be divorced for analytical purposes. The post-war experience of the auto, steel, electronics and many other industries shows that policy and industrial structure are inextricably intertwined. To try to understand a little more about precisely how they are connected, the second section draws on the foregoing case studies to identify those characteristics most commonly associated with changes in public policy or with policy initiatives. And, finally, the concept of industry strategies is examined in the light of the way firms in each of the industries just described have tried to alleviate the problems besetting them.

New uses of the TNC

A point which emerges from the evidence for the oil refining and auto industries is that TNCs are increasingly sought-after as a marketing arm by firms just entering an industry. Recognising that the worth of potential comparative advantage is undermined if it is thwarted by tariff and non-tariff barriers, such firms as China Steel's new car-manufacturing concern in Taiwan and the prospective national petrochemical and refining firms in the OPEC member states are turning to established TNCs in order to benefit from their distribution experience and market access. In turn, even the most sophisticated TNCs will probably wish, to an increasing degree, to buy merchandise from others, gaining in part from the protection afforded to their home market, while simultaneously benefiting from overseas firms that have distinct cost advantages in certain product lines. The clearest illustration comes from the auto industry where, in mid-1982, it became apparent that the latest chapter in Detroit's twenty-five-year history of the economy car will bring GM to import complete Japanese cars from its Isuzu affiliate, and will also entail joint production with Toyota. The US firm cannot produce these cars cheaply enough for the American market. Instead, it will use the leeway provided by the VER on all Japanese car imports, while simultaneously trying to capture at least some of the rent that lower-cost overseas competitors can earn by buying-in cars as a wholesaler to sell in the high-priced US market. Japanese firms have borne the brunt of GM's new marketing priorities. After August 1981 Japanese firms' exports of fully-assembled cars fell month by month in the face of mounting import restrictions. In the first six months of 1982 Japanese car exports totalled only 2.4 million units, a 9.5 per cent reduction compared with the same period in 1981. This decline intensified the search by Japanese firms – particularly Toyota – for a toe-hold in the US market. The GM–Toyota joint venture talks in mid-1982 were reportedly given added urgency by the local content laws being discussed in Washington at that time. As one report put it, 'a content law is a recurring nightmare for Toyota' (*BW*, 2 Aug. 1982, p. 59).

Closely allied to the US auto industry is the steel industry. And there, too, Japanese firms, which until 1982 owned very little steelmaking capacity in the US, began the search for defensive investments to forestall more stringent import restrictions. In mid-1982 Nippon Kokan, Japan's second-largest steelmaker, entered negotiations to buy the ninth-biggest steel facility in the USA. Ironically, that facility, the Rouge Steel Co., is owned by the Ford Motor Co. Japanese officials explained the bid in terms of their growing need 'to continue and maintain their longstanding relations with their customers in the US' (*WSJ*, 23 July 1982). Had the deal gone ahead, American auto firms would probably have bought steel from the plant at lower prices than those that currently prevail in the US market. Although the deal did not help the rest of the beleaguered American steel industry, it would have afforded some cost relief to car producers. Even in the worst times of 1981 and 1982, US car producers were reluctant to source significant amounts of their steel needs in Japan while they were simultaneously calling for protection against imports of assembled Japanese cars. They were also reluctant to be seen undercutting the efforts of the special trade representative and lobbyists in Washington who, during 1981 and 1982, were pressing foreign steelmakers to reduce shipments to the USA.

The significance of the TNC in its guise as marketing agent undermines the importance of ownership, for what matters in this context is access to otherwise circumscribed markets rather than actual ownership of the marketing apparatus. Some years ago Franko (1971) considered the likelihood that US-based TNCs would willingly enter into forms of co-operation other than full ownership. He concluded that, initially, joint ventures were tolerable for most manufacturers but went on to suggest that they would eventually want to be outright owners – particularly firms that were involved in narrow product lines. More recently, however, the spate of joint ventures in the auto industry has prompted a reappraisal of Franko's analysis. Peter Drucker, for example, has argued that the shape of world industry in the making is one of autonomous partnerships, linked in a confederation rather than through common ownership. Instead of ownership from a central plant, 'no one unit will be the "parent" . . . the relationship is one of mutual dependence' (*Industry Week*, 11 Jan. 1981). Relating his argument to the car industry, Drucker cited the links GM forged with other suppliers (Suzuki in 1981 and Toyota in 1983) as among the most significant recent events in international business.

This view of TNCs and their usefulness to new producers of industrial goods, particularly in LDCs and in the socialist countries, suggests that the more conventional interpretations of the TNC's post-war importance may need to be refined although by no means abandoned. Hitherto, the literature on the TNC has stressed its dominance in manufacturing rather than other types of economic activity, and the tendency for firms based in Canada, the UK, the USA and West Germany to be particularly active as TNCs (*UN*, 1978, pp. 39–45). Common ground in virtually all studies has been the importance of ownership. According to many interpretations, the *raison d'être* of the TNC was private access to its own R & D, technologies or human skills. So well-guarded was this private ownership that potential host countries which insisted upon taking shares in overseas branches were sometimes excluded from the TNC's plans. India provided several well-known examples of this type of dispute, prompting companies like IBM and Coca-Cola to leave the country in 1978 rather than submit to 'Indianisation'. After Mrs Gandhi's return to power in January 1980, there was some liberalisation of foreign investment, and inflows from the USA responded favourably although, by mid-1981, India still accounted for only 0.3 per cent of total US overseas investment (*BW*, 1 Mar. 1982, p. 31). Elsewhere, governments of LDCs have insisted on so-called performance requirements which TNCs are also unwilling to concede. In 1982 Data General Corporation rescinded a decision to produce in Brazil because the firm would have been required to cede control of some of its technologies to a Brazilian-owned affiliate (*NJ*, 22 May 1982).

A pioneering study of TNCs owned and operated from LDCs by Wells (forthcoming) has underlined the importance of the joint venture in comparison with full ownership. In a sample of 602 subsidiaries of TNCs, Wells found that only 57, or 9 per cent, were wholly-owned (*International Management*, Jan. 1982, pp. 39–40). Although he identifies five major reasons for the rise in joint ventures between TNCs and firms based in LDCs, Wells finds a particularly strong motivation in the desire to evade trade barriers. In these cases, however, it is not that, for example, footwear firms based in Hong Kong want to gain an entrée to the footwear market in Mauritius, but that quotas on Mauritian exports of footwear to third markets will not be so constraining as those imposed on exports originating in Hong Kong.

The declining importance of ownership which is suggested by much of the evidence gathered here returns the debate on TNCs to the state it was in in the 1950s and 1960s. At that time the overseas expansion – particularly into Europe – of US-based TNCs was thought to be governed by motives similar to those prevailing before the Second World War. In particular, it was said to be 'often impossible to obtain effective market penetration with exports from the USA' (Wilkins, 1974, pp. 379–83).

Industrial adjustment and public policy

Previous chapters have stressed a number of points with regard to public policy. First, it is clear that public policy deliberations are not only influential at the margin or in a small portfolio of industries; there are entire tracts of world industry whose very existence is due to government decisions. But it is equally clear that public ownership of manufacturing capacity is in practice a very different issue from that of public influence. Some illustrations are provided by Japan and the NICs. In Japan, there is no doubt that public policy, particularly as implemented by MITI, is an important voice in restructuring. This act is not, as a matter of record, a new or even a post-war phenomenon; rather it can be seen as a contemporary outgrowth of a century-long tradition. As Brown (1980, p. 59) has noted, 'ever since the Meiji restoration in November 1867, government and business have worked very closely together in mapping the development of the economy . . . in the period up to World War I, rapid westernisation of the economy and enormous expenditures on capital formation were all coordinated by the state'.

There is little doubt that in industries like steel, automobiles and electronics, the present structure and performance of the Japanese firms owe a great deal to MITI initiatives. It is often assumed that the absolute value of Japanese exports of manufactures is abnormally large, but this is incorrect. In 1980 and 1981, the country was still only the third largest exporter of manufactures, after West Germany and the USA. One consequence of MITI's careful nurturing is that even now exports of manufactures are concentrated in a relatively narrow range of goods – some of which have been noted in the industries scrutinised earlier. None the less, despite widespread intervention, public ownership is modest while the share of public expenditure in GDP is only two-thirds as large as in other Western countries.

Among the NICs, a somewhat different pattern tends to apply – with both public intervention and public ownership being widespread. Ironically, many Western observers imagine that the NICs are countries where *laissez-faire* principles are pursued rigorously and unrelentingly. Indeed, this argument, in its 'exploitation of labour' guise, usually forms part of the appeal by Western trade unions for protection against exports from the NICs. Yet there has always been extensive public intervention in these countries. In South Korea, the government has used its influence in the banking system to curtail borrowing by firms whose wage awards are 'too high': planners fear that already the country's 14 million labourers may be undercut, as export markets are lost to other Asian countries (*WSJ*, 22 July 1981). Planners in both South Korea and Taiwan began ten years ago to push their economies into more capital-intensive industries. The Taiwanese government has invested heavily in infrastructure and industry including steel, shipbuilding and the petrochemical industry (which is now the third largest in Asia after Japan and

China). But Singapore provides the most striking example. Not only is the state's control over political activity extremely tight – virtually no formal opposition is tolerated – but the government also arrogates to itself responsibility for macroeconomic and industrial policy at the highest level. In mid-1979 a major policy decision was taken to force the most labour-intensive industries out of Singapore in the hope of preserving the state's constrained labour supply to produce goods having a higher income elasticity of demand than traditional 'early' industries like textiles. By widening the export base, the authorities also hope to avoid the worst elements of Western protectionism, as well as avoiding any increase in the 100,000-strong pool of guest workers. The National Wages Council and the Economic Development Board have plans for rapid development of eleven specific industries in the 1980s, led by optical and electronic instruments and precision engineering. So far the plan is reportedly a success: the growth of industrial productivity has re-accelerated, and, over the 1978–80 period, value added per worker was doubled in high technology fields such as metal products and precision equipment, reaching US$30,000 (*FT*, 12 Nov. 1981).

A second point about industrial policy and industrial performance arising from the discussion in Chapters 6 and 7 concerns the influence of full or partial public ownership on adjustment. Is it correct to argue, as many commentators have done on *a priori* grounds, that public ownership or control necessarily delays or obstructs adjustment by an industry, or that, when adjustment does eventually take place, it is all the more convulsive for having been retarded?

The evidence for these propositions is by no means overwhelming. Looking first at the auto industry, national policy approaches have always tended to differ. The US government's relationship with the auto firms has been that of a regulator while in Europe, governments are owners; in Japan the government's role has been one of a promoter and in the LDCs, governments have acted as an initiator (Pearce, 1980, p. 259). Yet in Chapter 6 there was little evidence to suggest that publicly-owned firms have been any slower or less efficient in adjusting to the emerging Japanese competitive threat than have private firms that are subject to government regulation. European carmakers, chiefly because of higher petrol prices, have always built a product that was more substitutable for Japanese output than have US-based firms. But in the speed and extent of their reaction to the Japanese competitive threat, the US firms cannot be said to be clearly ahead of the Europeans. Governments in both markets have imposed *de facto* import controls. Although the US controls came relatively late, and were superimposed on a lower *ad valorem* tariff (2.9 per cent compared to 10.9 per cent in the EEC), they were enacted when the Japanese import penetration began to approach broadly similar levels: around 20 per cent in the US market and an average of 10–13 per cent in various European markets. In addition, it can easily be shown that Ford and Chrysler made fundamental errors of judgement in the late 1970s regarding the model mix for the American market, while GM made rather fewer errors and was accordingly better placed to deal with the oil scare of 1979. In Europe, by contrast, the quest for fuel efficiency and for the other qualities allegedly admired in Japanese products (chiefly quality of assembly and competitive prices) was not relaxed. On the other hand, it is clear that European firms have tended to be slower than US firms in slimming their work-forces and introducing new equipment. Direct employment in the US car industry was slashed drastically after 1978, 'on a scale that would make European workers blanch' (*The Economist*, 15 Aug. 1981, p. 13). General Motors' hourly paid employment fell by 18 per cent between 1979 and 1981, with 84,000 workers laid off, while its world-wide payroll fell by 13 per cent in the same period to 741,000 (GM, 1982).

Another of the industries examined earlier, oil refining, has experienced a pattern of state involvement that is an almost complete reversal of that observed for autos. Here it is the USA that has created the most state-dependent capacity. The long and enormously complex history of government involvement in the American oil industry is of course at the root of this. By contrast, substantial public ownership in Europe can be found only in Italy, where the charismatic character of Mattei induced the government to greater involvement in the oil business (Turner, 1978, p. 214) and in France, Portugal and Spain. Rather than public ownership being uniquely associated with sluggish reactions to adjustment pressures, it appears that the entire spectrum of oil refiners – irrespective of the form of ownership – have postponed change and prevaricated. At the other end of the business, in the producing countries which still control the bulk of world trade in crude oil, state involvement in managing and refining oil is virtually ubiquitous. But this is in the nature of the industry in OPEC, given the huge leverage over patronage, industrial linkages – real or imagined – and revenue that oil provides. Although, as in Libya, public ownership is sometimes seen as an objective in its own right, its appearance elsewhere among Arab countries probably reflects the refining industry's importance. For Arab industrialisation has tended to be *ad hoc* in its planning and in its execution. As Aliboni (1978, p. 66) has observed, 'in most Arab countries there is actually no national industrial strategy to speak of . . . (and evidence shows) the lack of a sustained, consistent and implemented strategy, and indus-trialisation attempts launched rather sporadically and unorganically'.

Electronics firms have of course operated in yet another type of environment as far as public policy is concerned – one that is at once intensely influenced by state policy in some areas and far less in other areas. With the exception of MITI's initiative in the late 1950s, state involvement in the consumer electronics industry has been minimal. Nevertheless, adjustments to international shifts in competitive ability have been comparatively rapid, being aided by the TNC's global marketing network for its own farflung production sitings. In the semiconductor industry the TNCs' ability to circumvent public policies through their world-wide pricing and marketing networks (Sciberras, 1977, p. 289) often means that the state's attempts to act as a regulator are thwarted.

A third feature of industrial restructuring and the policy environment is the great diversity of views regarding the appropriate involvement of public agencies in the adjustment processes of different industries and at different times. The steel industry is a field with considerable state involvement, not just through ownership but, as in the USA, through trade policy initiatives. Similarly, in electronics, intervention is extensive in R & D-intensive fields, notably through public procurement policies, while it is weak at the level of consumer goods.

These observations suggest a need to revise the interpretation of post-war industrial policy offered in an extremely thoughtful essay by Vernon in 1974. In that work, Vernon believed he had identified two discernable trends within European governments' thinking as regards industrial change. First, he observed that France had consistently pursued a different path from all the other countries. Long accustomed to intervention at the level of individual industries, the French private sector rarely questioned the legitimacy of state involvement. More recently, however, Brown (1980, p. 67) has suggested that planning was acceptable in France because the climate of the 1950s was 'relatively simple' and that 'the vacuum created by the chronic political instability of the Fourth Republic meant that the plan's prescriptions went relatively unchallenged'. Second, notwithstanding the idiosyncrasy of French interventionism, Vernon argued that there were clear signs of a convergence of attitudes to industrial planning throughout Europe. Led by France, even the traditionally liberal states of the UK and West Germany were increasingly inclined to imitate at least certain elements of the French experiment. Until the mid-1960s, the idea of the comprehensive plan enjoyed some vogue in many states. In the next few years, concentration on key industries or regions was the watchword while, after 1973, there was something of a rediscovery of the efficacy of free markets.

It is always attractive to try to impose some kind of order upon economic history in this way. But at present it is not likely that the convergence in policy which Vernon believed he detected is occurring. Instead, the 1980s may witness a growing disparity, both with respect to the intellectual debate regarding the appropriate relationship of policy to industry, and with respect to the practicalities of public intervention. For the evidence presented in Chapters 6 and 7, as well as information available elsewhere, suggests that henceforth there will be two, partially inconsistent and conflicting, attitudes to policy as it affects industry. The fact that there will necessarily be tensions between these attitudes points to a certain volatility in industrial policy; it also suggests that a renewed disparity in the industrial policies of different countries may be unavoidable.

One approach that is likely to retain adherents in virtually all countries is that of deliberate, intensive and prolonged state support focused on specific industries. Referred to in the context of Japanese firms' export strategies as the 'laser' approach, these policies are likely to be identified with fields that are technology- or capital-intensive, very probably dominated by an oligopoly or even a monopoly in each country. The classic example is aerospace, and, in particular, defence equipment within the aerospace industry. Some years ago Sampson analysed the interaction of state agencies, producers and major clients in this business and christened it 'Pentagon capitalism'. The approach is identifiable owing to the extreme degree of intimacy pervading the relationship between government, producer and client: 'as the Pentagon contacts became bigger and fewer, and the companies more precarious, the relationship was hard to recognise as any traditional kind of free enterprise' (Sampson, 1977, p. 101). In this type of policy environment the interaction, or direction, of causation among the various groups may start when the client demands something exceptional from the producer, and relies on the government for security; alternatively the government, intent on prestigious developments from its domestic producers, may encourage the acquisition of clients. In France, 'successive French governments were determined to catch up with the industry in Britain and America, as an assertion of national independence' (p. 108) and firms were supported by the full patronage of the state. But so successful was this emulation led by the entrepeneur Dassault, that, 'in the course of the 1960s, Dassault was able to show the British and American industries just how effective that formula could be' (p. 112).

In this case, then, the imitator's success transcended that of the initiator. In another respect, too, governments have copied one another in concentrating a battery of official apparatus on selected firms and industries. A clear instance is the increasing use of official diplomatic contracts to foster commercial relationships: 'the new game is commercial diplomacy – a mix of politics, finance and aid in exchange for trade' (*S. Times*, 4 Apr. 1982). A version of this approach that appears likely to take root throughout the advanced countries – although to varying degrees – is not so much industry-specific or product-specific but process-specific. Thus, state agencies are likely to encourage, finance and otherwise induce process innovations as a means by which industries can be rejuvenated. A French planner involved in the Mitterrand-inspired push for re-industrialisation observed that 'there are no condemned sectors. Innovation allows all sectors to be competitive' (*WSJ*, 29 Mar. 1982). Central to this theme is the use of electronics to help cut unit costs in 'threatened' industries. In July 1982 the French government announced a FF140 billion ($20 billion) programme to make France, in the words of Mitterrand's special advisor, M. Jacques Attali, 'a great technology power'. Net import penetration is to be cut back and some 80,000 jobs created. Since the main companies in such areas as mainframe computers, office equipment, information systems and space activities were brought under government control in 1981 and 1982, the plan should at least be fairly easy to agree upon (*FT*, 29 July 1982).

In contrast with this deliberate and relatively well-articulated policy, however, the 1980s are also likely to see the simultaneous pursuit of selective protectionist devices, occasioned by panic and short-term expediency. The growth of lobbyists and their power, described in Chapter 3, suggests that the institutional wherewithal to push for such *ad hoc* policy amendments exists. But under what circumstances might these policy amendments actually be granted? The following discussion attempts to identify the factors most likely to be associated with state intervention to slow down the pace or alter the pattern of change.

In the tables summarising the strategies open to firms in the industries examined in Chapters 6 and 7, at least one of the options open to each industry involved government action. In the case of the auto industry in the USA, for instance, it was suggested that a quota on Japanese imports coupled with or leading to US local content rules would provide one form of relief for the embattled auto manufacturers, their employees and their suppliers. Under what circumstances will firms attempt to pursue this option and, equally important, under what circumstances are their efforts likely to meet with success? The evidence from the five industries examined here, as well as from other research, strongly suggests that there are at least four industrial characteristics that may increase the likelihood of public intervention so as to retard or postpone the adjustments which firms would otherwise be compelled to implement.

Industrial characteristics prompting public intervention

Intuition and a great deal of evidence suggest that the larger the plant and/or industry that is threatened with collapse, the less likely it is that the government will tolerate its disappearance or drastic slimming. In the US auto industry, the sheer number of the workers involved – up to 2.5 million for the entire auto and suppliers complex – argued for import controls, particularly at a time when unemployment was 10 per cent nation-wide and 18 per cent in Michigan. Similar considerations would apply to the American steel industry, which laid off 114,000 workers between 1980 and mid-1982. In the UK, the work force of British Steel, the nationalised supplier, was nearly halved between 1979 and 1982. However, a large proportion of this labour-shedding took the form of voluntary redundancies induced by extremely attractive payments that were partly financed by the European Community and were therefore more palatable to employees and government alike.

By contrast, the refining industry has been able to command relatively little government support during its difficulties. This is true despite the fact that the industry is extremely capital-intensive. For instance, in 1981 refining firms in the USA were second only to oil drilling firms in terms of their assets per employee; these amounted to $315,000, compared to a figure of $52,000 in the auto industry, $46,200 for producers of electronics in electronics firms and an average for all industries of $60,437 (*Fortune*, 3 May 1982, p. 283). Thus in terms of the refining industry's substantial dollar assets, lobbyists might have expected the government's response to their difficulties would be favourable. A clear distinction between the refining and auto industries, however, is the size of their labour force: in 1982 refineries employed barely 100,000 people in the USA, and the main union, the Oil, Chemical and Atomic Workers, reported only 55,000 members to be working in refineries. Shutdowns, lay-offs and substantial unilaterally-imposed cuts in wages and pension rights by employers were a feature of most of 1981 and 1982 and prompted no response from state – much less federal – government (*BW*, 5 July 1982, p. 26).

The sophistication of an industry's lobbying apparatus and its skill in mobilising a public relations campaign constitutes a second factor which is important, although difficult to appraise. It is reasonable to expect that those industries which anticipate severe problems will inevitably organise themselves, so that there will be a close correlation between the extent of an industry's difficulties and the sophistication of its lobbying and public affairs apparatus. Earlier in this book the sophistication of the US steel firms' lobbying effort was noted.

Similar trends were noted among American auto firms, although in that case the conflicts between various parts of the industry limited overall effectiveness. Once the UAW's position on restricting imports began to be undermined by firms that were keen to adopt a strategy of captive imports, the conflicts between the various proponents of different positions reduced the pressure on the federal government.

A third factor identified by Walter and Jones (1980, p. 25) as an important determinant of the propensity to seek state aid through trade protection is the existence of a vested interest in the public industrial policy apparatus. In the case of the US steel industry, they find that 'as steel interests become more and more entrenched in the policymaking apparatus, the protection of producer interests by restrictions on trade become vested government interests' (p. 27). On *a priori* grounds this view would seem to be logical, although in fact the industries examined in this book provide little supporting evidence. For instance, the oil refining industry, with no public ownership in the USA but characterised by a great deal of public intervention, has been allowed to run down very significantly. The US auto industry, with rather greater public involvement in the form of the Chrysler support scheme, has been awarded a measure of protection, while in countries with greater public ownership – notably in Europe – a very considerable degree of protection has been awarded to it.

Finally, it is reasonable to expect that if firms have a choice of alternative products, or alternative ways of making the same products, the adjustment pressures resulting from a drop in demand for the accustomed product-mix will be less intense. But identifying ways of maintaining profitability are, obviously, not easy. It was suggested in Chapter 1 that some of the research associated with the long wave theory of economic development cast doubt on the inevitable decline of industries once the growth in demand for their main product or products slowed or contracted. Instead, a number of strategies could be deployed to regenerate interest in the original product, to stimulate interest in a related product, or, indeed, to adopt a combination of these and other strategies. The third section of this chapter discusses the question of industry strategies for escaping collapse.

Industry strategies for survival

Chapters 6 and 7 made frequent reference to policies which firms have instituted in an attempt to forestall bankruptcy or increase profitability at a time of intense competition. This section attempts to categorise such policies and note similarities and differences in the policy options open to various industries.

In Chapter 1 it was noted that, during the 1970s, businesses made increasing use of portfolio matrix analysis, which helped, under some circumstances, to order planners' thinking about the strength and weaknesses of their operations. As firms or their constituent operating divisions move between parts of the matrix they tend to display recognisable patterns. The product life-cycle is a well-known pattern of this sort, for which considerable empirical evidence exists. A study of the sales histories of 754 ethical drug products by Cox (1967), for instance, identified only six fundamental patterns at work. Whenever sales decelerated or began to fall in absolute terms, the product managers would act to buoy up interest in their product again as far as possible. Since relatively few options are open in practical business, it is not surprising to find a certain set of patterns being repeated again and again. Among the economists who have gone furthest recently in categorising the stages of firms' and products' evolution is van Duijn. The fundamental notion upon which van Duijn's schema is based assumes that the 'innovation life cycle' can be represented by an S-shaped curve. Four phases of this cycle, each of them referring to a successive period in demand for the good created by an innovation, are hypothesised. In the first, introductory, phase, there is a large number of product innovations and little is known about the nature of demand. In the second, growth, phase, customers have grown accustomed to the product and standardised technologies have allowed cost-cutting process innovations. There are, however, fewer product innovations. In the third phase, that of maturity, the growth of demand (and output) decelerates, and product differentiation becomes the vehicle of competition as each firm struggles to expand its market share. In the fourth and final phase, sales may fall. The firms which decide to retain a commitment to the industry try to escape from this phase of contracting sales by changes in technology or indeed any number of changes. At this point four further options open up, as shown in Figure 8.1.

The first option is one of substitution – firms introduce a new product to replace the original one. The second is extension of the first product's life by minor updating. The third involves changes in technology which trigger renewed periods of growth in demand, probably – although not necessarily – due to lower costs and thus price. The fourth represents a phase of extended maturity, in which stable demand persists. From all this van Duijn's conclusion is that 'a simple law of industrial growth does not exist'. Although 'the S-shaped growth curve may be a valid conceptualization of industry growth up to the maturity phase . . . anything may happen beyond this phase' (van Duijn, 1980, p. 33).

There is, of course, a fifth possibility which is absolute decline not

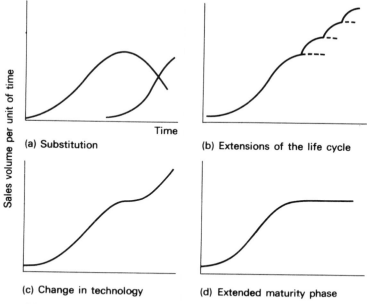

(a) Substitution   (b) Extensions of the life cycle

(c) Change in technology   (d) Extended maturity phase

Figure 8.1   *Industry strategies for evading a decline in sales*

followed, as in the first option, by the successful introduction of a new product. In some industries this can come about quickly and devastatingly. As Robinson (1981, p. 3) has noted, 'technological change can have an important effect on economic capacity – the building of railways quickly made most of Britain's canal capacity uneconomic'. And, following the introduction of the transistor, 'there is no salvation in price cutting, since valve radios are virtually unsaleable at any price'.

However, recalling the evidence for the industries dealt with earlier in this book, the four-fold schema proposed by van Duijn may not be a completely adequate representation of the options facing firms. In particular, this schema cannot satisfactorily deal with the shifts in international comparative advantage which underlie many of the problems facing the firms in the industries examined in Chapters 6 and 7. Because of the international character of modern industry there are very few industries that face a global contraction of demand or are everywhere being replaced by a fundamentally new set of products. This is because there are so many countries at different stages of economic development that, somewhere in the world, there is scarcely a product that is not at the growth phase of development. In the steel industry, for instance, whatever the problems faced by American and European firms, demand in LDCs will still be growing strongly for the foreseeable future.

Looking again at the five industries examined in Chapters 6 and 7, it is possible to assess which industries face the greatest array of choices. Table 8.1 summarises these possibilities which correspond to the options depicted in Figure 8.1. Although this figure refers to work carried out by van Duijn, the categories represented there are by no means uniquely his, and are common ground to many observers. Column A in Table 8.1 shows that the option of substitute product lines is not feasible except in certain parts of the electronics industry. Because of its nature as a purveyor of durable goods, the auto industry can hardly be expected to create totally new product groups. Firms in the industry certainly can be expected to redefine their products' positions in the market, and to take other profit-enhancing measures which were discussed earlier. What is clear is that at this level of aggregation there is little to offer in strategy A. The same comments apply, by and large, to the steel industry. Although special steel products could be seen as offering substitution possibilities for some firms, the relatively small importance of such items within the industry as a whole means that they cannot yield much more than a slight respite from the industry's problems. In any case, it is precisely in the specialty steels area that US and European producers have been experiencing the most tensions over international trade. During the first eight months of 1982, imports of specialty items such as alloy tool steel and stainless bar, rod, plate, sheet and strip steel accounted for up to 50 per cent of total US domestic sales. Late in 1982 President Reagan was considering taking action under the 1974 Trade Act to stem this growth of imports (*WSJ*, 17 Nov. 1982). In the oil refining industry, diversification was certainly an option exercised by the oil firms with windfall profit gains in 1979–81, but again this process slowed as cash reserves dwindled with the erosion of the real oil price during 1982. The other strategy which appears to offer relatively little hope is that of extended maturity. Unless the steady state of sales is at a level where virtually all profit has been eliminated from the industry, new entrants (chiefly from overseas, of course, where firms would still have economies of scale and learning curves to exploit) would put pressure on prices. Strategy B, extending the products' life by innovations, appears to offer some more hope, particularly if later stages of the product life-cycle offer higher unit profit than was possible at earlier stages. The option of strategy C varies considerably between industries. The clearest candidate for this would obviously be electronics, where successive rounds of technical innovation have cut prices and raised sales volume.

Table 8.1 *Industry strategies open to firms in autos, steel, electronics and refining*

Industry	A Substitution	B Extensions of the life cycle	C Changes in technology	D Extended maturity phase
Automobiles	Not feasible, though once attracted to electric cars, public transport provision, etc., as supplements to car production	Tradition of product obsolescence makes this readily available	Being attempted now	Very difficult owing to intensive price competition
Steel	Not possible	Possible if emphasis is on processed products	Being attempted through process innovations	ditto
Electronics	Available as new products arise, often using established components	Possible through new product and process innovation	In tradition of industry as costs fall	ditto
Oil refining	Profits once allowed diversification, but this has not gone very far. So small option	Possible if firm moves downstream to specialty products	Possible to some extent as improved efficiency, but overall demand likely to be flat	Possible due to locational characteristics

Further disaggregation of these strategies is, however, possible. A framework which is increasingly popular is the notion of 'generic strategies' associated with Porter (1980), among others. Referred to as 'a few over-arching game plans that work in one industry after another' (*Fortune*, 19 Oct. 1981, p. 181), these have the great merits of simplicity and universality. Each is simply a plan or series of man-oeuvres drawn up by participants in an industry who wish to build on their strengths so as to shape a defendable position within their indus-try. First there is the strategy of 'overall cost leadership', whereby one maximises profits by being the lowest price producer. A second strategy is 'differentiation', whereby a firm's product is perceived as sufficiently different to command a price premium and thus allow the firm to enjoy long-standing profits. The third strategy is 'focus', in which a particular client group or region is concentrated upon, using one or both of the preceding two strategies. The good or service then being offered is of sufficient merit to the target group so that, again, long-term profitability is likely. This schema draws on earlier work (Porter, 1979) in which it was suggested that companies in an industry must identify and cope with five fundamental factors in their operat-ing environments: the threat of new entrants; the jockeying for mar-ket share among the firms already in the industry; customers' bar-gaining power; suppliers' bargaining power; and the threat of the market being eroded through the appearance of substitute products.

These three generic strategies may be adopted singly or in com-bination. Firms unable to move towards any of them are unlikely to achieve profitability. Looking again to the industries dealt with in Chapters 6 and 7, this time in the light of the generic strategies approach, yields the results shown in Table 8.2.

It is immediately apparent from column A of Table 8.2 that firms producing in advanced countries can not secure long-term profitabil-ity through the pursuit of overall cost leadership. Productivity is simply too low, with the possible exception of certain parts of the electronics industry. As noted in Chapter 7, price-competitiveness in R & D-intensive electronics products tends to be relatively unimpor-tant at the initial phases of product development. Instead, the discus-sion in this chapter has suggested that increasing use of international marketing agreements may allow overall cost leadership to be retained even if domestic costs of production are internationally uncompetitive. The means of resolving this problem is by sponsoring imports from a lower-cost source to be sold in the host country's higher-priced markets.

A strategy of differentiation appears to be markedly more applic-able. In some industries, such as machine tools, this has always been the way of doing business, yet it has not prevented net import

Table 8.2 Industry strategies, based on the 'generic strategies' approach, open to five industries

	A Overall cost leadership	B Differentiation	C Focus
Automobiles	Virtually impossible for US and European firms in view of Japanese advantages	Too many firms for all to be successful. In any case, Japanese producers, in addition to (A), are pursuing (B) with up-market autos	Scale of operation of big three US firms is too large for this. Smaller firms, e.g. BMW, may attempt this strategy
Steel	ditto	ditto	Possible, but implies divesting from much of crude steel capacity and labour force
Electronics (i) consumer goods	May still be retained	Depends on extraordinary inventiveness being maintained	Improbable, given increasingly large scale of mainstream producers and retailers
(ii) capital goods	ditto	ditto	ditto
Oil refining	Access to crude oil inputs at cost of production allows OPEC-located facilities actual or potential cost advantage which owners can not match	More sophisticated downstream products may be a solution, e.g. in pharmaceutical goods	Regional markets could be served, e.g. by gasoline retail network

penetration in the countries with the longer-established tools firms, such as the USA or West Germany, from rising quickly. Implicit in many differentiation strategies is the relinquishing of mass-marketing. Rather than maintaining an assault on the entire scope of a market, differentiation strategies stress the profit possibilities of focusing on niches. The literature on market share and its relation to profitability has grown rapidly and has tended more and more to the view that pursuit of market share may frequently be, in Fruhan's (1972) words, a 'pyrrhic victory'. Instead, there is greater emphasis on the attraction of a deliberate low market share strategy. Such a strategy encourages the firm to 'segment, segment, segment' (Hamermesh *et al.*, 1978, p. 98) by carefully selecting its target market and its product range. As far as the auto industry is concerned, a number of firms can hope to follow a 'harvest' strategy, gradually relinquishing the cheaper segments of the market while concentrating resources in more carefully-defined segments. However, with twenty-five major international firms in the industry, all attempting some form of segmentation, there are unlikely to be many high unit profit niches that are not already claimed. Similar comments apply to steel and to the high value-added chemicals and pharmaceuticals.

Generally, versions of the strategies of focus and differentiation offer the best hope for firms threatened with stagnating overall demand and intensifying price competition from overseas. All this suggests a need for more careful market opportunity analysis than has perhaps characterised many firms in the now-beleaguered smokestack industries of Europe and the USA. Above all, the discussion points to the need for diligent efforts to develop more subtly-designed and conceived products, which would be aimed at more carefully defined markets than has been the case.

Summary and conclusions

Today's map of world industry looks very different from the one which prevailed in 1945. Much of the political effort during that period was intended to foster change and to achieve some measure of economic interdependence between Western countries. However, the gradual extension of interdependence was accompanied by an erosion of economic power among the world's leading industrial countries and, in this sense, the present industrial map is also far different from the one imagined by the negotiators of the original policy framework. Almost all economies demonstrated a remarkable degree of flexibility in accommodating and responding to these sweeping changes. But, at the same time, a steadily growing system of industrial interdependence meant that the impetus for adjustment had shifted as external forces came to overshadow domestic ones. One consequence is that, today, countries rather than industries or companies are perceived as the real competitors in world markets. An increasingly important policy criterion is the impact on the competitive position of domestic industries in international markets.

There is another sense in which the sorts of changes documented in foregoing chapters reflect deliberate public policy decisions rather than tendencies which are more or less inherent in economic growth and development. Many of these decisions, made in the capitals of the West as well as in several of the newly-independent LDCs, led to the appearance of substantial tranches of industrial capacity. The new capacity created during much of the 1950s and 1960s tended to be for the replacement of imports by indigenously-produced goods. But as the domestic markets for some of these products approached saturation (at least at the price levels then prevailing), more and more firms were encouraged to turn to exporting. More recently, renewed interest in the beneficial consequences which more liberal trade regimes may bring for LDCs has fostered a series of policy reforms. India, some large Latin American countries, and many Asian NICs, are among the countries where to a greater or lesser extent policymakers are increasingly embracing the new liberalism. Simultaneously, the socialist countries were also undertaking far-reaching changes in their economic structure. There, too, very substantial industrial capacity was built up so that, by 1980, these countries accounted for around a quarter of the world's manufacturing value added.

Naturally, such sweeping changes in the character of world industry involved the construction of billions of dollars of new plant capacity in many countries. The fact that the very existence of much of this capacity is now jeopardised or is being run down can not be attributed solely to the current economic slump. Substantial over-investment in existing technologies occurred during the 1960s and early 1970s, although the consequences are now more obvious when industries and economies compete on a worldwide scale as never before. Thus excess capacity is prevalent among several of the industries discussed here – automobiles, steel, oil refining and even semiconductors – as well as among others. Present economic conditions have only served to dramatise some of the more difficult problems associated with this dramatic build-up in the world's industrial capacity and the problems associated with it. Ultimately, the explanation for the collapse of firms in these industries can not really be attributed to misguided monetary and fiscal policies but are the result of much more basic, deep-seated causes.

The growing involvement of the state in this process of industrial expansion was seldom accompanied by any new institutional arrangements for co-ordination. A variety of interest groups have found this dispersion of authority to be useful in the sense that industrial policies are now more susceptible to special-interest pressure. These tactics, like others discussed in this book, are not particularly unique to the present phase in the development of world industry. As Philip Wicksteed observed in 1910, 'Every man who lives by supplying any want dreads anything which tends either to dry up that want or supply it more easily and abundantly. . . . If all the world turned sober, it would indefinitely increase its well-being but countless publicans, brewers, distillers and hop and vine growers would be thrown out of employment'. Because the cost of running down a sizeable portion of the uncompetitive capacity created in the 1960s is so great, today's pressure groups are perhaps better organised and more active than ever before. As this phenomenon has spread, groups of firms acting in concert with labour interests and government officials have added a political dimension to the traditional range of economic and corporate decisions that were previously regarded as the responsibility of the industrial firm.

A consequence is that much of the debate regarding industrial change in the 1970s and early 1980s focused upon immediate or short-term problems while adopting an apocalyptic tone, with crises and confrontation being the touchstones of discussion. Much of the material presented in the latter part of this book shows clearly that such an approach is inadequate. The governments of advanced countries have reacted in different ways to these sorts of tactics, but they have all conceded ground to the mounting pressure of industrial lobbies. Although the Japanese record of successes and failures is, perhaps, more impressive than that of other advanced countries, there is little reason to expect that this approach to industrial policy-making would be easily transferable to other economies and societies. However, one underlying principle of the Japanese approach which does provide an instructive contrast to other countries is the fact that economic considerations have generally taken precedence over political ones while the reverse has been true elsewhere.

To sum up, it is clear that the dispersion of industrial activity, so ardently sought by the Allies after 1945, has begun to gather pace and would be difficult, if not impossible, to reverse. Since 1963, the share of the older established industrial powers has declined from 46 per cent to 33 per cent of world MVA. There is scarcely an industry where their dominance is not being challenged by competitors in other advanced countries or in LDCs. Yet real income *per capita* has continued to grow. Indeed, 'these structural changes have not simply coincided with the great growth and unprecedented levels of income in the democratic industrial countries – they have made that prosperity possible' (Diebold, 1978, p. 573). There is nothing in this book to suggest that this process is no longer applicable. What has been suggested is that the well-publicised interruptions to this process should not blind one to the enormous changes that are taking place in world industry; to ignore these changes, or to attempt to thwart them, and in the process keep the price of manufactured goods unnecessarily high, would be of benefit to no one in the long run.

Bibliography

Abernathy, W. J. (1978) *The Productivity Dilemma: Roadblock to Innovation in the Automobile Industry* (Baltimore, Md.: Johns Hopkins University Press).

AISI (American Iron and Steel Institute) (1978) *The Economic Implications of Foreign Steel Pricing Practices* (Washington DC: AISI).

AISI (1980) *Steel at the Crossroads: The American Steel Industry in the 1980s* (Washington DC: AISI).

AISI (annual), *Annual Statistical Report* (Washington DC: AISI).

Akrasanee, N., Viseskul, C. and Sophastienphong, S. (1981) *Comparative Advantage of Iron and Steel, Petro-chemical and Plastic Products Industries in Thailand* (Tokyo: Institute of Developing Economies).

Aliboni, R. (ed.) (1978) *Arab Industrialization and Economic Integration*, (London: Croom Helm).

Allen, G. C. (1981) 'Industrial policy and innovation in Japan' in C. Carter (ed.) *Industrial Policy and Innovation* (London: Heinemann) pp. 68–87.

Anderson, R. G. and Kreinin, M. E. (1981) 'Labour costs in the American steel and auto industries', *The World Economy*, vol. 4, no. 2, pp. 199–205.

Bacon, R. and Eltis, W. (1976) *Britain's Economic Problem: Too Few Producers*, (London: Macmillan).

Baer, W. (1969) *The Development of the Brazilian Steel Industry*, (Nashville, Tenn.: Vanderbilt University Press).

Baer, W. (1972) 'Import substitution and industrialization in Latin America: experiences and interpretations', *Latin American Research Review*, vol. 7, no. 1, pp. 95–122.

Baer, W. and Samuelson, L. (1981) 'Toward a service-oriented growth strategy', *World Development*, vol. 9, no. 6, pp. 499–514.

Balassa, B. (1968) 'Tariff protection in industrial countries: an evaluation', repr. in R. E. Caves and H. G. Johnson (eds) *Readings in International Economics*, vol. xi, (Homewood, Ill.: Richard D. Irwin).

Balassa, B. (1971a) 'Effective protection: a summary appraisal' in H. G. Grubel and H. G. Johnson (eds) *Effective Tariff Protection* (Geneva: GATT and Graduate Institute of International Studies.

Balassa, B. (ed.) (1971b) *The Structure of Protection in Developing Countries* (Baltimore, Md.: Johns Hopkins University Press).

Balassa, B. (1977) *Policy Reform in Developing Countries* (New York: Pergamon Press).

Balassa, B. (1978a) 'The new protectionism and the international economy', *Journal of World Trade Law*, vol. 12, no. 5, September, pp. 409–36.

Balassa, B. (1978b) 'Export incentives and export performance in developing countries: a comparative analysis', *Weltwirtschaftliches Archiv*, Band 114, Heft 1, pp. 24–51.

Balassa, B. (1980) *The Newly-Industrializing Countries after the Oil Crisis* (Washington DC: World Bank, Staff Working Paper no. 437).

Ballance, R., Ansari, J. and Singer, H. (1982) *The International Economy and Industrial Development* (Brighton: Harvester Press).

Batchelor, R. A., Major, R. L. and Morgan, A. D. (1980) *Industrialization and the Basis for Trade* (Cambridge: Cambridge University Press for the National Institute of Economic and Social Research).

Beenstock, M. and Warburton, P. (1980) 'UK imports and the international trading order' (London: London Business School, Discussion Paper no. 83).

Behrman, J. N. (1972) *The Role of International Companies in Latin American Integration: Autos and Petrochemicals* (Lexington, Mass.: D. C. Heath).

Bennett, D., Blackman, M. J. and Sharpe, K. (1978) 'Mexico and multinational corporations: an explanation of state action' in J. Grunwald (ed.) *Latin America and the World Economy: A Changing International Order* (London: Sage).

Bergsman, J. (1979) 'Industrial priorities in Brazil', in UNIDO, *Industrial Priorities in Developing Countries* (New York: United Nations).

Berry, A.. (1978) 'A positive interpretation of the expansion of urban services in Latin America, with some Colombian evidence', *Journal of Development Studies*, vol. 14, pp. 210–31.

BIS (Bank for International Settlements), *Annual Reports*, various issues.

Blackaby, F. (1979) 'Introduction' in F. Blackaby (ed.), *Deindustrialization* (London: Heinemann).

Blondel, J. (1979) *Voters, Parties and Leaders* (Harmondsworth: Penguin, rev. ed.).

BLS (Bureau of Labor Statistics), *Monthly Labor Review* (Washington DC: BLS, various issues).

BP (British Petroleum) (1982) *BP Statistical Review of World Energy, 1981* (London: BP).

Brown, C. J. F. (1980) 'Industrial policy and economic planning in Japan and France', *National Institute Economic Review*, no. 93, August, pp. 59–75.

Brown, L. *et al.* (1979) *The Future of the Automobile in an Oil-Short World* (Washington DC: Worldwatch Institute, Worldwatch Paper no. 32).

Carter, C. (ed.) (1981) *Industrial Policy and Innovation* (London: Heinemann).

Chenery, H. B. (1960) 'Patterns of industrial growth', *Industrial Economic Review*, vol. 50, September, pp. 624–54.

Chenery, H. B. and Taylor, L. (1968) 'Development patterns: among countries and over time', *The Review of Economics and Statistics*, vol. 50, no. 4, November, pp. 391–415.

Chenery, H. B. and Sirquin, M. (1975) *Patterns of Development 1950–70* (London: Oxford University Press).

Clark, C. (1940) *The Conditions of Economic Progress* (London: Macmillan).

Cooper, R. N. (1973) 'Trade policy is foreign policy', in R. N. Cooper (ed.) *A Reordered World Emerging from International Economic Problems* (Washington DC: Potomac Associates).

Corden, W. M. (1974) *Trade Policy and Economic Welfare* (Oxford: Clarendon Press).

Cox, W. E. (1967) 'Product life cycles as marketing models', *Journal of Business*, October, pp. 375–84.

Cyert, R. M. and Hedrick, C. L. (1972) 'Theory of the firm: past, present and future: an interpretation', *Journal of Economic Literature*, vol. 10, no. 2, pp. 398–412.

de Bandt, J. (1981) 'France' in G. Renshaw (ed.) *Employment, Trade and North-South Co-operation* (Geneva: ILO).

Desai, P. (1969) 'Alternative measures of import substitution' *Oxford Economic Papers*, vol. 21, no. 3, pp. 312–23.

Diebold, W. (1972) *The United States and the Industrial World* (New York: Praeger).

Diebold, W. (1978) 'Adapting economies to structural change: the international aspect', *International Affairs*, October, pp. 573–88.

Donges, J. (1976) 'A comparative study of industrialization policies in fifteen semi-industrialized countries', *Weltwirtschaftliches Archiv*, Band 112, pp. 626–59.

Dosi, G. (1981) *Technical Change and Survival: Europe's Semiconductor Industry* (Brighton: European Research Centre).

Duijn, J. J. van (1980) 'Another look at industry growth patterns' (College of Commerce, University of Illinois at Urbana-Champaign, Faculty Working paper no. 667).

Duijn, J. J. van (1981) 'Fluctuations in innovations over time', *Futures*, vol. 13, no. 4, August, pp. 264–75.

Duijn, J. J. van (1983) *The Long Wave in Economic Life* (London: George Allen and Unwin).

ECE (Economic Commission for Europe) (1976) *Long-Term Prospects for Steel Consumption until 1985 and Outlook for 1990, and Past Trends in Production and Trade* (Geneva: United Nations).

ECE (1977) *Structure and Change in European Industry* (Geneva: United Nations).

ECE (1981) *Economic Survey of Europe in 1980* (Geneva: United Nations).

Emery, R. (1967) 'The relation of exports and economic growth', *Kyklos*, vol. 20, pp. 470–86.

Fane, G. (1973) 'Consistent measures of import substitution', *Oxford Economic Papers*, vol. 25, no. 2, pp. 251–61.

Federal Trade Commission (1977) *Staff Report on the United States Steel Industry and Its International Rivals: Trends and Factors Determining International Competitiveness* (Washington DC: US Government Printing Office).

Fei, J. C. H. and Ranis, G. (1964) *Development of the Labour Surplus Economy, Theory and Policy* (Homewood, Ill.: Richard D. Irwin).

First Chicago Bank (1981) *World Report*, March (Chicago: First Chicago Bank).

Fisher, A. G. B. (1939) 'Production, primary, secondary and tertiary', *Economic Record*, vol. 15, pp. 24–38.

Fishlow, A. (1978) 'The mature neighbour policy: a proposal for a United States economic policy for Latin America' in J. Grunwald (ed.) *Latin America and the World Economy* (London: Sage).

Fong, C. D., Lim, K. C., Cheong, K. C. and Lin, T. Y. (1981) *Comparative*

Advantage of Iron and Steel, Petro-chemical and Plastic Products Industries in Malaysia (Tokyo: Institute of Developing Economies).

Frank, I. (1961) *The European Common Market: An Analysis of Commercial Policy* (New York: Praeger).

Franko, L. G. (1971) *Joint Venture Survival in Multinational Corporations* (New York: Praeger).

Freeman, C. (ed.) (1981) special issues of *Futures*, August and October.

Fruhan, W., Jr. (1972) 'Pyrrhic victories in fights for market share', *Harvard Business Review*, September–October, pp. 100–107.

Fuchs, V. R. (1968) *The Service Economy* (New York: Columbia University Press).

GATT (1979) International Trade 1978/79 (Geneva: GATT).

GATT (1980) International Trade 1979/80 (Geneva: GATT).

GATT (1981) International Trade 1980/81 (Geneva: GATT).

Gilpin, R. (1975) *U.S. Power and the Multinational Corporation* (London: Macmillan).

Ginman, P. J., Pugel, T. A. and Walter, I. (1980) 'Mixed blessings for the third world in codes on non-tariff measures', *The World Economy*, vol. 3, no. 2, September, pp. 217–33.

GM (General Motors) (1974) 'Competition and the motor vehicle industry' (Washington DC: submitted to the Sub-Committee on Antitrust and Monopoly of the US Senate).

GM (1982) *Annual report.*

Gomez-Ibanez, J. and Harrison, D. (1982) 'Imports and the future of the U.S. automobile industry', *The American Economic Review, Papers and Proceedings*, vol. 72, no. 2. pp. 319–23.

Gomulka, S. (1971) *Inventive Activity, Diffusion and the Stages of Economic growth* (Aarhus: Skrifter fra, Aarhus Universtets Okonomiske Institut).

Griffin, K. B. and Enos, J. L. (1970) *Planning Development* (London: Addison-Wesley).

Gwynne, R. N. (1980) 'The Andean group automobile programme', *Bank of London and South America Review*, August, pp. 160–8.

Hallwood, P. and Sinclair, S. (1981) *Oil, Debt and Development: OPEC in the Third World* (London: George Allen and Unwin).

Hammermesh, R. G., Anderson, M. J. and Harris, J. E. (1978) 'Strategies for low market share business', *Harvard Business Review*, May, pp. 95–102.

Healy, M. J. (1982) 'Plant closures in multi-plant enterprises: the case of a declining industrial sector', *Regional Studies*, vol. 16, no. 1. pp. 31–5.

Heathcoat Amory, D. (1981) 'Government and industry' (London: Bow Paper, the Bow Group).

Helleiner, G. K. (1972) *International Trade and Economic Development* (Harmondsworth: Penguin).

Helleiner, G. K. (1973) 'Manufactured exports from less-developed countries and multinational firms', *Economic Journal*, vol. 83, March, pp. 21–47.

Hewer, A. (1980) 'Manufacturing industry in the seventies: an assessment of import penetration and export performance', *Economic Trends* (London: Central Statistical Office) June, pp. 97–109.

Hibberd, J. and Wren-Lewis, S. (1978) 'A study of the UK imports of manufactures' (London: Government Economic Service Working Paper no. 6, August).

Hirsch, S. (1975) 'The product cycle model of international trade – multi-country cross-section analysis', *Oxford Bulletin of Economics and Statistics*, vol. 37, no. 4, pp. 305–17.

Hirschman, A. O. (1958) *Strategy of Economic Development* (New Haven, Conn: Yale University Press).

Hirschman, A. O. (1968) 'The political economy of import-substituting industrialization in Latin America', *Quarterly Journal of Economics*, vol. 82, no. 1, February, pp. 1–32.

Hoffman, W. G. (1958) *The Growth of Industrial Economies* (Manchester: Manchester University Press).

Hoover, C. (1946) 'The future of the German economy', *American Economic Review*, vol. 36, no. 2, May, pp. 642–49.

Hufbauer, G. C. (1970) 'The impact of national characteristics and technology on the commodity composition of trade in manufactured goods', in R. Vernon (ed.) *The Technology Factor in International Trade* (New York: National Bureau of Economic Research).

Hughes, H. and Waelbroeck, J. (1981) 'Can developing country exports keep growing in the 1980s?', *The World Economy*, vol. 4, no. 2, June, pp. 127–48.

IDE (Institute of Developing Economies) (1980) *The Electronics Industry in Japan* (Tokyo: IDE).

IISI (International Iron and Steel Institute) (1980) *Projection 90* (Brussels: IISI, IISI/ECON/100).

IISI (1981) *Steel Statistical Yearbook, 1981* (Brussels: IISI).

IISI (1982) *World Steel in Figures, 1982* (Brussels: IISI).

IMF (International Monetary Fund) (annual) *International Financial Statistics Yearbook* (Washington DC: IMF).

IMF (1982) *World Economic Outlook* (Washington DC: IMF, Occasional Paper no. 9).

Institute of Petroleum (1981) *Petroleum Statistics* (London: Institute of Petroleum).

Interfutures (1979) *Facing the Future: Mastering the Probable and Managing the Unpredictable* (Paris: OECD).

JAMA (1982) (Japan Automobile Manufacturers Association), *Motor Vehicle Statistics of Japan, 1982* (Tokyo: JAMA).

JETRO (Japanese External Trade Organization) (1976) 'The Automobile Industry in Transition', *Now in Japan*, May, no. 21.

Johnson, B. F. and Mellor, J. W. (1961) 'The role of agriculture in economic development', *American Economic Review*, September, pp. 571–81.

Johnson, C. (1982) *MITI and the Japanese Miracle: The Growth of Industrial Policy, 1925–1975* (Stanford: Stanford University Press).

Johnson, H. G. (1967) *Economic Policies Toward Less Developed Countries* (Washington DC: Brookings Institution).

Jones, D. T. (1981) *Maturity and Crisis in the European Car Industry: Structural Change and Public Policy* (Brighton: European Papers no. 8).

Jones, D. T. (1980) 'The metalworking machine tool industry in Western Europe and government intervention' (Brighton: paper for the Sussex University Working Group on Structural Adjustment).

Jones, K. (1979) 'Forgetfulness of things past: Europe and the steel cartel', *The World Economy*, vol. 2, no. 2, pp. 139–54.

Jones, L. P. (1975) *Public Enterprise and Economic Development: The Korean Case* (Seoul: Korean Development Institute).

Kaldor, N. (1966) *Causes of the Slow Economic Growth of the United Kingdom* (Cambridge: Cambridge University Press).

Kawahito, K. (1981) 'Japanese steel in the American market: conflict and causes', *The World Economy*, vol. 4, no. 3, pp. 229–50.

Keesing, D. (1978) 'World trade and output of manufactures: structural trends and developing countries' exports' (Washington DC: World Bank, mimeo).

Kefauver, E. (1965) *In a Few Hands: Monopoly Power in America* (Harmondsworth: Penguin).

Kemp, T. (1978) *Historical Patterns of Industrialization* (London: Longman).

Killick, A. (1980) 'Trends in development economics and their relevance to Africa', *The Journal of Modern African Studies*, vol. 18, no. 3, pp. 367–86.

Kotler, P. (1980) *Marketing Management: Analysis, Planning and Control* (Englewood Cliffs, NJ: Prentice-Hall).

Krause, L. B. (1968) *European Economic Integration and the United States* (Washington DC: Brookings Institution).

Kravis, I. (1970) 'Trade as a handmaiden of growth: similarities between the nineteenth and twentieth centuries', *Economic Journal*, December, pp. 850–72.

Krueger, A. (1974) 'The political economy of the rent-seeking society', *American Economic Review*, vol. lxiv, no. 3, pp. 291–303.

Kuznets, S. (1957) 'Quantitative aspects of the economic growth of nations', II: 'International distribution of national product and labour force', *Economic Development and Cultural Change*, vol. 5, suppl.

Ladd, E. C. (1980) 'How to tame the special interest groups', *Fortune*, October 20, pp. 66–80.

Lal, D. (1979) 'Industrial priorities in India', in UNIDO, *Industrial Priorities in Developing Countries* (New York: United Nations).

Lary, H. B. (1968) *Imports of Manufactures from Less Developed Countries* (New York, NY: National Bureau of Economic Research).

Levitt, T. (1965) 'Exploit the product life cycle', *Harvard Business Review*, November–December, pp. 81–94.

Lewis, S. R. and Guisinger, S. E. (1968) 'Measuring protection in a developing country: the case of Pakistan', *Journal of Political Economy*, vol. 76, no. 6, pp. 1170–98.

Lewis, W. A. (1951) *Principles of Economic Planning* (Washington DC: Public Affairs Press).

Lewis, W. A. (1980) 'The slowing down of the engine of growth', *The American Economic Review*, September, vol. 70, no. 4, pp. 555–64.

Lewis, W. A. (1981) 'The rate of growth of world trade, 1830–1973' in S. Grassman and E. Lundberg (eds) *The World Economic Order Past and Prospects* (London: Macmillan).

Lipton, M. (1976) *Urban Bias: Why Poor People Stay Poor* (London: Temple Smith).

Little, I. M. D., Scitovsky, T. and Scott, M. F. G. (1970) *Industry and Trade in Some Developing Countries: A Comparative Study* (London: Oxford University Press).

Maddison, A. (1979) 'Per capita output in the long run', *Kyklos*, vol. 32, fasc. 1/2, pp. 412–29.

Mabro, R. and Radwan, S. (1976) *The Industrialization of Egypt, 1939–1973, Policy and Performance* (Oxford: Clarendon Press).

Majumdar, B. (1979) 'Innovations and international trade: an industry study of dynamic comparative advantage', *Kyklos*, vol. 32, pp. 559–68.

Maizels, A. (1968) *Exports and Economic Growth of Developing Countries* (Cambridge: Cambridge University Press).

Maxcy, G. (1981) *The Multinational Motor Industry* (London: Croom Helm).

Mensch, G. (1975) *Das Technologische Patt: Innovationen uberwinden die Depression* (Frankfurt: Umschau).

Michaely, M. (1977) 'Exports and growth, an empirical investigation', *Journal of Development Studies*, vol. 4, pp. 49–53.

MIJ (Machine Industries of Japan) (1978) 'Machinery industries of Japan – Investigation by industries' (Tokyo: MIJ) pp. 1–7.

Mogridge, M. J. H. (1978) 'The effect of the oil crisis on the growth in the ownership and use of cars', *Transportation*, vol. 7, pp. 45–67.

Mohnfeld, J. M. (1980) 'Changing patterns of trade', *Petroleum Economist*, August, pp. 329–32.

Morawetz, D. (1977) *Twenty-five Years of Economic Development 1950–1975* (Baltimore, Md.: Johns Hopkins University Press for the World Bank).

Morawetz, D. (1980) *Why the Emperor's New Clothes Are Not Made in Colombia* (Washington DC: World Bank, Staff Working Paper no. 368).

MVMA (Motor Vehicle Manufacturers Association) (1977) *Motor Vehicle Facts and Figures* (Detroit, Mich.: MVMA).

Murrell, P. (1982) 'The comparative structure of growth in the major developed capitalist nations', *Southern Economic Journal*, vol. 48, no. 4, April, pp. 985–95.

National Institute for Economic and Social Research, *Review* (London: NIESR) various issues.

Newhouse, J. (1982) *A Sporty Game* (New York: Knopf).

Nurske, R. (1958) 'The conflict between balanced growth and international specialization', *Lectures on Economic Development* Istanbul University, repr. in G. Meier (ed.) *Leading Issues in Development Economics* (1964) (New York: Oxford University Press) (pp. 250–4).

OECD (Organization for Economic Co-operation and Development) (1975) *The Aims and Instruments of Industrial Policy: A Comparative Study* (Paris: OECD).

OECD (1980) 'Steel in the 1980s, an OECD symposium', *OECD Observer*, no. 103, pp. 3–10.

OECD (1981a) *Main Economic Indicators* (Paris: OECD) various issues.

OECD (1981b) *Economic Outlook* (Paris: OECD) July.

Olson, M. (1965) *The Logic of Collective Action* (Cambridge, Mass.: Harvard University Press).

Olson, M. (1982) 'Stagflation and the political economy of the decline in productivity', *American Economic Review, Papers and Proceedings*, vol. 72, no. 2, pp. 143–8.

OPEC (Organization of Petroleum Exporting Countries) (1981) *OPEC National Oil Company Profiles* (Vienna: OPEC).

Ozawa, T. (1980) 'Japan's new resource diplomacy: government-backed group investment', *Journal of World Trade Law*, vol. 14, no. 1, pp. 3–13.

Paretti, V. and Bloch, C. (1956) 'Industrial production in Western Europe and the United States, 1901 to 1955', *Banca Nazionale del Lavoro Quarterly Review*, no. 39.

Pearce, M. C. (1980) 'International competition in the world automotive industry' in D. H. Ginsburg and W. J. Abernathy (eds) *Government, Technology and the Future of the Automobile* (New York: McGraw-Hill).

Peston, M. (1981) 'The integration of monetary, fiscal and incomes policy', *Lloyds Bank Review*, no. 141, July, pp. 1–13.

Porter, M. (1979) 'The structure within industries and companies' performance', *Review of Economics and Statistics*, vol. 61, pp. 214–27.

Porter, M. (1980) *Competitive Strategy* (New York: The Free Press).

Prebisch, R. (1959) 'Commercial policy in the underdeveloped countries', *American Economic Review, Papers and Proceedings*, May.

Price, V. C. (1980) *Unemployment and Other Non-work Issues* (London: Trade Policy Research Centre, Thames Essay, no. 25).

Pyo, Y. P., Il, K. T., Sun, P. J. and Ho, J. S. (1980) *Comparative Advantage of Iron and Steel, Petro-chemical and Plastic Products Industries in Korea* (Tokyo: Institute of Developing Economies).

Rahman, A. H. M. M. (1973) *Exports of Manufactures from Developing Countries, a study of comparative advantage* (Rotterdam: Rotterdam University Press).

Reich, R. B. (1982) 'Making industrial policy', *Foreign Affairs*, Spring, pp. 852–81.

Reynolds, L. G. (1977) *Image and Reality in Economic Development* (New Haven, Conn., and London: Yale University Press).

Robinson, B. (1981) 'The manufacturing recession and structural change', *Economic Outlook 1980–1984*, London Business School Forecast Release, August, pp. 1–4.

Rosenstein-Rodan, P. (1961) 'Notes on the theory of the big push', in H. Ellis (ed.), *Economic Development for Latin America* (New York: St Martin's Press).

Rostow, E. V. (1948) *A National Policy for the Oil Industry* (New Haven, Conn.: Yale University Press).

Rowthorne, R. (1975) 'What remains of Kaldor's Law?', *Economic Journal*, vol. 85, December, pp. 10–19.

Runciman, W. G. (1972) *Relative Deprivation and Social Justice* (London: Routledge and Kegan Paul).

Sabolo, Y. (1975) assisted by J. Garde and R. Wery, *The Service Industries* (Geneva: ILO).

Sachs, J. (1982) 'Stabilization policies in the world economy: scope and skepticism', *American Economic Review, Papers and Proceedings*, vol. 72, May, pp. 56–61.

Sampson, A. (1977) *The Arms Bazaar* (London: Hodder and Stoughton).

Schumpeter, J. (1939) *Business Cycles: A Theoretical, Historical and Statistical Analysis of the Capitalist Process* (New York: McGraw-Hill).

Schydlowsky, D. (1972) 'Latin American trade policies in the seventies: a prospective appraisal', *Quarterly Journal of Economics*, vol. 86, May.

Sciberras, E. (1977) *Multinational Electronics Companies and National Economic Policies* (Greenwich, Conn.: JAI).

Scitovsky,T. (1954) 'Two concepts of external economies', *Journal of Political Economy*, repr. in A. Agarwala and S. Singh (eds) *The Economics of Underdevelopment* (1963) (New York: Oxford University Press, pp. 295–308).

Segal, R. (1968) *America's Receding Future* (Harmondsworth: Penguin).

Shepherd, G. (1981) 'The Japanese challenge to Western Europe's new crisis industries', *The World Economy*, vol. 4, no. 4, December, pp. 375–90.

Singer, H. W. and Mahmood, R. A. (1982) 'Is there a poverty trap for developing countries? Polarization: reality or myth?', *World Development*, January, pp. 19–22.

Singh, A. (1977) 'UK industry and the world economy: a case of de-industrialization?', *Cambridge Journal of Economics*, vol. 1, no. 2, June, pp. 113–36.

Soligo, R. and Stern, J. (1965) 'Tariff protection, import substitution and investment efficiency', *The Pakistan Development Review*, vol. V, no. 2. pp. 249–69.

Spero, J. E. (1974) 'Energy self-sufficiency and national security' in R. H. Connery and R. S. Gilmour (eds) *The National Energy Problem* (Lexington, Mass.: Lexington Books).

Streeten, P. (1979)'Multinationals Revisited', *Finance and Development*, vol. 16, no. 2, June, pp. 39–42.

Sugiarto, S. (1981) *Comparative Advantage of Iron and Steel, Petro-chemical and Plastic Industries in Indonesia* (Tokyo: Institute of Developing Economies).

Sutcliffe, R. B. (1971) *Industry and Underdevelopment* (London: Addison-Wesley).

Taniura, T. (1971) *Comparative Advantage of Iron and Steel Industries in Asia* (Tokyo: Institute of Developing Economies).

Tanzer, M. (1969) *The Political Economy of International Oil and the Underdeveloped Countries* (Boston, Mass.: Beacon Press).

Tate, R. H. and Morgan, D. R. (1980) 'Gasoline taxation in selected OECD countries 1970–79', *IMF Staff Papers*, June, vol. 27, no. 2, pp. 349–79.

Thirlwall, A. P. (1982) 'Deindustrialization in the U.K.', *Lloyds Bank Review*, April, no. 144, pp. 22–37.

Turner, L. (1978) *Oil Companies in the International System* (London: George Allen and Unwin).

Turner, L. (1982) 'An Overview' in L. Turner and N. McMullen (eds) *The Newly Industrializing Countries: Trade and Adjustment* (London: George Allen and Unwin).

Tyler, W. G. (1981) 'Growth and export expansion in developing countries', *Journal of Developing Economies*, vol. 9, no. 1, pp. 121–30.

UN (monthly), *Monthly Bulletin of Statistics* (New York: UN).

UN (annual), *Yearbook of Industrial Statistics: General Industrial Statistics* (New York: UN) vol. I.

UN (annual), *Yearbook of Industrial Statistics: Commodity Production* (New York: UN) vol. II.

UN (annual), *Yearbook of International Trade Statistics* (New York: UN).

UN (1963a) *Growth of World Industry, 1938–1961* (NewYork: UN).

UN (1963b) *A Study of Industrial Growth* (New York: UN).

UN (1964) *Economic Bulletin for Latin America* (New York: UN) vol. 9, no. 1, March.

UN (1978) *Transnational Corporations in World Development: A Re-examination* (New York: UN).

UNCTAD (1969) *Handbook of International Trade and Development Statistics* (Geneva: UNCTAD).

UNCTAD (1976) 'The dimensions of the required restructuring of world manufacturing output and trade in order to reach the Lima target' (Geneva: UNCTAD, TD/185/Supp. 1).

UNCTC (1980) 'Transnational corporations in food and beverage processing' (New York: UN, ST/CTC/19).

UNIDO (1969) *Industrial Development Survey* (New York: UN).

UNIDO (1974) *Industrial Development Survey* (New York: UN) special issue for the Second General Conference of UNIDO.

UNIDO (1976) *World-wide Study of the Iron and Steel Industry: 1975–2000* (Vienna: UNIDO, UNIDO/ICIS.25).

UNIDO (1978a) 'The Manufacture of Low-Cost Vehicles in Developing Countries' (New York: UN, Development and Transfer of Technology Series, no. 3).

UNIDO (1978b) *The World Iron and Steel Industry* (Vienna: UNIDO, UNIDO/ICIS.89 p. 42).

UNIDO (1979) *World Industry Since 1960: Progress and Prospects* (New York: UN) special issue of the Industrial Development Survey for the Third General Conference of UNIDO.

UNIDO (1980) *Picture for 1985 of the World Iron and Steel Industry* (Vienna: UNIDO, UNIDO/ICIS.161).

UNIDO (1981a) *World Industry in 1980* (New York: UN), a biennial issue of the Industrial Development Survey.

UNIDO (1981b) *Restructuring World Industry in a Period of Crisis – The Role of Innovation* (Vienna: UNIDO, UNIDO/IS.285).

UNIDO (1982a) *A Statistical Review of the World Industrial Situation, 1981* (Vienna: UNIDO, UNIDO/IS.292).

UNIDO (1982b) *Changing Patterns of Trade in World Industry: an Empirical Study on Revealed Comparative Advantage* (New York: UN).

UNIDO (1982c) *Handbook of Industrial Statistics* (New York: UN).

Velasco, E. T. and Almario, E. S. (1981) *Comparative Advantage of Iron and Steel, Petro-chemical and Plastic Products Industries in the Philippines* (Tokyo: Institute of Developing Economies).

Verndoorn, P. J. (1949) 'Fattori che regolano lo sviluppo della produttività del lavoro', *L'Industria*.

Vernon, R. (ed.) (1974) *Big Business and the State* (London: Macmillan).

Vernon, R. (1974) 'Enterprise and government in Western Europe' in R. Vernon (ed.) *Big Business and the State* (London: Macmillan) pp. 3–24.

Vernon, R. (1981) 'International economic relations in transition', *The*

World Economy, vol. 4, no. 1, p. 17–28.

Walter, I. (1979) 'Protection of industries in trouble – the case of iron and steel', *The World Economy*, vol. 2, no. 2, pp. 155–88.

Walter, I. and Jones, K. (1980) 'Industrial adjustment to competitive shocks: a tale of three industries', paper submitted to the International Symposium on Industrial Policies for the 1980s, Madrid, 5–9 May.

Walters, K. D. and Mansen, R. J. (1979) 'State-owned businesses abroad: new competitive threat', *Harvard Business Review*, March-April, pp. 164–71.

Warnecke, S. J. (ed.) (1978) *International Trade and Industrial Policies, Government Intervention and an Open World Economy* (London: Macmillan).

Weiss, F. and Wolter, F. (1975) 'Machinery in the United States, Sweden and Germany – an assessment of changes in comparative advantage', *Weltwirtschaftliches Archiv*, vol. 111, no. 2, pp. 282–309.

Wells, L. T. (1972) 'International trade: the product life cycle approach' in L. T. Wells (ed.) *The Product Life Cycle and International Trade* (Cambridge, Mass.: Harvard University Graduate School of Business Administration) pp. 3–33.

Wells, L. T. (forthcoming), study on LDC-based TNCs (Boston, Mass.: MIT Press).

Wilkins, M. (1974) *The Maturing of Multinational Enterprise* (Cambridge, Mass.: Harvard University Press).

World Bank (1976) *The Philippines: Priorities and Prospects for Development* (Washington DC: World Bank).

World Bank (1979) *The Changing Composition of Developing Country Exports* (Washington DC: IBRD, Staff Working Paper no. 314).

World Bank (1981) *Industrial Prospects and Policies in the Developed Countries* (Washington DC: IBRD, Staff Working Paper no. 453).

Journals and Newspapers
Arabia (London)
(AN) Automotive News (Detroit)
(BW) Business Week (New York)
Courier (Brussels)
L'expansion (Paris)
(FEER) Far Eastern Economic Review (Hong Kong)
(FT) Financial Times (London)
Fortune (New York)
(IW) Industry Week (Cleveland, Ohio)
(IHT) International Herald Tribune (Frankfurt)
(IM) International Management (London)
(ISE) Iron and Steel Engineer (Pittsburgh)
(ISI) Iron and Steel International (Guildford, Surrey)
NIESR Review (London)
(NJ) National Journal (Washington DC)
(NYT) New York Times (New York)
OPEC Bulletin (Vienna)
(PE) Petroleum Economist (London)

(PR) Petroleum Review (London)
(ST) Steel Times (Redhill, Surrey)
(S. Times) Sunday Times (London)
The Economist (London)
The Guardian (London)
The Times (London)
(USNWR) US News and World Report (Washington DC)
(WSJ) Wall Street Journal (New York)
(WAW) Ward's Auto World (Detroit)

Index